CRITICAL PEDAGOGY

This accessible text provides a clear overview of the contemporary themes and challenges within critical pedagogy, and suggests a path towards a more conscientious world for all through education. Boronski encourages us to imagine radical alternatives to current approaches, not merely for ideological reasons, but due to increasing necessity for environmental and sociological perspectives.

With case studies, discussion tasks and exemplars from global history woven throughout, each chapter considers a prominent societal and educational issue, tackling some difficult and unsettling areas. Embedded in this exploration is an understanding and application of key concepts, such as justice, equality, rights and power, and how these relate to a range of topics in UK schooling. These include the role of teachers in an age of hyper surveillance and performance monitoring, alternative approaches to education and the growing fear of the 'other'.

Essential reading for Education Studies students at undergraduate and Master's level, this comprehensive text will also be of interest to students of Social Policy, Sociology and Politics programmes.

Tomas Boronski is former Senior Lecturer and Programme Leader for Education Studies at University of East London, UK. He has worked in education at all levels from Primary to Higher Education, and has authored publications on a range of topics within Education.

CRITICAL PEDAGOGY

An Exploration of Contemporary Themes and Issues

Tomas Boronski

LONDON AND NEW YORK

First edition published 2022
by Routledge
2 Park Square, Milton Park, Abingdon, Oxon, OX14 4RN

and by Routledge
52 Vanderbilt Avenue, New York, NY 10017

Routledge is an imprint of the Taylor & Francis Group, an informa business

© 2022 Tomas Boronski

The right of Tomas Boronski to be identified as author of this work has been asserted by him in accordance with sections 77 and 78 of the Copyright, Designs and Patents Act 1988.

All rights reserved. No part of this book may be reprinted or reproduced or utilised in any form or by any electronic, mechanical, or other means, now known or hereafter invented, including photocopying and recording, or in any information storage or retrieval system, without permission in writing from the publishers.

Trademark notice: Product or corporate names may be trademarks or registered trademarks, and are used only for identification and explanation without intent to infringe.

British Library Cataloguing-in-Publication Data
A catalogue record for this book is available from the British Library

Library of Congress Cataloging-in-Publication Data
Names: Boronski, Tomas, author.
Title: Critical pedagogy: an exploration of contemporary themes
and issues / Tomas Boronski.
Description: Abingdon, Oxon; New York, NY: Routledge, [2022] |
Includes bibliographical references and index. |
Identifiers: LCCN 2021007159 (print) | LCCN 2021007160 (ebook) |
ISBN 9781138105416 (hardback) | ISBN 9781138105423 (paperback) |
ISBN 9781315101811 (ebook)
Subjects: LCSH: Critical pedagogy—Great Britain. | Social justice and education—Great Britain. | Education—Aims and objectives—Great Britain.
Classification: LCC LC196 .B676 2022 (print) | LCC LC196 (ebook) |
DDC 370.11/5—dc23
LC record available at https://lccn.loc.gov/2021007159
LC ebook record available at https://lccn.loc.gov/2021007160

ISBN: 978-1-138-10541-6 (hbk)
ISBN: 978-1-138-10542-3 (pbk)
ISBN: 978-1-315-10181-1 (ebk)

Typeset in News Gothic BT
by codeMantra

For Catherine and Josef

CONTENTS

Preface   viii

1 Introduction: A pedagogy for change   1
   with Nasima Hassan

2 Imagining an alternative world   21
3 Alternative ways of being and educating   40
4 Austerity in a time of spectacular wealth   57
5 Decolonising the curriculum and society   76
6 Higher education as a site of liberatory practice   96
7 Schools and the pursuit of social justice   113
8 Critical pedagogy and promoting social justice   132

Index   *151*

PREFACE

At the time of writing, Britain, and indeed much of the rest of the world, was in the grip of one of the worst pandemics since the 1918 influenza outbreak which, at that time, affected an estimated five hundred million people and killed at least fifty million (Gunderman, 2018). Such virus-type pandemics have long been predicted by scientists to occur at least once a century, so the COVID-19 pandemic was not something unexpected and governments have had fair warning to prepare for it (Murdoch, 2020). However, many politicians, particularly those in neoliberal economies, chose to ignore these warnings. What such global crises do is to expose the inherent weaknesses in existing systems of government, economic and social policies, as well as the disproportionately negative impact they tend to have on the poor and most vulnerable members of society. The COVID-19 pandemic, which began in China in late 2019, is no exception. Whilst this health crisis threatens us all, the initial evidence reveals that it is indeed the poor, those with disabilities, the elderly and minority ethnic groups that have been most affected, particularly in some of the most affluent societies that claim to be liberal democracies and have the most advanced medical and scientific knowledge and technologies (Boseley, 2020). This clearly highlights the limits of scientific progress as a means of assessing human social progress. While the full impact of the pandemic may well be revealed in due course in national and international enquiries, what is clear is that we have an opportunity to reflect on the injustices that exist in the world relating to continuing and growing inequalities, be they in health, income, wealth or education, and their interrelated nature, that have been thrown into high relief by the crisis.

What the science reveals, however, is that the prevailing economic, environmental and political systems that dominate some of the most affluent societies of the Northern hemisphere are becoming so unsustainable as to threaten the viability of the planet and thereby the very future of humanity. In other words, there are likely to be more of such major crises, and they are expected to become more frequent (Murdoch, 2020). However, no matter how much scientific evidence is produced, there is a growing number of political leaders who deny or reject it and place their own narrow economic and national interests above those of all other global and international concerns (Schaller and Carius, 2019). This persisting tendency of powerful nations to put their own interests, in particular those of their most wealthy and powerful citizens, above those of others, must be challenged and replaced by a global approach that gives priority to the weaker and most vulnerable communities. In order to do this, there needs to be a wholesale re-evaluation of how we think about and understand our place and responsibilities on this fragile planet. Narrow-minded nationalism and the obsessive promotion of the interests of the wealthy, as well as endless economic growth, regardless of its consequences, are proving to be some of the biggest obstacles to creating a more humanising and sustainable existence. A key part of this re-evaluation relates to education and the importance of listening to all citizens, including children, minority ethnic groups as well as the weakest and most vulnerable, who are often subjected to discriminatory policies and whose voices are generally silent because our politicians and the powerful dominate the political agenda as well as most sectors of the media. The prescriptive curriculum needs to be replaced with dialogue and collaboration with all relevant groups – teachers, parents, children, students, academics and, of course, politicians.

We all have the right to a start in life that enables us to reach our full potential, to earn sufficient income not to have to worry about whether or not we are able to feed our children, and to reach the end of our lives in a dignified manner. Moreover, young people have a not unreasonable expectation to inherit a planet that will be healthy and safe for them as well as their own children. These are not unrealistic, given the potential humanity has to be able to meet them. If we do not think in terms of alternative ways of living, we will be unable to tackle the huge challenges we face that need to be addressed now and not at some distant time in the future when it may be too late. There are signs that young people around the world are becoming increasingly aware of the threats we all face and are also becoming more active. They want to play a part in deciding their future, and this includes enabling them to act and speak freely and openly about the failures of our existing political and economic systems and to imagine alternative ways of doing things, be it producing food, investing in health and education or deciding on energy policies. They also want an education system and curriculum that reflects this freedom and opportunity for dialogue and gives voice to all groups, not just those of the powerful and wealthy whose narrow commercial and economic interests have tended to prevail.

It is perhaps no coincidence that with a growth in the activism of young people in political, environmental and economic issues, governments around the world including the US, Britain, Hungary, Russia and Poland have been enacting legislation that enforces strongly nationalist, paternalistic and patriotic policies along with the promotion of free-market ideologies. In Britain, the Conservative government has issued guidelines stating that schools should under no circumstances use resources produced by organisations that promote 'extreme' political positions. Under the heading 'extreme', it includes not only views that advocate the abolition of democracy or free elections but also those that challenge capitalism (Gov.UK, 2020). Moreover, it has been promoting highly nationalistic and racist policies in relation to the treatment of its own citizens of non-white British origin, such as through the implementation of a national curriculum that limits the voices of Black British citizens, and the creation of a 'hostile environment' for Black people in terms of their status as British citizens. Young people in Britain are effectively being banned from freely thinking about their world and imagining something better, and racism is becoming increasingly institutionalised and accepted as a key element of government policy.

Never has there been a more appropriate time to examine critically the consequences for us all of the continuing growth in the influence of neoliberal capitalism around the world, as well as the increasing tolerance of racism and the glorification of colonialism and empire. It is a system that constantly reveals itself as anti-democratic, anti-intellectual, lacking in humanity and is relentless in its promotion of the interests of the rich and powerful and contemptuous of the consequences of selfish capitalist accumulation on the planet. These are the key issues covered in this book, which does not propose to provide single answers or solutions in terms of dealing with them; instead the book is designed to encourage dialogue and reflection. It seeks to stimulate a debate regarding what might be considered some of the most pressing issues that concern humanity now and are likely to face us for decades to come. Much of the evidence suggests that such problems as global warming, racial injustice and inequalities in terms of wealth and income are getting progressively worse for a huge proportion of the populations of both less developed and most developed societies.

Such perverse logics are central to the debates raised in this book whose aim is to encourage us to think more critically about conventional intellectual as well as common sense assumptions which dominate what we are taught at school and university. Young people should be encouraged to engage in critical thinking, exercise autonomy, question conventional wisdom and be able to recognise injustices where they exist as well as propose solutions that address such injustices. This advice applies just as much to the adult population, many of whom have become stuck in ways of thinking that it seems they are self-evident 'truths'. Yet many of these long-held assumptions may be the main obstacles to much needed change.

References

Boseley, S. (2020) 'Pre-existing inequality led to record UK Covid death rate, says health expert'. *The Guardian*. 15 December.

Gov.UK. (2020) 'Plan your relationships, sex and health curriculum'. *Guidance: Department for Education.* 24 September. Available at: https://www.gov.uk/guidance/plan-your-relationships-sex-and-health-curriculum#choosing-resources (Accessed 12 January 2021).

Gunderman, R. (2018) 'The "greatest pandemic in history" was 100 years ago – but many of us still get the basic facts wrong'. *The Conversation*. Available at: https://theconversation.com/the-greatest-pandemic-in-history-was-100-years-ago-but-many-of-us-still-get-the-basic-facts-wrong-89841 (Accessed 12 December 2020).

Murdoch, D. (2020) 'The next once-a-century pandemic is coming sooner than you think – but COVID-19 can help us get ready'. *The Conversation*. Available at: https://theconversation.com/the-next-once-a-century-pandemic-is-coming-sooner-than-you-think-but-covid-19-can-help-us-get-ready-139976 (Accessed 12 December 2020).

Schaller, S. and Carius, A. (2019) *Convenient Truths. Mapping Climate Agendas of Right-Wing Populist Parties in Europe.* Berlin: Adelphy Consult.

1 Introduction

A pedagogy for change

(with Nasima Hassan)

Introduction

In an attempt to broaden the approach of critical pedagogy, this book aims to challenge hegemonic views of contemporary social, political and economic issues and to provide alternative ways of looking at them, in particular using the ideas of critical pedagogy to see the world from the perspective of the powerless including children and young people, the poor elderly and those in need of social care, those on low incomes, the homeless, marginalised minorities and those with impairments. Such groups, for one reason or another, tend to rely on others to speak for them and where there is no one to speak for them, they are silent and therefore do not 'exist'. And if they do not exist, we need not concern ourselves with them. In those cases where someone does speak on their behalf, they are usually only partially heard or their position is not effectively presented because of vested interests or claims to 'professional neutrality' (see Barnes and Mercer, 1997; Boronski and Hassan, 2015). This book does not claim to speak for these groups, but it does suggest alternatives to the current official and hegemonic perspectives and offers more critical ways of thinking about the world and the assumptions we take for granted. Nor does it intend to engage in a detailed examination of the origins of critical pedagogy or a detailed explanation of the theoretical debates in the field. These are already covered in a number of works (see Darder et al., 2009). The purpose of this book is to encourage the development of a 'language of possibility' (Giroux, 2001).

A 'language of possibility'

Critical pedagogy is an approach to education which emerged in the 1980s from a conviction that there is a need to build more just, equitable and democratic societies. It is based on a variety of philosophical traditions all of which have been concerned with the role of mainstream education in maintaining social inequalities and the oppression of powerless groups. A key aim of critical pedagogy from its origins has been to create a 'language of possibility' (Giroux, 2001). The term captures the significance of language and its role in the process of enabling poor and oppressed groups to challenge the hegemonic ideas and definitions of the world through a more critical approach to teaching and learning. However, as Seehwa Cho (2013) points out, these possibilities have not generally been articulated as clearly as they might be. Cho believes that terms such as democracy, justice and equality are often presented in ways that are too broad and abstract. In the following chapters, it is hoped that such possibilities will be more clearly identified and the ways in which critical insights and consciousness, developed through a critical education, can help to inform political, social and economic action, in order to bring about real change in all aspects of human life. It should be pointed out then that the discussions and analyses in the present and following chapters will be informed by and replete with ideas and concepts as well as theories associated with critical theory and critical pedagogy.

The need to prioritise the weak, the poor and the vulnerable

The consequences of existing policies and political structures are becoming increasingly clear in the growing body of evidence on the effects of poverty on children (RCPCH, 2017), the growing crisis in social care (Stewart and Walker, 2017) and the shortage of affordable housing (Madden, 2016). Despite these and other issues, all of which are linked, governments in neoliberal countries such as England continue to deny any responsibility resorting instead to blaming the poor for their 'lifestyle choices' (Jones, 2011; Smyth and Wrigley, 2013), the inefficient use of resources in the public sector and, more recently, the 'foreign threat'. Despite evidence to the contrary (Dustmann and Frattini, 2014; Asthana, 2016), the government has been devoting much of its energy and scarce resources to promoting the idea that many of these problems lie in our relationship with Europe. The public has been led to believe that the shortage of housing, the growing pressures on education and the health service as well as poor wages lie not with the government's long-term neglect of the welfare of its people and the low wages paid by employers, but with the erosion of British sovereignty caused by membership of the European Union (EU) and the negative effects of the free movement of labour.

A key feature of this nationalism is an 'imagined' concept of community (Anderson, 2006) in which all British citizens in England, Northern Ireland, Wales and Scotland are seen as equal and have a common cause against a threat that comes from outside such as the EU. The defeat of this threat is seen as imperative in order to banish our problems and to make the nation 'great' again. It is this imagined unity of one nation with a common set of values and identity as well as the belief in magical solutions that enables political leaders to convince their citizens to 'fight' for their nation rather than against the inequalities and injustices they may be experiencing. However, rather than unite the nation it has instead begun to lay bare even more starkly than ever the fault lines within the so-called United Kingdom, not just between England and the other nations of the union, but also within England. This was demonstrated clearly in the campaign for devolution in Scotland and outcome of the British referendum on continued membership of the EU in 2016, in which the Scots voted with a large majority to remain (Jackson-Preece, 2016). The rhetoric of British national identity and sovereignty serves ultimately as a distraction from the real problems that lie instead within our borders and have been caused by the political and economic leaders who claim to care for their citizens whilst in reality showing little evidence of doing so in terms of ensuring access to decent pay and affordable housing, children's right to a happy childhood and education, the right to a well-funded and functioning health service free at the point of use, the right to a comfortable old age free from the worries of loneliness and neglect, the right of people with impairments to live lives as rewarding and fulfilling as any other citizen, the right to affordable childcare and properly funded parental leave for mothers and fathers, the right of minority ethnic groups to feel secure and safe in a country to which they contribute their labour and taxes (Dustmann and Frattini, 2014). These are not the unreasonable expectations of radicals and revolutionaries or indeed the politics of envy (Johnson, 2013). They could be seen as the expectations of anyone who wants to live in a humane and caring society where not just the fit and strong prosper, but so also do the weak and vulnerable. It is suggested that there is an urgent need for the humanisation (Freire, 1996) of the nation as well as for a reform to the political system that will guarantee protection for all members of society regardless of economic conditions or the political party in power.

Victims of a so-called free society

The voiceless and powerless are in effect victims of a so-called free society, in a 'nation' where freedom of speech and of the press is considered sufficient guarantee to a fair hearing. Those who benefit from this situation are able not only to employ a range of political, economic, philosophical and 'common sense' arguments to justify their privilege and power (see Johnson, 2013), they also either own or have access to the most influential media outlets and information systems and, if they choose, are able to control or suppress the flow of information (Dutta, 2013). This is why it is suggested that we need critical theory such as critical pedagogy and critical literacy in order to give voice to the powerless and to enable them to rename a world which has already been predefined for them by those with an interest in keeping things as they are. In addition, new ways of thinking are required to challenge apparently common-sense assumptions.

Perverse logics

In this book the notion of *perverse logics* is employed to highlight the consequences of applying apparently self-evident and generally accepted beliefs in ways which may result in widespread injustices or harm. These can be seen in slogans and neologisms to which it is assumed there is no riposte, such as: 'There is no alternative' (TINA) to fiscal consolidation, i.e. government cuts to services which affect the most vulnerable and the increasing privatisation of public services, despite there being many possible options to austerity; that although we are all supposed to be 'in this together', the rich and already highly paid need to be incentivised to be more productive through lower taxes and ever higher pay, whilst those on low incomes, the poor and those with disabilities, who are accused of having become too dependent on the state, should be penalised by cuts to their benefits and welfare services. So, rather than pathologise the rich for their obsession with excessive wealth, we demonise the poor and weak for being dependent on welfare or for simply 'being poor'. Such assumptions are usually linked to certain rights and obligations that are considered so inalienable that few, other than those branded as 'radical subversives', are prepared to challenge them, thus shutting down the opportunity for legitimate debate. Instead of witnessing a sense of concern or moral outrage, for example, at the huge pay differentials between Britain's corporate bosses and ordinary workers (Wyporska, 2017), and the levels of poverty in Britain, there is a tendency to view the rich and high earners as virtuous, productive and deserving, and the poor and low paid as lazy, unproductive and reliant on benefits (Bamfield and Horton, 2009; Harrington, 2018). Indeed, there seems to be no real appetite to cap the incomes or raise taxes of high earners, even within the Labour Party (Mason, 2017) which purports to represent the poor. What appears even more problematic than the growing gap between the rich and the poor in Britain is that there appears to be little in the way of any debate about what seems to be a tacit acceptance of the right of individuals to *infinite* wealth. This raises some important ethical and moral questions relating to the rights of individuals in a society where there is poverty and a lack of basic services for ordinary citizens.

In essence, perverse logics are the building blocks of ideologies that together provide the supporting values, common sense assumptions and myths which result in unjust relations. They are most effective when combined with stories of ancient institutions such as the monarchy or ideas of national identity and sacred legends of origin and destiny. In elevating the nation to something sacred (Durkheim, 1912) there is an expectation of unquestioning loyalty from the citizens/subjects to policies and decisions that are alleged to be in the 'national interest' but which tend to actually benefit a minority of the wealthy and privileged. However, any attempt to question such decisions is usually met with accusations of a lack of patriotism and loyalty to the nation. In such situations the weaker and relatively powerless members of society ultimately collude in their own oppression.

A pedagogy for change

The chapter will set the scene for this book in terms of its approach to issues of education: what it is for, what it could be and how this transformation can be achieved. In particular, it examines the role of education and schooling in a global context and the current climate of growing neoliberalism and the 'economism' upon which it is based, as well as the ideological role it plays in the reproduction and perpetuation of injustice such as the growing inequality between the rich and poor within and between nations globally (Wilkinson and Pickett, 2009, 2018; Dorling, 2011; Piketty, 2020). It will not propose new ideas about how to deal with such injustices but will suggest that there is an urgent need for a debate in this country, and globally, about some of the fundamental principles upon which our everyday beliefs and actions are based. It is hoped that such a debate will identify how the priorities of governments and educators need to change in order to turn schools and universities into sites which can be part of a process of dialogue, social transformation and engaged citizenship. In particular, the design and delivery of the curriculum requires radical rethinking of economic relations (who creates the wealth and how it should be distributed?) and political processes (what is the purpose of education and the values that motivate funding and guide policy?) which will inform the reader about the place and value of critical pedagogy and its potential impact on the process of education. This chapter captures the fluid nature of education policy and practice and in turn opens the world of dialogue and philosophical thinking to responsible citizens as well as to pupils and students as the basis of a pedagogy for change.

Many on the political right will ask whether such a debate is necessary given that, as they claim, the argument has been won (Fukuyama, 1989; Berlinski, 2007). However, there is sufficient evidence to convince all but the most hard-line neoliberals that a debate does need to be had on some of the fundamental questions about the trajectory of global politics, economics and the consequences of the relatively unfettered spread of neoliberal policies (Ostry et al., 2016). Moreover, it is in the interest of all humanity to address such issues before we reach a tipping point beyond which the situation becomes irretrievable.

Evidence of the negative impact of neoliberalism on the education system in England is increasing. It has become all too familiar to read of how unhappy our children are. In report after report we read about how children in England lag behind those in other countries in terms of well-being (UNICEF, 2007, 2011, 2013; Pople et al., 2015; PISA, 2015b), and yet no matter how many of these are published or the weight of evidence collected, the government refuses to accept that there is a crisis, not just in the education system, but also of childhood. If the evidence regarding the mental health and well-being of our children are anything to go by, then ignoring the voices of our children could be seen as negligence at best and cruelty at worst. Prime Minister Theresa May's initiative in 2017 (Gov.uk, 2017) to tackle the growing issue of mental illness among young people (IPPR, 2016) is effectively the medicalisation (Illich, 1976; Szasz, 1977; Tamimi, 2010) of the wider issue of our children's unhappiness brought about by government welfare and education policy and not as a result of a sudden or random epidemic of mental illness. There is a pattern here which takes the form of governments identifying problems and providing palliatives rather than accepting the links between them which stem from the effects of ideologically driven policies of neoliberal reform. Tamimi (2010) refers to this as the 'McDonaldisation' of childhood in which the declining mental health of our children results in the pathologisation of children, their parents and schools, rather than an acknowledgement by policy makers of the consequences of the increasing pressures faced by children and families caused by neoliberal capitalism and austerity.

The arguments for change

Ever since the ideas of neoliberalism gained a hold on the policy process in Britain during the late 1970s a number of things have become clear. In particular, that Britain has become one of the most unequal of the developed nations (Piketty, 2014, 2020; Savage et al., 2015) and that the effects of such inequalities are likely to affect us all adversely, not just the poor and disadvantaged (Wilkinson and Pickett, 2009, 2018). A further consequence is that education has become one of the key policy areas used by the government to pursue its neoliberal agenda (Ball, 2013). Wilkinson and Pickett (2009) present an argument for greater income equality in countries such as Britain using an 'evidence-based politics' from which they conclude that more equal societies in general do better in terms of a range of social and welfare criteria including lower health and social problems such as mental illness, lower homicide rates and levels of imprisonment, and higher overall achievement in education than less equal societies. Their findings seemed to have moved the debate away from an ideologically based justification for greater equality of income to one based on objective scientific criteria.

The evidence is compelling and it seemed to capture the spirit of the time in the aftermath of the financial collapse of 2008 when bankers and city traders epitomised all that is wrong with the current system of unrestrained and deregulated finance capitalism. At first politicians from both ends of the political spectrum welcomed it as ground-breaking. Michael Gove, the education minister at the time, described it as a 'fantastic analysis' (Booth, 2010). Even David Cameron referred to it in his 2010 election addresses on the Big Society. However, when the initial enthusiasm had died down and the full implications of *The Spirit Level* became apparent, there was a huge *volte face* by politicians and policy analysts on the right. Indeed, a number of right-wing think tanks (Sanandaji et al., 2010; Saunders, 2010; Snowdon, 2010) produced swingeing attacks on the findings branding them socialist propaganda with one detractor suggesting that Wilkinson and Pickett are part of the movement of 'anti-wealth egalitarianism' (Niemietz, 2013 cited in Snowdon, 2010).

The moral and ethical void that is neoliberal economics

The findings of Wilkinson and Pickett (2009) suggest that extreme levels of inequality that are a growing feature of neoliberal economies such as Britain are undesirable not just for the poor, but because they affect all members of society adversely. However, for libertarian economists such as Friedman and Friedman (1980), freedom of the individual is compromised by any attempts to limit or moderate inequality resulting from the free market economy: individual freedom is seen as sovereign regardless of the consequences for others. So, it is on this assumed foundational principle Nozik (1974) claims that an individual has an absolute right to keep all earnings, lawfully acquired, without limitation. Any state that attempts to reduce inequality by increasing taxes specifically on the riches acquired lawfully by the rich is seen as infringing their fundamental rights. It is these ideas, which will be examined in more detail later in Chapter 4, that are the basis of President Donald Trump's riposte during the 2016 US presidential campaign, after Hilary Clinton accused him of avoiding hundreds of millions of dollars of taxable income: 'Honestly, I have brilliantly used those laws ... I have a responsibility to pay as little tax as legally possible' (Dearden, 2016). Ultimately, liberal, and more recently, neoliberal economists present the economy as a neutral system which has no morality associated with it, such as the notion of redistributive justice that Rawls (1999) might propose. Indeed, for Robbins (1932), ethics and economics exist in different dimensions and do not meet. It is this desire to divorce economic action from morality and ethics that this book wishes to challenge.

It is convenient for advocates of neoliberalism to justify such a position on the grounds that for the economy to function at its optimum level of efficiency there should be as little government interference and regulation as possible. This is a myth which effectively acts as a licence for the owners of business to act as they wish by paying their employees as little as they can and to impose conditions over which workers have no say or protection, and it is a world where morality has no place: extreme inequalities are merely seen as the inevitable consequences of a competitive market system in which workers' wages are seen as reflecting the true value of their labour: 'If workers are poor, therefore, it must be because they are not very productive. In other words, it's their own fault' (Stanford, 2015: 56).

To argue that morality and ethics have no place in economic relations is in itself perverse and intellectually unsound in the extreme. Morality affects all relations and indeed there are few if any aspects of human social, political and economic interaction where a moral dimension is absent. Employers who fail to pay their employees a 'living wage' despite their companies making healthy profits, or who impose unreasonable conditions of work on employees, are acting immorally and cannot hide behind the idea of 'market forces'. Governments that impose fiscal policies which adversely affect the poor and vulnerable whilst at the same time cutting taxes for the already wealthy are acting immorally. Corporate bosses who use the lax and ineffectual tax laws to avoid paying taxes on all their income are acting immorally. These actions and policies inspired by neoliberal ideology lack humanity. In countries such as Britain, corporate regulation and tax laws are designed by the wealthy to benefit the wealthy, and their administration as well as enforcement is similarly biased. In the aftermath of the financial crisis in 2008 which was caused by the reckless and immoral acts of a number of global financial institutions, we can see evidence for such claims.

The degradation of education

A further consequence of the encroachment of neoliberalism in Britain and England in particular is that education has become one of the key policy areas used by the government to pursue its neoliberal agenda. The result has been a shift in the notion of education as something inherently human and of intrinsic merit in itself in helping to develop moral and engaged citizens, to one in

Case study 1.1: The financial crash of 2008

In 2014 the *New York Times* asked:

> why the largest man-made economic catastrophe since the Depression resulted in the jailing of a single investment banker – one who happened to be several rungs from the corporate suite at a second-tier financial institution.
>
> (Eisinger 2014)

Eisinger goes on to speculate about the reasons for this, identifying a Justice Department ill- prepared for such cases, poor coordination of the legal resources at its disposal and the ability of high-profile bankers suspected of illegal financial activities to play the system and do what they do best: gambling. In this case, the charges against them were so complex and time-consuming to pursue that they would not hold up in court, and they won. Though providing a critique of the of corporate prosecution process in the US, Eisinger does not challenge the nature and morality of finance capitalism. There is merely a sense of frustration at the oversight of the system and the resulting lack of justice.

A similar story can be told about the lack of prosecutions of bankers and financial services executives in Britain for such crimes. Despite billions of pounds being lost due to the reckless behaviour of traders and bankers during the financial crash in which millions of people globally lost their jobs as well as their homes, few bankers have faced prosecution (*The Economist*, 2013). Nevertheless, it is the taxpayer who was forced by the government to pay billions of pounds to bail out these banks that were deemed too big to fail, and it is the ordinary tax payer who has been expected to endure the austerity measures which the government insists are necessary to pay for these bailouts. However, *The Economist* (2013) takes a similar line to the *New York Times* suggesting that it is very difficult to prove wrongdoing in such matters and warns against adopting an excessively punitive approach to these crimes as that may 'discourage risk-taking altogether' (*The Economist*, 2013). This was seen by *The Economist* as prudent and sound advice concerning what Eisinger has already described as the 'largest man-made economic catastrophe since the Depression' (Eisinger, 2014). There are, however, signs of unease and frustration regarding the dominance of neoclassical economics, the intellectual and academic foundations of neoliberalism and its narrative regarding the global economic system, especially its rejection of ethical and political considerations. A number of student-led groups such as *Rethinking Economics*, an international organisation made up of economics students, and the *Post-Crash Economics Society* set up by undergraduate economics students at Manchester University are demanding a more critical approach to economics for university students:

> Economics degrees are characterised by a lack of critical thinking, a lack of alternative perspectives, a lack of real world application and a lack of ethical and political context.
>
> (Rethinking Economics, 2017)

This is an important and encouraging development and clearly shows there is support for a curriculum in which 'critical economics' should play a key role.

8 Introduction

> **Case study 1.2: The civil unrest of 2011 in the UK**
>
> It is instructive to compare the treatment of these errant and criminally culpable bankers and traders with the way offenders are treated at the other end of the socio-economic class spectrum. In the aftermath of the civil unrest during the summer of 2011 when thousands of people took to the streets after the killing by the police of Mark Duggan, there was understandable shock and concern at the damage caused which amounted to an estimated three hundred million pounds in London alone (Dodd, 2011). However, the response of the government and the justice system in this instance was altogether more active, robust and punitive. Despite the evidence to show that the violence was triggered by an act of protest against police racism, a general feeling of injustice resulting from government austerity measures as well as the scandal surrounding MPs' expenses (*Guardian*, 2011), politicians such as David Cameron and the Justice Minister, Kenneth Clarke, insisted on referring to the participants as 'mindless' and to the 'shocking reminder of how broken a society ours is' (*Guardian*, 2011).
>
> Moreover, in terms of the police response to the urban unrest of 2011 there seems to have been a much higher level of activism that was conspicuously absent in their pursuit of the 'rogue traders' whose actions had caused many billions of pounds worth of losses and ruined the lives of millions. Lightowlers and Quirk (2014: 5) found evidence to suggest that there was a degree of 'zealous advocacy' on the part of the Crown Prosecution Service (CPS) and an overzealous prosecution of offenders for relatively minor offences as part of a policy of making an example of those involved in the riots, as opposed to taking each case on its own merits.

which children are measured primarily in terms of their use-value to the economy, where they are encouraged to see greed and individualism as the only ways to find fulfilment and recognition in life. Moreover, education is being transformed from being 'a public good to a private commodity' to be bought and sold for profit (Ford et al., 2015). This has led to the reduction of education to a tool of the powerful with which to control the minds of citizens who are trained to become compliant worker consumers rather than critically thinking citizens able to question and challenge injustices and oppressive practices.

This dehumanises us all, not just the vulnerable and weak, but also the rich and powerful who become desensitised to the needs of others. It is also an act of deception which is limiting education to a series of assessments and performance criteria in which children are led to believe that truth can be found through the banking system (Freire, 1996) of education rather than as part of an ongoing process of dialogue between teachers and learners in which each learns from the other. If education is about discovering what it means to be human, then our education system can be seen as a denial of this. For Freire humanisation is 'humankind's central problem' (Freire, 1996: 25). This involves asking fundamental questions about what it means to be human and moving away from the amoral ideology of humanity currently being imposed on us. Instead, we should be moving towards a world where to be authentically human is to eliminate all forms oppressive relationships based on self-interest and individual freedom of the wealthy and powerful few which denies any responsibility to others. There would be a 'preferential option' for the weak and vulnerable who would be prioritised in terms of the provision of the resources for a decent quality of life. A humanising society would moreover promote relations in schools and a curriculum based on the principles of mutual respect and dialogue where all have a voice. It would eschew policies of threat, sanctions and the stigmatisation of schools, teachers and children who are assessed and measured against criteria devised by Treasury economists rather than educational practitioners (NUT, 2016).

The continuing role of education in reproducing class privilege

The state of our current system of education encourages us to ask: What is education and what is it for? How should our children be educated? At present, we have a one-dimensional system of training for a future of work in a low-paid, increasingly unequal and precarious labour market for the majority of pupils, and an elitist, highly resourced system for those privileged to have a private or grammar school education. We are led to believe that there are equal opportunities and that hard work and dedication to passing assessments are the route to employment success. Much of the evidence however suggests that these claims are not borne out by the facts which even the government acknowledges but is doing little to address other than by tinkering with the system (Cabinet Office, 2009, 2011). The ideology of meritocracy suggests that the solution lies in 'opening doors, breaking barriers' (Cabinet Office, 2011) supported by strong leadership and discipline in schools (Gove, 2012). Ultimately the tendency is to blame the victims for poor educational attainment which is a further instance of perverse logic given the class divisions of the education system in England and the palpable advantage conferred on some children at the expense of others (Ball et al., 1996; Ball, 2002; Smyth and Wrigley, 2013). However, in a strange line of argument, suggesting more than a hint of perversity in his logic, Michael Gove, a former education minister in the coalition government (2010–2015), admits that English public schools are places of great privilege that produce a disproportionate number of the English elite, be it in sport, entertainment, the law, journalism, business and politics, but instead of accepting that this is an inevitable consequence of such privilege and of proposing a significant increase in resources for state schools, he claims that this is no excuse for the lower achievement of poorer children in state schools. Sweeping aside the wealth of evidence which suggests otherwise, Gove asserts all that is needed is 'hard work and good teaching' (Gove, 2012).

The desire by the Prime Minister Theresa May to pass legislation in England to allow the creation of more grammar schools is one of the more recent manifestations of the stated intention of increasing meritocracy through greater social mobility despite the evidence which shows that selection actually serves to promote and reinforce class divisions (Boronski, 2016; Burgess et al., 2017). The continuing existence of grammar schools and their possible growth in the future together with the relatively untouched and almost sacred status of English public schools symbolise an abiding respect for ancient traditions regardless of their consequences for the wider society. This, together with a renewed emphasis on choice in education through the introduction of a quasi-market, a *laissez faire* approach to government regulation of such markets and the emphasis on the individual's freedom to accumulate and spend their wealth as they wish, will only serve to guarantee the persistence in inequalities we are currently experiencing, rather than leading to a more meritocratic society (Pickett and Wilkinson, 2018).

Once again, there is a strange line of reasoning associated with this approach to education in which the government simultaneously promotes the notions of social mobility and meritocracy as well as an elitist system which supports privilege and exclusivity based on an ability to pay rather than merit. This uniquely English approach to fairness and opportunity in education is the product of powerful ideological, cultural and social class forces (see Boronski and Hassan, 2015: 188). Despite the claims that class is dead (Pakulski and Waters, 1996), the evidence shows a continued and ever-growing obsession with class in England, particularly amongst the 'elite' (Savage et al., 2015), as well as the exclusivity inherent in ancient institutions which preserve a hierarchical system in which everyone knows their place. This belief is not confined to the ruling class but appears to be tacitly accepted by many at the bottom of the class system, even if they don't quite understand how such ancient institutions work (Kynaston and Kynaston, 2014).

This is a key element of their success: the notions of mystery and wonder regarding ancient institutions of which the independent schools and grammar schools are a part, and the monarchy the ultimate symbol. Any suggestion that private schools, especially the ancient public schools, should be abolished is met with accusations of cultural and academic vandalism. Indeed, private schools are bastions of educational excellence in the traditional sense of the term (Yorke, 2017). The British 'establishment' is reluctant to bring an end to the independent schools that many of them have themselves attended, as they are seen as the 'Crown Jewels' of English education. Moreover, to these establishment figures private schools represent quintessentially what it means to be English. They effectively produced the (mainly) men who built and led an empire which was once the envy of the world. To abolish them would be viewed by such people as a betrayal of this legacy.

The allure of nation

This very English and elitist approach persists as part of our imagined concept of nation. It is one in which national identity is seen as more important than any other dimension of identity such as class, gender or ethnicity and demands supreme loyalty. Moreover, it imagines a mythical community where all are seen as equal citizens united by a common cause and destiny in which all must play their part. This is a powerful narrative which has been the unifying force behind the rise of empires over the millennia and was the inspiration for Plato's solution to saving Athens in the *Republic*. From such a position, education is the servant of the nation, rather than a humanising process based on moral or ethical principles that have no geographical boundaries. As a servant of the nation the education system is constructed in such a way as to require great sacrifice and conformity from ordinary citizens for the 'good of the nation' rather than meeting the needs of individual groups or wider ethical, moral or environmental considerations. This issue will be examined in more detail later in Chapter 5.

In addition to the emphasis on loyalty and sacrifice for the nation, there is the belief by the neoliberal state in the need to compete ruthlessly in a global economy rather than to cooperate with other nations (Hazzard, 2017). In fact, the key measures of national success have now become economic and financial rather than other criteria. Economic growth and yet more economic growth is the aim. The citizen is programmed at school to be assessed and to perform on a regular basis and learns from an early age to value others on the basis of such performance data. The narrative of government and school leaders is becoming one dominated by notions of employability and standardised criteria into which all children must fit. These objective instrumental measures of education have taken over all other criteria and rendered moral and human factors redundant. In the process, the individual learner is reconfigured from a social and political citizen whose status is based on a mutually beneficial social contract with the state in which education and other public services are viewed as aspects of the public good, to consumer citizen who is motivated by their own self-interest (Ford et al., 2015). It is these atomised and consumer-driven individuals that the neoliberal state sees as the nation's future citizens. Failure to achieve the required standards of success is seen as the fault of the individual to take full advantage of the opportunities offered by the system rather than the education system which is claimed to be rational and efficient.

A confused and confusing system

The reality is quite different for most pupils. What we have in England's education system is a strange amalgam of traditional and newly created institutions supposedly driven by a quasi-market imposed on children and parents who are governed by performance and management principles rather than pedagogical ones. This is a confused and confusing experience for all concerned not least because of the constant changes which are introduced as well as the variety of types of school that are supposed to represent a choice in the market which does not really exist. To add further to the confusion is the continuing assumption in England that children can from the age of ten or eleven be categorised as having different intellectual characteristics: they are either academic or practical in orientation, and this can be managed through a selective system in which children are allocated to schools according to the results of intelligence tests. This view and the belief that selective grammar schools are the motors of social mobility are unsupported by the evidence (Boliver and Swift, 2011; Burgess et al., 2017), and yet despite this the government has proposed legislation to create more of them. Whilst our politicians make such policies based on specious science and an ideological commitment to neoliberal economics, our children are becoming increasingly unhappy and stressed with no evidence that the current policies are working (PISA, 2013, 2015a, 2015b; Adams et al., 2017). The dependence on so-called objective criteria for assessing pupils is reducing teachers to the level of mere technicians who spend most of their time preparing children for tests, administering them and then labelling children accordingly, rather than developing authentic relationships of mutual trust and genuine learning.

An alternative approach

So, what is the alternative to this unjust and gloomy picture conjured up by the education system in England? This would involve asserting some very basic assumptions that would start from the belief that education is a right and not a commodity to be bought and sold: there is no place for the market in education. By reducing it to just another form of economic exchange corrupts its essence and turns the relationship between teacher and learner into one of performance measurement rather than an authentic human relationship. Utility and value become the main criteria for assessing such relationships rather than those of mutual existential understanding. Moreover, children and other vulnerable groups should never be exposed to such economic relations that are based primarily on competition and the selfish desire for profit. Furthermore, all children, of whatever background, are of equal importance and therefore deserve the same respect and the same level of resources allocated to their education. Moreover, they should all be viewed as having unlimited potential (Hart and Drummond, 2014), rather than be labelled at an early age as either 'failures' or 'successes'. Above all, education should be seen as a sacred thing, in the Durkheimian (1912) sense, to be treated with the utmost reverence and respect, rather than be sullied by the ideological motives of the rich and powerful who wish primarily to preserve the right to define the world in their own interest and to control and consume a disproportionate amount of global resources for their own benefits rather than for the good of all.

Education as a sacred thing

The notion of education as a sacred thing is neither extravagant nor overstated. It is one of the foundations upon which our relationship with our children is based and in which they are expected to place their trust in adults to treat them fairly and without discrimination to prepare them for their future lives and to become responsible, reflective and ethical beings. This was certainly recognised by Bertrand Russell, one of the foremost English philosophers of the twentieth century, much of whose writings espoused the 'sanctity of human relations, and especially those involving children as something sacred' (Russell, 1916, cited in Park, 2013: 136). However, neither the state nor, arguably, many established religions provide an education in the spirit of such reverence, instead employing compulsion and a desire to control children's minds and thinking about issues which should be the subjects of independent thought, debate and deep reflection. Moreover, Russell advocated more autonomy and creative freedom for teachers in deciding the curriculum as well as shorter working days for pupils and teachers. For pupils he also recommended opportunities to develop their self-discipline and autonomy as well as radical changes to the examination system (Park, 2013).

The variety of alternative approaches to education

A variety of alternative contemporary views capture the notion of the creative curriculum as demonstrated by the Montessori Method and Steiner Waldorf education (Dahlin, 2009) which offer a child-led approach to schooling. The Montessori Method promotes independent thinking in a creative environment and which aligns closely with Freire's concept of critical consciousness and is the anti-narrative to a curriculum embedded in standardised testing. It could be argued that the aim of nurturing freethinking in pupils also has the added bonus of cultivating social consciousness (Giroux, 2009). Similarly, Steiner schools are co-educational, fully comprehensive, mixed ability and apply the creative curriculum approach giving equal attention to the physical, emotional, intellectual, cultural and spiritual needs of each pupil. Values education and a heightened focus on a child's spiritual development also feature heavily in this setting. To what extent these alternative schooling options deliver on critical thinking, exercising autonomy, questioning established conventions and recognising injustices which are significant elements in critical pedagogy from a classroom perspective remains the focus of continued research; however, it is important to note that well-established alternatives do exist and are recognised in the workplace.

A further example of the alternative view from a global perspective is popular education, originating from the Latin American source 'of the people'. Popular education requires the learners to define what they need in order to learn and as such follows a classic Freirean pedagogy as it is non-hierarchical and the boundaries between learners and teachers are intentionally unclear so that an equitable power dynamic is established with each teaching the other according to their personal skills, knowledge and lived realities (Crowther et al., 1999). Essentially, popular education is structured and designed to raise the consciousness of its participants and to allow them to become more aware of how personal experiences are connected to larger societal problems.

Walters and Manicom (1996: 2) explore the elements of Popular education stating that:

> It involves an inherently self-reflective, reflexive and non-dogmatic approach. It works to make space for the collective production of knowledge and insight, and builds on what emerges from the experiences of those actively participating. The richness of the approach lies, therefore in the thought and implicit analysis that has gone into the design of the specific educational events or programmes, and in the spontaneous, sometimes serendipitous, process it unfolds at a particular moment, yielding even more challenges and possibilities.

This quote illustrates a commitment to creativity which in practical terms is rooted in the teaching of art and the creation of culture as a means of shaping a way of life. This example of curriculum design aims to reinforce and shape cultural expression and also offers an insight into ways in which creativity can be the foundation stone of a more holistic, transformational education system. Popular education is increasingly important in UK-based higher education where university-based teachers and researchers have come together to refocus on equality and social justice despite the overwhelming pressures which erode any notion of autonomy and creativity. The International Popular Education Network (PEN) was established in 1997 and now operates in 57 institutions of higher education. Academics who feel that they too, occupy the margins (of their institutions) have come together to prioritise community-based activism and social action, to be critical of the political drivers which maintain the status quo and to embrace progressive political action.

To illustrate how the status quo can be challenged, a resource on citizenship entitled 'Renewing Democracy in Scotland' (Crowther et al., 2005a,b) explores the practical implementation of democracy in Scotland as a social and cultural process that is transmitted and sustained through learning, in particular via the curriculum. Topics include the legal system, gender, identity, homelessness, civic life, language, welfare and the Asian experience in Scotland reflecting the comprehensive and fluid nature of what it might mean to be an active citizen in Scotland. The authors of this resource would argue that they are embracing the civic mission of their higher education institutions (HEIs) whilst at the same time investing in social and political movements with global HEIs, described as an 'in and against' position (Crowther et al., 2002). A collective that engages in dialogue and publications against the surveillance of academics and the market-driven performance indicators (Blackmore, 2001) that dominate workloads and addresses the potential for societal transformation through the creation of a critical culture amongst the student body is a concrete example of an alternative view of education through the vehicle of academic solidarity. A re-investment in community education as a social enterprise is a stepping stone in the process of creating a critical culture which takes on the lived experiences and day-to-day challenges of exploited and oppressed groups, whilst at the same time offering an anti-narrative to the 'academic capitalism' (Slaughter and Leslie, 1999) of the post-modern HEI.

Critical pedagogy in the classroom

Moving beyond theory and considering what critical pedagogy might look like in the classroom reflects the natural progression of the discussion into alternative approaches to education. In essence, critical pedagogy in the classroom supports the notions that both teachers and students are creative, autonomous individuals and, as hooks (1994: 88) argues, students should be viewed as whole people with their own lived experiences which should form part of their learning culture, stating that

> You can't deny that students have experiences and you can't deny that these experiences are relevant to the learning process even though you might say these experiences are limited, raw, unfruitful or whatever. Students have memories, families, religions, feelings, languages and cultures that give them a distinctive voice.

Similarly, Shor and Freire (1987: 8) would argue that knowledge is 'created and re-created by students and teachers in their classrooms' thus reinforcing an open and equitable relationship of dialogue and engagement, as opposed to the passive student and the privileged teacher of the banking model of education (Shor, 1987). Therefore, the classroom is understood as a connected space to society and the learning that takes place therein is part and parcel of culture formulation. Creating opportunities to reflect on and question power played out by the state (what is taught in the curriculum) and in the context of the classroom authority figures in the immediate setting (when the school day begins and ends) provides opportunities to expose students to ideas about privilege and disadvantage. In turn, this dialogue and reflection may impel them to a political awakening and in time support their understanding of education as a vehicle that may bring about much needed social change (Egan, 2008). As Katz (2014) argues, it is the responsibility of the student to grapple with these opportunities and how the experience as an embedded part of their schooling might encourage them to work towards such change.

Critical pedagogy in the contemporary era

The previous discussion considered the position that the classroom as an influential discursive space for the enactment of critical pedagogy, suggesting that the power dynamic therein is both inherently political and therefore the basis to explore inequality, social justice and reproduction. The classroom is also a space that offers real-life connections to how society functions, the ideological and economic drivers and the potential to be a change maker therein is also considered. A further important factor is the role of the teacher which key thinkers (Ladson-Billings, 2006; Smyth, 2011) have argued occupy the role of intellectuals bringing about (potential) social change in the efforts to construct and deconstruct knowledge production. Freire (1996) provides a more profound idea of schooling arguing that radical critical teaching is needed where teachers are able to examine how schools are engaged in shaping the ideological and material conditions that contribute relationships embedded in domination and struggle. To explore this point further, Giroux (2011) supports the position that education is driven by political interests that aim to empower and legitimise particular ways of life through school structures which reinforce specific values and perspectives that are the domain of the privileged. Essentially, this describes a form of cultural imperialism where the values and perspectives of non-privileged and non-dominant groups are rendered invisible (Delpit, 2006). This is a powerful exemplar of critical pedagogy in action. The imposed school curriculum displaces or overlooks other knowledge(s), advantages dominant groups and is celebrated by society. Therefore, critical pedagogy is noted as a movement that aims to bring about change or to motivate collective action to achieve change by investing in the endeavour to teach others to think critically in order to question and challenge an unjust status quo.

Raising critical consciousness

From a classical perspective, for Freire, critical pedagogy is understood as a movement that supports the development of *conscientizacao*, usually translated as critical consciousness. Liberation from the oppressive status quo, for Freire, begins with the acknowledgement of a system of unequal relations and one's own place in that system. The function of critical pedagogy is to bring members of an oppressed group (non-dominant groups in society) to a critical consciousness of their own situation as a starting point of their liberatory *praxis*. Praxis can be understood as acts which shape and change the world or the steps people take to act on their emerging critical consciousness; thus, a greater sense of awareness or thoughtful examination of taken-for-granted assumptions can be two further illustrations of praxis. Taking this exemplar back to the classroom setting momentarily, the teacher provides a curriculum which helps students to question ideologies and practices considered oppressive (including those at school) and encourage liberatory collective and individual responses to the actual conditions of their own lives. Students begin the process as members of society with its established institutions of power and conformity. Exposure to an alternative view of education can lead to a point of revelation where they begin to view their society as unjust and reflect on their potential to act towards making a change. The purpose of critical pedagogy is therefore one of engagement of learners in the act of conscientizacao (Freire, 1996), hopefully leading to heightened intellectual power. Giroux (1994) talks of the illuminating nature of this knowledge:

> Critical pedagogy . . . signals how questions of audience, voice, power, and evaluation actively work to construct particular relations between teachers and students, institutions and society, and classrooms and communities. . . . Pedagogy in the critical sense illuminates the relationship among knowledge, authority, and power.
>
> (Giroux, 1994: 30)

Thus, a Frierian outlook would combine this recognition of a critical consciousness with the need for concrete action. As students become aware of how social, economic and political systems work and also become conscious of themselves as agents, they can identify and critique this form of domination and control. This ideology has shaped contemporary notions of transformation (Wrigley et al., 2012; Gale and Parker, 2014; El Bouhali, 2015) which, in turn, have influenced the concept of 'pedagogical action' – the belief that all students bring something of value to the learning space, hence the need for a pedagogic curriculum which incorporates and draws on all these sources of knowledge (Moll et al., 1992). Dei (2010: 98) writes of 'epistemological equity' as a movement to counter the ways in which some knowledges are deemed more important than others by the creation of 'spaces where multiple knowledges can co-exist in the western academy is central especially as Eurocentric knowledge subsumes and appropriates other knowledges without crediting their sources' (Dei, 2010: 98).

Conclusion

In the following chapters there will be an examination of critical pedagogy as a means of both imagining a fairer, more ethically just world and as a way of educating hope for a better future for all. Schools and universities have traditionally been seen as sites of cultural and economic reproduction of capitalist relations and class inequalities (Bowles and Gintis, 1976; Bourdieu and Passeron, 1977); however, as Giroux (1992: 218) claims this domination is 'always only partial', thus providing space for teachers and students to challenge hegemonic power. This involves not only raising consciousness of alternatives to the present system but also to develop within individuals the ability to act as agents of change for a more democratic society rather than to merely resign themselves to what is generally seen as the inevitable growth and dominance of neoliberal capitalism.

Points for reflection and consideration in this chapter

This chapter has provided an outline of the nature of the neoliberal state and the perverse logics that arise from an ideology that renders the weak and powerless as insignificant. The notion of education as a public good that is sacred has been proposed, but it is suggested that this has been corrupted and usurped by the wealthy and powerful for their own ends. Alternatives to the current education system have also been identified that restore the importance and centrality of every child, and not just those of the privileged.

- What are your views on the way the neoliberal states such as Britain treat their poor and vulnerable groups?
- Do you think that education is essentially about preparing young people for their future jobs, or should it be about much more than that?
- Can equality of opportunity in education exist in a system that includes the right of the wealthy to pay for an exclusive education for their children?
- Can schools alone ensure that children are able to achieve their full potential?

References

Adams, R., Weale, S., Bengtsson, H. and Carrell (2017). 'UK Schools fail to climb international league table'. *The Guardian*. Available at: https://www.theguardian.com/education/2016/dec/06/english-schools-core-subject-test-results-international-oecd-pisa (Accessed 18 April 2017).

Anderson, B. (2006) *Imagined Communities: Reflections on the Origins and Spread of Nationalism*. London: Verso.

Asthana, A. (2016) 'Theresa May accused of trying to alter immigration report before BREXIT vote'. *The Guardian*. Available at: https://www.theguardian.com/politics/2016/sep/27/theresa-may-accused-trying-to-alter-immigration-report-before-brexit-vote (Accessed 11 February 2017).

Ball, S. (2002) *Class Strategies and the Education Market Place: The Middle Classes and Social Advantage*. London: RoutledgeFalmer.

Ball, S. (2013) *The Education Debate*, 2nd edn. Bristol: The Policy Press.

Ball, S.J., Bowe, R. and Gerwitz, S. (1996) 'School choice, social class and distinction: The realisation of social advantage in education'. *Journal of Educational Policy*. Vol. 11, No. 1, pp. 89–112.

Bamfield, L. and Horton, T. (2009) *Understanding Attitudes to Tackling Economic Inequality*. London: JRF.

Barnes, C. and Mercer, G. (1997) 'Breaking the Mould? An introduction to doing disability research', in C. Barnes and G. Mercer (eds.), *Doing Disability Research*. Leeds: The Disability Press, pp. 1–14.

Berlinski, C. (2007) *'There Is No Alternative': Why Margaret Thatcher Matters*. New York: Basic Books.

Blackmore, J. (2001) 'Universities in crisis? Knowledge economies, emancipatory pedagogies, and the critical intellectual'. *Educational Theory*. Vol. 51, No. 3, pp. 353–371.

Boliver, V. and Swift, A. (2011) 'Do comprehensive schools reduce social mobility?' *British Journal of Sociology*. Vol. 62, No. 1, pp. 211–230.

Booth, R. (2010) 'The spirit level: How "ideas wreckers" turned book into political punch bag'. *The Guardian*. 14 August.
Boronski, T. (2016) 'Grammar schools: A very English solution to a very English problem'. *The Conversation*. Available at: https://theconversation.com/grammar-schools-a-very-english-solution-to-a-very-english-problem-65389
Boronski, T. and Hassan, N. (2015) *Sociology of Education*. London: Sage.
Bourdieu, P. and Passeron, J. (1977) *Reproduction in Education, Society and Culture*. London: Sage.
Bowles, C. and Gintis, H. (1976) *Schooling in Capitalist America: Educational Reform and the Contradictions of Economic Life*. New York: Basic Books.
Burgess, S., Crawford, C. and Macmillan, L. (2017) 'Grammar Schools: Why academic selection only benefits the very affluent'. *The Conversation*. Available at: http://theconversation.com/grammar-schools-why-academic-selection-only-benefits-the-very-affluent-74189 (Accessed 12 April 2017).
Cho, S. (2013) *Critical Pedagogy and Social Change: Critical Analysis on the Language of Possibility*. New York: Routledge.
Crowther, J., Martin, I. and Shaw, M. (eds.) (1999) *Popular Education and Social Movements in Scotland Today*. Leicester: National Institute of Adult Continuing Education.
Crowther, J., Martin, I. and Shaw, M. (2002) 'Re-inventing the civic tradition: In and against the state of higher education', Paper presented at SCUTREA, 32nd Annual Conference, 2–4 July 2002, University of Stirling.
Crowther, J., Galloway, V. and Martin, I. (eds.) (2005a) *Popular Education: Engaging the Academy*. Leicester: NIACE.
Crowther, J., Martin, I. and Shaw, M. (eds.) (2005b) *Renewing Democracy in Scotland: An Educational Source Book*. Leicester: NIACE.
Dahlin, B. (2009) 'On the path towards thinking: Learning from Martin Heidegger and Rudolf Steiner'. *Studies in the Philosophy of Education*. Vol. 28, pp. 537–354.
Darder, A., Baltodano, M.P. and Torres, R.D. (2009) *The Critical Pedagogy Reader*, 2nd edn. London: Routledge.
Dearden, L. (2016) 'Donald Trump boasts of "brilliant" use of US laws to pay as little tax as is legally possible after Hilary Clinton's attack'. *The Independent*. 4 October 2016. Available at: http://www.independent.co.uk/news/world/americas/donald-trump-income-taxes-tax-return-presidential-race-documents-brilliant-use-little-as-possible-a7343751.html (Accessed 27 February 2017).
Dei, G.J.S. (2010) *Teaching Africa: Towards a Transgressive Pedagogy*. Dordrecht: Sense Publisher.
Delpit, L. (2006) *Other People's Children: Cultural Conflict in the Classroom*. New York: New York Press.
Dodd, V. (2011) 'Cost of English riots higher than at first thought, Met Police report says'. *The Guardian*. Available at: https://www.theguardian.com/uk/2011/oct/24/england-riots-cost-police-report (Accessed 10 March 2017).
Dorling, D. (2011) *Injustice*. Bristol: The Policy Press.
Durkheim, E. [1912] (1976) *The Elementary Forms of Religious Life*. London: Allen & Unwin.
Dustmann, C. and Frattini, T. (2014) 'Fiscal impact of immigration to the UK'. *The Economic Journal*. Vol. 124, pp. 593–643.
Dutta, K. (2013) 'Government delays EU migration report because it is too positive'. *The Independent*. Available at: http://www.independent.co.uk/news/uk/politics/government-shelves-eu-immigration-report-because-it-is-too-positive-8994264.html (Accessed 11 February 2017).
Egan, K. (2008) *The Future of Education: Reimagining our Schools from the Ground Up*. New Haven, CT: Yale University Press.
Eisinger, J. (2014) 'Why only one top banker went to jail for the financial crisis'. *The New York Times*. Available at: https://www.nytimes.com/2014/05/04/magazine/only-one-top-banker-jail-financial-crisis.html?_r=0 (Accessed 5 March 2017).
El Bouhali, C. (2015) 'The OECD neoliberal governance', in A.A. Abdi and T. Pillay (eds.), *Decolonising Global Citizenship*. Rotterdam: Sense Publishing, pp. 119–129.
Ford, D.R., Porfilio, B. and Goldstein, R.A. (2015) 'The news media, education and the subversion of the neoliberal social imaginary'. *Critical Education*. Vol. 6, No. 7, pp. 1–23.
Freire, P. (1996) *Pedagogy of the Oppressed*. London: Penguin.
Friedman, M. and Friedman, R. (1980) *Freedom to Choose*. San Diego, CA: Harcourt Brace and Jovanovich.
Fukuyama, F. (1989) 'The End of History?' *The National Interest*. Vol. 16, pp. 3–18.
Gale, T. and Parker, S. (2014) 'Navigating change: A typology of student transition in higher education'. *Studies in Higher Education*. Vol. 39, No. 5, pp. 734–753.
Giroux, H. (1992) *Border Crossings: Cultural Workers and the Politics of Education*. London: Routledge.
Giroux, H. (1994) *Disturbing Pleasures: Learning Popular Culture*. New York: Routledge.

Giroux, H. (2001) 'Utopian Thinking Under the Sign of Neoliberalism: Towards a Critical Pedagogy of Educated Hope'. *Democracy and Nature*. Vol. 9, No.1, pp. 91–105.

Giroux, H. (2009) 'Critical theory and educational practice', in A. Darder and M.P. Baltodano, and D. Torres, (eds.) *The Critical Pedagogy Reader*, 2nd edn. London: Routledge, pp 27–51.

Giroux, H. (2011) *On Critical Pedagogy*. London: Bloomsbury.

Gov.uk. (2017) 'Prime Minister unveils plans to transform mental health support'. *Press Release*. Available at: https://www.gov.uk/government/news/prime-minister-unveils-plans-to-transform-mental-health-support (Accessed 13 April 2017).

Gove, M. (2012) 'Education Secretary Michael Gove's speech to Brighton College'. Available at: www.gov.uk/government/speeches/education-secretary-michael-goves-speech-to-brighton-college (Accessed 14 January 2015).

Guardian Datablog. (2011) 'England riots: was poverty a factor?' Available at: http://www.guardian.co.uk/news/datablog/2011/aug/16/riots-poverty-map-suspects (Accessed 21 October 2011).

Harrington, B. (2018) 'The bad behavior of the richest: what I learned from wealth managers'. *The Guardian*. 19 October. Available at: https://www.theguardian.com/us-news/2018/oct/19/billionaires-wealth-richest-income-inequality (Accessed 12 April 2020).

Hart, S. and Drummond, M.J. (2014) 'Learning without limits: Constructing a pedagogy free from determinist beliefs about ability', in L. Florian (ed.), *The Sage Handbook of Special Education*. London: Sage, pp 439–458.

Hazzard, K. (2017) 'Empire 2.0 and Brexiteers' "swashbuckling" vision of Britain will raise hackles around the world'. *The Conversation*. Available at: https://theconversation.com/empire-2-0-and-brexiteers-swashbuckling-vision-of-britain-will-raise-hackles-around-the-world-76101 (Accessed 21 April 2017).

Her Majesty's Government. (2009) *Unleashing Aspiration: The Final Report of the Panel on Fair Access to the Professions (the Milburn Report)*. London: Cabinet Office.

Her Majesty's Government. (2011) *Opening Doors, Breaking Barriers: A Strategy for Social Mobility*. London: Cabinet Office.

hooks, b. (1994). *Teaching to Transgress: Education as the Practice of Freedom*. New York: Routledge.

Illich, I. (1976) *Medical Nemesis: The Expropriation of Health*. New York: Pantheon Books.

Institute for Public Policy Research. (2016) *Education, Education, Mental Health: Supporting Secondary Schools to Play a Central Role in Early Intervention Mental Health Services*. London: IPPR.

Jackson-Preece, J. (2016) 'Is nationalism to blame for the post Brexit vote divisions?' *LSE Blog*. 29 June. Available at: https://blogs.lse.ac.uk/brexit/2016/06/29/is-nationalism-to-blame-for-the-post-brexit-vote-divisions/ (Accessed 21 July 2020).

Johnson, B. (2013) 'Boris Johnson: 3rd Margaret Thatcher Lecture (FULL)'. Available at: www.youtube.com/watch?v=DzIgrnr1ZB0 (Accessed 15 December 2015).

Jones, O. (2011) *Chavs: The Demonization of the Working Class*. London: Verso.

Kane, L. (2001) *Popular Education and Social Change in Latin America*. London: Latin America Bureau.

Katz, L. (2014) *Teachers' Reflections on Critical Pedagogy in the Classroom*. file:///C:/Users/nasima.hassan/AppData/Local/Packages/Microsoft.MicrosoftEdge_8wekyb3d8bbwe/TempState/Downloads/eScholarship%20UC%20item%202c6968hc.pdf (Accessed August 2017).

Kynaston, D. and Kynaston, G. (2014) 'Education's Berlin Wall: The private school Conundrum'. *New Statesman*. Available at: http://www.newstatesman.com/2014/01/education-private-schools-berlin-wall (Accessed 14 April 2017).

Ladson-Billings, G. (2006) '"Yes, but how do we do it?": Practicing culturally relevant pedagogy', in J. Landsman and C.W. Lewis (eds.), *White Teachers/Diverse Classrooms*. Sterling, VA: Stylus, pp 29–42.

Lightowlers, C. and Quirk, H. (2014) 'The 2011 English "riots": Prosecutorial zeal and judicial abandon'. *British Journal of Criminology*. Vol. 54(5): 65–85.

Madden, D. (2016) 'Don't blame foreign investors: The problem lies closer to home'. *The Guardian*. 4 October. Available at: https://www.theguardian.com/commentisfree/2016/oct/04/foreign-investors-housing-crisis-sadiq-khan-london (Accessed 2 February 2017).

Mason, R. (2017) 'Corbyn calls for wage cap on bosses at government contractors'. *The Guardian*. 10 January. Available at: https://www.theguardian.com/politics/2017/jan/10/corbyn-proposes-maximum-wage-for-all-government-contractors (Accessed 10 February 2017).

Moll, L., Amanti, C., Neff, D. and Gonzalez, N. (1992) 'Funds of knowledge for teaching: Using a qualitative approach to connect homes and classroom'. *Theory into Practice*. Vol. 31, No. 1, pp. 132–141.

Nozik, R. (1974) *Anarchy, State and Utopia*. Oxford: Blackwell.

NUT. (2016) *The Mismanagement of Learning: How Tests Are Damaging Children and Primary Education. Reclaiming Schools: The Evidence and the Arguments.* London: NUT Communications Department.

Ostry, J., Loungani, P. and Furceri, D. (2016) *Neoliberalism: Oversold?* Washington, DC: International Monetary Fund.
Pakulski, J. and Waters, M. (1996) *The Death of Class*. London: Sage.
Park, J. (ed.) (2013) *Bertrand Russell: On Education*. London: Routledge.
Pickett, K. and Wilkinson, R. (2017) 'Without equality of income there can be no equality of opportunity'. *The Conversation*. Available at: https://theconversation.com/without-equality-of-income-there-can-be-no-equality-of-opportunity-80488 (Accessed 15 August 2017).
Piketty, T. (2014) *Capital in the Twenty-First Century*. Transl. Arthur Goldhammer. Cambridge, MA: Belknap Harvard University Press.
Piketty, T. (2020) *Capital and Ideology*. Transl. Arthur Goldhammer. Cambridge, MA: Harvard University Press.
PISA. (2013) *Education at a Glance: OECD Indicators*. Paris: OECD Publishing.
PISA. (2015a) *Programme for International Student Assessment (PISA) Results from PISA 2015. Country Note: United Kingdom*. Paris: OECD Publishing.
PISA. (2015b) *Programme for International Student Assessment (PISA) Results from PISA 2015 Students' Well-being. Country Note: United Kingdom*. Paris: OECD Publishing.
Pople, L., Rees, G., Main, G. and Bradshaw, J. (2015) *The Good Childhood Report*. London: The Children's Society.
Rawls, J. (1999) *A Theory of Justice: Revised Edition*. Cambridge, MA: Belknap/Harvard University Press.
Rethinking Economics. (2017) 'Reforming the curriculum'. Available at: http://www.rethinkeconomics.org/get-involved/why-reform-the-curriculum/ (Accessed 5 March 2017).
Robbins, L. (1932) *An Essay on the Nature and Significance of Economic Science*. London: Macmillan.
Royal College of Paediatrics and Child Health. (2017) *State of Child Health Report 2017*. London: RCPCH.
Sanandaji, N., Malm, A. and Sanandaji, T. (2010) *The Spirit Illusion: A Critical Analysis of How "The Spirit Level" Compares Countries*. London: The TaxPayers' Alliance.
Saunders, P. (2010) *Beware False Prophets: Equality, the Good Society and the Spirit Level*. London: Policy Exchange.
Savage, M., Cunningham, N., Devine, F., Friedman, S., Laurison, D., McKenzie, L., Miles, A., Snee, H. and Wakeling, P. (2015) *Social Class in the 21st Century*. London: Pelican.
Shor, I. (1987) *Freire for the Classroom*. Portsmouth, NH: Boynton, Cook Publishers.
Shor, I. and Freire, P. (1987) *A Pedagogy for Liberation: Dialogues on Transforming Education*. Westport, CT: Bergin & Garvey Publishers.
Slaughter, S. and Leslie, L. (1999) *Academic Capitalism: Politics, Policies and the Entrepreneurial University*. Baltimore, MA: John Hopkins University Press.
Smyth, J. (2011) *Critical Pedagogy for Social Justice*. London: Continuum Press.
Smyth, J. and Wrigley, T. (2013) *Living on the Edge: Rethinking Poverty, Class and Schooling*. Oxford: Peter Lang.
Snowdon, C. (2010) *The Spirit Level Delusion: Fact-Checking the Left's Theory of Everything*. London: Little Dice.
Stanford, J. (2015) *Economics for Everyone: A Short Guide to the Economics of Capitalism*, 2nd edn. London: Pluto Press.
Stewart, H. and Walker, P. (2017) 'Social care crisis: MPs put May under pressure to act fast'. *The Guardian*. Available at: https://www.theguardian.com/society/2017/jan/06/social-care-crisis-theresa-may-under-pressure-to-act-fast (Accessed 2 February 2017).
Szasz, T. (1977) *The Manufacture of Madness*. Syracuse: Syracuse University Press.
Tamimi, S. (2010) 'The McDonaldisation of childhood: Children's mental health in neo-liberal market cultures'. *Transcultural Psychiatry*. Vol. 47, No. 5, pp. 686–706.
The Economist. (2013) 'Why have so few bankers gone to jail?' Available at: http://www.economist.com/blogs/economist-explains/2013/05/economist-explains-why-few-bankers-gone-to-jail (Accessed 5 March 2017).
UNICEF. (2007) *Report Card 7: Child Poverty in Perspective: An Overview of Child Well-Being in Rich Countries*. Florence: UNICEF Innocenti Research Centre.
UNICEF. (2011) *Child Poverty in the UK*. London: UNICEF. Available at: www.unicef.org.uk/Documents/Publications/Child%20poverty%20in%20the%20UKUNICEF%20UK%20Information%20Sheet.pdf (Accessed 15 January 2015).
UNICEF. (2013) *Report Card 11: The Well-Being of Children: How Does the UK Score?* Florence: UNICEF Innocenti Research Centre.

Walters, S. and Manicom, L. (eds.) (1996) *Gender in Popular Education. Methods for Empowerment*. London: Zed Books.

Wilkinson, R. and Pickett, K. (2009) *The Spirit Level: Why More Equal Societies Almost Always Do Better*. London: Penguin.

Wilkinson, R. and Pickett, K. (2018) *The Inner Level: How More Equal Societies Reduce Stress, Restore Sanity and Improve Everyone's Well-being*. London: Allen Lane.

Wrigley, T., Lingard, B. and Thomson, P. (2012) 'Pedagogies of transformation: Keeping hope alive in troubled times'. *Critical Studies in Education*. Vol. 53, No. 1, pp. 95–108.

Wyporska, W. (2017) 'Welcome to "Fat Cat Wednesday" – The day that marks when FTSE 100 CEOs have already earned your entire salary for 2017'. *The Independent*. Available at: http://www.independent.co.uk/voices/fat-cat-wednesday-what-is-it-ftse-100-ceos-executive-pay-earned-average-british-salary-2017-a7508531.html (Accessed 13 February).

Yorke, H. (2017) 'A level results 2016: The top 100 secondary schools'. *Daily Telegraph*. 19 January. Available at: http://www.telegraph.co.uk/education/2017/01/19/level-results-2016-top-100-secondary-schools/ (Accessed 18 April 2017).

2 Imagining an alternative world

Introduction

In the previous chapter, we saw how the free market has been portrayed almost as a natural force operating outside the field of morality and ethics, just as the forces of nature, in which any attempt to intervene is seen by its proponents as interfering in the natural order that can only end in disaster such as totalitarian government. So, any state policies designed to address the social injustices that are a consequence of unfettered market capitalism are branded as the desire to take us back to the dark days of Soviet-style Communism. Resorting to such extreme dichotomies clearly reduces the debate to a simplistic set of alternatives in which any attempt to tackle the growing injustices caused by the growing gap between the rich and the poor is branded as 'the politics of envy' or an attack on the so-called wealth creators who should instead, as Boris Johnson (2013) claims, be hailed as heroes.

The possibility of alternatives

There are, however, many possible alternatives to the current neoliberal capitalist path, and fairer and more socially just societies can not only be imagined and aimed for, but already exist. Evidence collected by Wilkinson and Pickett (2009, 2018) over four decades on the most affluent market democracies suggests that levels of inequality within these societies greatly influence the overall welfare of their all their citizens, rich and poor. Using a wide range of international data relating to health, life expectancy, educational attainment, the environment and crime, Wilkinson and Pickett (2009, 2018) found that in the most unequal societies not only do the less well-off do badly, but so also does the rest of the population when compared to the least unequal societies. Highly unequal societies are, on the basis of this objective evidence, generally less pleasant places to live for the majority. In this respect it is suggested that the American Dream is a myth, as the US is one of the most unequal societies in the developed world. If American citizens wish to live in a society where they and their children are most likely to achieve their full potential in terms of education and employment, Richard Wilkinson (Ted-ED, 2013) claims that they should move to Denmark, one of the least unequal market democracies. If better is possible, at least in terms of objective criteria, a key obstacle is the belief that there is no alternative to the present system and that any other views are seen as 'utopian' or as an attack on enterprise and individual freedoms. Indeed, utopianism has been branded as not just unrealistic but potentially dangerous (Hayek,

1944; Shklar, 1957; Popper, 1962; Gray, 2007). Writing at the end of the Second World War, Popper (1962) presents a scathing attack on any attempt to provide a blueprint for a society, stating that no matter how carefully planned, it will inevitably encounter unforeseen obstacles. As a consequence, Popper believes that the only way such an ideal state can be achieved is through a powerful centralising authority that will inevitably result in dictatorship. So, for Popper, the rigidity of a strong utopian blueprint is incompatible with the inevitable consequences of unknown obstacles that are likely to arise. Popper's approach to utopianism is based on an anti-utopian belief in the dangers of systemic definitions that identify specific places to be created:

> It is the sweep of Utopianism, its attempt to deal with society as a whole, leaving no stone unturned. It is the conviction that one has to go to the very root of the social evil, that nothing short of a complete eradication of the offending social system will do...
>
> (Popper, 1962: 164)

As a consequence, Popper brands Plato's *Republic* as the prototype for all totalitarian systems that followed and in *The Open Society and Its Enemies* (vol. 1, Popper, 1962) carries out a comprehensive assault on Plato's historicist utopian engineering, advocating instead a piecemeal social engineering approach to social change governed by a policy of trial and error in which we learn from the mistakes we make, rather than dogmatically following a preconceived vision of the future. In doing so Popper accuses Plato of betraying his teacher and mentor Socrates, whose critical reasoning is seen as the path to the *open society*.

Gray (2007) presents a similar position and suggests that utopias are based on a destructive mixture of the impossible belief in human perfectibility and the use of violence to achieve it that results in totalitarianism. This is a very narrow and gloomy view of what is possible for humanity to achieve, for even if we cannot reach perfection we should not restrict our ambitions to make a better world by either succumbing to a defeatist belief that there is no alternative and that any alternative is either an unrealistic romanticism or that such proposals will only lead to oppressive dictatorship. Moreover, these interpretations of utopian writing are misplaced and miss the point. Such works of the imagination, even comprehensive visions, are essential aspects of the human condition which involve self-reflection through literature, art, music, dance and poetry, all of which illustrate our ability to dream of different ways of living and organising ourselves politically, socially and economically (Ricoeur, 1986).

Adopting a utopian spirit

This chapter will examine the possibility of imagining something different to the continued and relentless marketisation of social, economic and educational systems, the ultimate logic of which leads to the subjugation of all humanity to a process of dehumanisation. It will do so by enlisting the support of a utopian spirit of thinking of the world differently, of making the familiar unfamiliar and of making the unfamiliar something to reflect on as a possible future. In doing this, there would need to be a process of disruption which would force us to reconsider our taken-for-granted assumptions (Garfinkel, 1967), for it is only when we actively reflect on our lives that we are able see the contradictions and injustices that exist and to take the next step, which is to change them. However, in terms of what we could be, there is no single blueprint for a better world because it would first require an informed dialogue between all groups in society and, second, because utopia is not an ultimate destination but an ongoing process of change and development based on this dialogue that is constantly required to meet the needs of new situations that may arise. As William Morris claims (Morris and Bax, 1893: 17–18), 'It is impossible to build a scheme for the society of the future, for no man can really think himself out of his own days'. The role of critical pedagogy is crucial here in terms of facilitating that dialogue and of educating hope.

Ernst Bloch (1986) suggests that there is something essentially human in longing for a better world or to fill a void which gives greater meaning to life. This restless desire, he claims, is only fulfilled by imagining dreams becoming a reality. For Bloch, this human longing is so natural that it manifests itself in all aspects of human culture, including art, literature, music, philosophy as well as science, all of which create utopian worlds of possibility. This requires, in the words of Abensour (1999), the 'education of desire', which emphasises the importance of imagining alternative ways of being, not as specific models of the future but as a necessary part of the process of bringing about change. In the current neoliberal system, we need to make strange the ideas and processes which we are beginning to take for granted and think of as normal: greed, unrestricted acquisitiveness, self-interest, individualism, human domination over nature and the belief that there is no alternative to the dehumanising system of neoliberal capitalism and the relentless exploitation of the world's resources. Without this we are unable to imagine alternatives. Such imaginings are therefore part of this education of desire and the beginning of any attempt to improve the world.

In *Pedagogy of Freedom* (2001) Paulo Freire also examines the nature of human longing that involves a consciousness of our having choices and of the 'unfinishedness' of our lives and existence. In being aware of this we develop the potential to learn and of our role in making the world which is also unfinished. Such an awareness suggests that there are options available to us and that things are not predetermined. They can take a number of possible courses which are effectively limited only by our imagination. However, there is the possibility that, rather than getting better, things can get worse and for critical pedagogy there is no teleological notion of the inevitability of a better and more humane future for all. What is inevitable for Freire, however, is the human desire for something better and that this can be stimulated through a pedagogy of hope which can transform the consciousness of individuals from that of compliant and silent acceptance of their oppression to one of a critical consciousness and the desire to change the world through *praxis* (Freire, 1997). The awakening of this hope is an essential element in creating the possibility of change, for without it 'instead of history we would have pure determinism. History exists only where time is problematized and not simply a given. A future that is inexorable is a denial of history' (Freire, 2001: 69).

Utopia's fall from grace

The twentieth century, however, was a period of disenchantment with utopias and utopian thinking that involved the collapse of Soviet-style communism and before that the defeat of Nazi Germany that foresaw a thousand years of fascist rule under the Third Reich. This is also reflected in philosophical approaches that reject concepts of the ideal state or other such grand narratives and instead focus on critiques of any attempts to impose ideas of truth and certainty. It is such modernist grand schemes and plans for the ideal society that lost credibility during the late twentieth century in much intellectual thinking and political life. With the relatively peaceful revolutions in Central and Eastern Europe in 1989 and the collapse of the Soviet Union in 1991, almost seventy-five years of socialism came to an end, the question arose as to what alternative was there to Western capitalism?

In Western Europe, commentators on the Left as well as Right were writing not only of the death of socialism as it existed but also of its ultimate successor: communism, as systems of beliefs and as futures to aim for (Dahrendorf, 1990; Garton Ash, 1990; Hobsbawm, 1990). There was little inclination generally to distinguish between the different types of socialism, especially by those on the Right, despite the attempts by democratic socialists to provide an alternative to the state socialism of the Soviet era. The Communist Party of Great Britain (CPGB) produced a *Manifesto for New Times* in 1989 as a response to the collapse of traditional state communism and the emergence of 'Post-Fordism' in Western capitalist economies that, it was suggested, required a new type of radical politics. What they were describing is the rise of neoliberal capitalism with its global reach and its successful assault on traditional class-based politics and the welfare state. Indeed, the CPGB had spent the previous decade assessing the reasons for the continuing resilience and growth of capitalism rather than its decline which Marx had predicted (Hobsbawm, 1978). In the *Manifesto* Hall and Jacques (1989) presented a way forward for an alternative future based on such policies as an internationalist and environmentally sustainable economy, a citizens' wage and devolved democratic and local politics supported by the new information technology. What is remarkable is that not only are these policies on the political agenda in countries such as the UK, but some are actually becoming a reality (Henderson, 2016; Sodha, 2017). However, within a couple of years the Soviet Union had collapsed and the CPGB too had folded. In Britain, as in other parts of Western Europe, a sense of ennui took hold with parties on the Left disbanding or erasing any reference to communism. These events effectively marked the end not only of socialism but also the end of utopia as a modernist project (Stedman Jones, 1990). For many, socialism epitomised the utopian vision of a secular heaven in which all other utopias had been subsumed. Utopia had become so closely tied to socialism that the death of one effectively meant the death of the other (Kumar, 1992).

In the struggle for freedom from Soviet-style 'utopianism' intellectuals such as Vaclav Havel spoke of a 'far-reaching ... central European scepticism about Utopianism of all colors about the slightest suggestions of Utopianism' (Havel, 1985). Whilst recognising that 'dreams of a better world are surely a fundamental aspect of authentic humanity' (Havel, 1985), Havel was speaking for many Eastern Europeans at the time when he warned of the tendency for 'fanatics' to take control and to create 'short cuts' to their better world. It is hardly surprising then that, having experienced their share of failed political experiments based on the blueprints of a string of fanatics, there was a desire in Eastern Europe for a more benign politics, an 'anti-political politics' which entails 'Politics "from below": Politics of man, *not of the apparatus*. Politics growing from the heart, *not from a thesis*' (emphasis added) (Havel, 1984).

The growing dominance of global capitalism together with the suspicion of utopias on both the political Right and the political Left has led to what some have called a 'crisis of hope' (Amsler, 2008) in which humanity has lost the desire to believe in alternatives to the present system. For Amsler (2008: 302), a key feature of this crisis is the 'reification of impossibility' in which utopianism is associated with naive romanticism. Jameson (2004: 41) refers to this 'revolt against utopia' as something which has been evident in both intellectual and political life. Few politicians wish to be associated with notions of the ideal society, and even those on the Left rarely use terms such as 'socialism' or 'communism', except as terms of warning or derision. In the field of utopian studies, there is a persistent awareness of the postmodern injunction to avoid presenting ideas which might be seen as systemic or telic (Amsler, 2008; Levitas, 2013).

And yet, it would seem that utopianism, as a literary form as well as political and social philosophy, continues to be revived to the point that it almost seems to be an eternal theme of human longing and desire to fill the 'scarcity gap' (Levitas, 1990: 209) in our lives, that is, the void between our desires and the satisfaction of those desires. Levitas proposes a broad approach to utopia which she suggests is the 'desire for a different, better way of being' (ibid., 2009) but shies away from the suggestion that this desire is an essential human trait as Marcuse (1955, 1968, 1970), Bloch (1961) and Freire (2001) would claim. Whilst it is clearly not possible to declare that it is an essential human trait to desire in such a way, what can be argued is the possibility as well as the necessity to educate human desire for such change. Moreover, it could be seen as essential if humanity is to think creatively and act effectively in order to avert the kinds of social, political, economic and environmental disasters that threaten us all.

The renewal of the utopian spirit

Whether it is viewed as an essential part of human nature or a culturally produced phenomenon, utopian literature and practice are in evidence throughout history since Ancient times to the present. It could be viewed as part of the moral consciousness of society that represents a recurring and restless desire to reassess its identity and place in the world. In his survey of utopian writing since 1516, when Thomas More's *Utopia* was first published, Sargent (2010) claims that there has been a regular and continuous output of utopian works by authors from various societies regarding issues deemed to be in need of urgent attention. Be it poverty and inequality, environmental protection, political and legal rights or a need for spiritual renewal, in general the desire is to create a better world.

However, as Sargent (2010) shows in his research, each epoch produces specific issues and problems that require urgent action and 'Utopias are reflections of the issues that were important to the period in which their author lived' (Sargent, 2010: 21). There is, to use the words of Weber (1949), a degree of 'value-relevance' to their choice and identification of such issues. The present is clearly no exception. The effects of neoliberal economic and welfare policies on the poor (UNHRC, 2019), the legacy of colonialism (Heleta, 2016), the threat of global warming and environmental destruction resulting from the continued and reckless use of fossil fuels (Davenport and Pierre-Lewis, 2018; National Geographic, 2019) and the refugee crisis resulting from regional wars and poverty (Paynter, 2019), to name but a few of the issues that currently take the form of what can only be identified as *super wicked problems* (Levin et al., 2012), have provoked utopian-like responses in the form of social and political action (Taylor-Collins, 2018; Youth Strike 4 Climate, 2019; Zero Hour, 2019) and dystopian as well as utopian literature (Willmetts, 2017).

This growing desire for a better world is reflected in the new approach to utopian theoretical and literary studies and the perceived purpose of utopian fiction. There has been a clear move away from blueprint utopianism that takes utopia as a single end point and towards a *processual utopianism* (Brincat, 2009) that is characterised by a continual drive to address the imperfections and injustices in society. As Fredric Jameson (2005), one of the foremost scholars of utopianism in both its literary and theoretical form suggests, utopianism's function is now *not* one of presenting us with models of the perfect society; instead, it reminds us about our own limitations and the importance of continuing our attempts to improve society through the ending of gender inequality, institutional racism and other oppressive hierarchical systems and environmental destruction from which weak and vulnerable groups suffer most. It is in this form that Jameson (2005: xii) claims 'Utopia seems to have recovered its vitality as a political slogan and a politically energizing perspective'.

The new utopian spirit and the education of desire

A key figure in developing *new utopian studies* is Miguel Abensour (1999), who has contributed greatly to making utopianism respectable again by rescuing it from attacks by anti-utopians who associate it with left-wing authoritarianism. His thesis, which only became available in English translation in 1999, was already making an impact through much of Europe during the 1970s and 1980s on the basis of his idea of the 'education of desire'. The term is now used widely by writers in the new utopianism, often with little reference to Abensour himself. As Nadir (2010: 50) notes, 'Their mentions ... demonstrate the permeation of the name "Abensour" throughout Anglo-American utopian studies without any reference to Abensour's actual written work'. In his writing, Abensour addresses the paradox that has long haunted utopianism through much of the twentieth century: why is it that utopian promises of emancipation lead to dystopian systems characterised by authoritarianism and oppression? This has been an essential step in Abensour's development of a new approach to utopianism. Using Adorno and Horkheimer's (1972) theory in *Dialectic of Enlightenment* in which they explain how the promise of liberation and freedom expected through the discovery of 'truth' and enlightened understanding of the world is reversed and becomes its opposite: domination and oppression, Abensour claims that within utopianism there lies a similar dialectic which he refers to as the *dialectic of emancipation* in which the emancipatory promise contained in utopia also contains the threat of becoming its opposite: of turning into oppressive totalitarianism. It is this paradox that Abensour claims the new utopian spirit has set itself the task of addressing (Abensour, 1999). So, although he has identified the significance of the new spirit in the education of desire, he also alerts us to the dangers of potentially dystopian outcomes.

This latter point is one that Nadir (2010) suggests has been overlooked by many new utopian scholars who tend to focus instead on a renewed utopia, liberated from its previous status as purveyor of static and totalising notions of a different future. For this more positive and optimistic approach, the shift is to see utopias as heuristic rather than systematic futures (Williams, 1978). It is now possible to desire without being accused of advocating unreasonable or impossible dreams because utopias act now as a means of educating desire rather than as specific systems to be created. This education is enacted through the analysis and critique of literary utopias as part of a process of stimulating new visions of the future and the desire for action to create a better world. However, Abensour is not content with the simple process of the critique of literary utopias, as he claims that the education of desire is not achieved merely by avoiding a focus on the 'perfect' society with a fixed end point. He suggests that the new utopianism should concern itself with the mechanisms by which the utopian spirit can transform itself from being a means of offering freedom and liberation to its opposite and with how to resist this 'dialectic of emancipation' (Abensour, 1999: 127). For Abensour utopia is constantly under threat from anti-democratic tendencies, and yet he suggests that modern democracy suffers from the lack of a utopian spirit. What is required, he claims, is for the new utopian spirit to be infused with a new democratic imagination. As he states in 'Utopie et démocratie', 'One of the essential questions of modernity ... [is how] to democratize utopia ... and utopianize democracy' (Abensour, 2001, cited in and translated by Nadir, 2010: 28). To this end, Abensour focuses on William Morris's (1891) romantic and 'marvelous' novel *News from Nowhere* to show how in this work and in its creation, Morris has developed a new and innovative form of presenting utopia and, in the process, Abensour claims, Morris manages to merge both the utopian and democratic imaginations and thereby educate desire.

Morris's method is to create a 'play' between the democratic imagination and the utopian romance in the book through the creation of a dialogic exchange between readers and the author. Instead of writing in the form of a fixed and 'closed medium of the book' (Abensour, 1999: 132), Morris published *News from Nowhere* over a ten-week period in 1890 through the medium of the socialist periodical *Commonweal*. The readership of committed socialists was invited to respond to the utopian story as it was being written and to submit their ideas for improvements and alterations, thereby collaborating in developing their own utopia that achieves a democratic awareness of the dangers of the fixed and closed system. As an open work it presents a utopia that is incomplete and dreamlike in a form that inspires the imagination and invites contributions from its readers. The author does not present a completed utopia but a medium by which space is created to allow others to identify how it can be made better. In doing so, the fragility of the utopia is constantly exposed and solutions proposed.

News from nowhere: plot, structure and method

News from Nowhere is an example of what Abensour (1999) describes as representing a new type of European literature that marks a break with traditional approaches to utopia characterised by presentations of perfect societies that are coherent and fully formed. The new utopian spirit coincides with the publication in 1848 of Marx and Engels's *Communist Manifesto* and the outbreak of revolutions throughout Europe at the time and is more open and speculative. The novel is an experiment in socialism that takes a literary form. The narrator William Guest who wakes up one morning to find himself two hundred years in the future, in an England that has experienced a socialist revolution and has settled into a post-revolutionary period of calm, relative peace and happiness: an 'epoch of rest'. There is no want, homelessness or exploitation by capitalist employers and landowners as the production of goods and services is carried out not for pay, as there is no money, but on the basis of need and craft production, though machines are available for such tasks. Work, both mental and manual, is not seen as a painful chore but as an activity to be done voluntarily, communally as well as through creative acts.

There are three parts to the book. The first is where William Guest is befriended by Dick and Clara and taken on a trip through the new London to meet Old Hammond. In the second part, Guest hears from Hammond about the revolution and how the new England came about and how it is run. The third part describes a three-day journey up the Thames from Hammersmith to the source of the river in Oxfordshire. On his travels Guest sees the dramatic changes to the environment in which industrial squalor is replaced by green fields and pleasant towns and villages where the population is evenly spread, rather than being concentrated in cities. Without private property no individual is able to control housing and deny another person the right to a place to live. With the abolition of private property and wealth, the need for a state that protects the rights of the rich declined and it has withered away. Administration and decision-making that relate to community interests and welfare take place at meetings of *the neighbours* known as *Motes*. Outcomes of debates are decided on the basis of majority rule, though in cases of a small majority the minority does have the opportunity to make its case at a future meeting. It is this section of the book which, though still quite thin in terms of detail, fits the more traditional approach to utopia. The third and final part of the book, according to Abensour, is the most utopian, imbued as it is with what he refers to as the 'utopian marvellous' (Abensour, 1999: 132). This is essentially a literary form common in the mediaeval world of chivalry in which romance and courtly love coincide with heroic tasks, such as the quest for the Holy Grail (communism?), through ethereal and often magical landscapes that provoke desire and imagination (Hamilton, 1990). The form this third part takes is implied in the subtitle of the book – *News from Nowhere; or, An Epoch of Rest, Being Some Chapters from a Utopian Romance* – and involves just such a romantic journey by Guest up the Thames in all its riparian beauty with his companion Ellen in a quest for something precious but elusive:

> This is the moment that News from Nowhere grasps, the epiphany that transforms England into an island of happiness. But this moment is fragile and necessarily ephemeral, for as soon as it is achieved, the threat of separation surges on the horizon as if in anticipation of the fading of the time of rest at nightfall, the protagonists of News from Nowhere were preparing for the experience of new tensions.
> (Abensour, 1999: 132–133)

In *News from Nowhere* Morris creates an experiment in socialism, not in a fixed and preconceived form, but as provisional and incomplete, with open spaces to stimulate the reader to imagine and indeed desire somewhere better. The focus is more specifically to provoke alternatives to traditional bourgeois concepts of happiness relating to wealth, control, ownership of possessions as well as to traditional Marxist approaches to socialism that focus on utilitarian matters of the economy and the centrality of work.

The originality of Morris's approach then, according to Abensour, is in his rejection of the classical utopian approach of constructing a preconceived model of a future society on which a new moral and social order can be based, with all of its political, juridical and economic structures and systems explained within a coherent doctrine. However, when it was published there was widespread criticism of *News from Nowhere* in the press and from socialist thinkers that it lacked an 'educational method', that is, a set of comprehensive guidelines for us to follow and learn from. This omission was deemed to be its main weakness. Nevertheless, Abensour suggests that far from being its weakness, this is in fact its strength, for *News from Nowhere* succeeds in the education of desire through its readers and critics pointing to its failings and lacunae, and who, by correcting or improving them, thereby alert us to the risks attached to any rigid 'monological principle of utopian socialism' (Abensour, 1999: 131).

The role of dialogue and the opportunity to question, challenge and contribute to a debate about a future society is an essential process in the education of desire and is crucial in what Abensour sees as the need to democratise utopia in order to prevent it from degenerating into dystopia.

Utopian literature and the education of desire

Abensour's new spirit of utopianism is particularly relevant in the context of the looming ecological crisis, for what it also suggests is the dialectic of emancipation extant in the current desire for a cleaner and more sustainable environment. The point is made clearly by Nadir (2010) in relation to her analysis of Ursula Le Guin's novel *The Dispossessed* (1974). The story is set on the worlds of Anarres and Urras, the former is an anarchist society beset with acute ecological problems and resource shortages, and the latter, dominated by two systems – one capitalist and the other left-wing authoritarian – is endowed with a wealth of natural resources. The occupants of Anarres address the issue of scarcity through two key systems. One is through what is called the Production and Distribution Coordination (PDC) organisation which manages the planet's natural resources. The second is that the conduct of daily life is based on an ideology known as Odonianism. This was developed by the philosopher Laia Odo who, though a Urrasian, her ideas were adopted by the anarchists of Anarres. Odo developed both an ecological theory and a socio-political theory that were merged to form a social system ostensibly geared to maximise resource security of the planet.

In this condition, the Anarresti are led to believe that their environmentalism inspired by Odo is based on necessity and scarcity but one which ultimately diminishes their opportunity to seek the fulfilment of needs that do not directly relate to the basic human requirements of food and shelter. In fact, the philosophy of selflessness and sacrifice become so dominant that aesthetic pursuits such as music and art are subjected to the arbitrary judgement of the PDC. Anything deemed to be of threat to ecological survival is banned. However, as Nadir (2010) points out, the position of the Anarresti is such that living in conditions of scarcity and environmental pressure makes them highly vulnerable to domination. The discourse of scarcity dominates all aspects of life to the point where questioning the prevailing ideas and practices of self-sacrifice are met with serious social sanctions, such as in terms of career progression. Indeed, this is what befalls the protagonist Shevek, a physicist whose discovery known as general temporal theory which had the potentially inestimable value of making space-time communication instantaneous. His research, however, falls foul of Odonianist principles of 'social organic utility', that is, of not being essential to survival. As a result, it is terminated by his superiors who justify their decision on the grounds of the danger posed from greater communication with outsiders may cause the young to question their abstemious and ascetic lifestyles. What is evident here is the ambiguity of this utopian society of Anarres, which is clearly implied in the subtitle of some editions of the book: *An ambiguous utopia*. In presenting Anarres as a place of imperfections and contradictions where the promise of freedom is cut off and controlled by oppressive ideologies and practices, there is a clear threat to turn such a promise of emancipation into a dystopia.

These points highlight the significance of *The Dispossessed* as an important contribution to the discussions relating to utopianism today and, more specifically, the dangers inherent in creating and living in 'ecotopias'. Indeed, much of Le Guin's philosophical and ecological influences come from the work of the post-scarcity anarchist Murray Bookchin (1991), who claims that environmentalism should be based on an awareness of creative human needs and not merely physical ones. He points to the dangers in which environmentalism can use the mantra of ecology and scarcity to dominate life; 'There is a point at which society begins to intervene in the formation of needs to produce a very special type of scarcity: a socially induced scarcity' (Bookchin, 1991: 68). Moreover, as Nadir (2010) points out, *The Dispossessed* anticipates a future in which ecotopias are not based on the principle of desire or 'willed transformation' (Williams, 1978) in which a temporary sacrifice is made in the hope of achieving a world of plenty and abundance, but instead, of a future world in which not only is such transformation forced upon us but requires continuous sacrifice if the planet and its inhabitants are to survive.

Addressing the dialectic of emancipation

The dialectic of emancipation is clearly a key issue in the development of a new utopian spirit; however, if an important function of the education of desire is to create a will to change and for a transformation of society, then how is this to be achieved in terms of Abensour's approach to the education of desire? Abensour claims that in *News from Nowhere* Morris creates the first utopian work to present a utopia that sets out to be self-critical and to invite the subversion of its own ideas, principles and institutions (Nadir, 2010). In this process of resisting the dialectic of freedom, the result is an 'endless experimentation and incompleteness' (Abensour, 1999: 156–157) in which we find ourselves in a process that 'endlessly defers utopia's realization'. Nevertheless, Allison (2018) suggests that Morris does provide some ideas as to how this problem can be overcome by claiming that he proposes a vision of the future that is shared by others: 'Yes, surely! and if others can see it as I have seen it, then it may be called a vision rather than a dream' (Morris, 1891: ch. 32). This vision, Allison (2018) suggests, constitutes a basis upon which to create a 'utopian party' within which a movement of disparate groups is able to organise itself, thereby shifting utopianism from merely a dream of a better world to a concrete movement that can move towards it. A party with a vision has potential to harness the individual hopes that are often lost in a sense of isolation, to form a group that has a sense of direction. As Matthew Beaumont (cited in Allison, 2018: 53) writes, 'Utopian fiction ... seeks to recruit its readers to a notional party of potential activists, a Party of Utopia'.

Utopianism and 'wicked' problems

Utopian thinking is particularly relevant and appropriate in addressing super *wicked problems* (Levin et al., 2012) such as the environmental crisis. This is because some of the issues we face at present are so pressing that not only do they need to be resolved immediately if we are to avoid potentially irreversible catastrophic consequences for humanity and the planet, they also require us to break from our current reality and to think in radically different but more humanising ways. Levin et al. (2012) suggest that such problems are usually characterised by irrational responses by those responsible for creating them. They seem incapable of acting in a positive and constructive manner and recklessly continue their policies and practices despite the evidence which suggests the need for fundamentally different courses of action. It is because the people and organisations responsible for solving these problems are usually the very same ones that have precipitated them in the first place and any effective solutions may go against their narrow interests. This certainly seems to be the case in relation to the major fossil fuel companies that, despite the evidence, seem incapable of reversing the promotion of highly damaging energy policies (Savage, 2019).

The urgency for change

Never before has there been a more appropriate time to imagine something better than the current state of national and international economic and political systems that seem to be increasingly dominated by global corporations as well as populist leaders who put their own narrow personal, political and economic interests above not only those of their citizens but also that of the planet (Giroux, 2017). In the case of environmental pollution, for example, Dibley (2018) estimates

Case study 2.1: Dreaming of a safer and cleaner world

It is perhaps the utopian thinking and actions of Greta Thunberg, the young Swedish environmental activist who has inspired millions of people, young and old, through her passionate attempts to highlight the very real threats to the future of the planet, that seem to have encapsulated the new utopian spirit in recent years. Her inability to comprehend how so-called responsible adults can not only have allowed such a situation to arise but that they continue to recklessly pursue their destructive economic and energy policies despite the extensive scientific evidence showing that continuing to do so is likely to raise planetary temperatures irreversibly, with the potential for disastrous consequences for us all. Thunberg's ability to imagine a different world as possible, her disruptive challenges to conventional economic and political thinking and her activism through her solo school strike, as well as her rejection of the Nordic Council's environment award for 2019 worth $52,000 with the words: 'The climate doesn't need awards' (Thunberg, cited in The Guardian, 2019), is the epitome of the utopian method, or what Levitas (2013: xi) calls the Imaginary Reconstitution of Society.

In particular, Thunberg seems to have made the leap from what Bloch (1955–1959) calls 'abstract utopia', that involves wishful thinking about a world which seems to be deficient or lacking in some way, to 'concrete utopia'; the pursuit of a better world through praxis. She is driven to action by a dream of a world that is not yet there but is something which is possible in the future if, indeed, we are able to act in time. Moreover, if, as Levitas (2013) suggests, utopianism involves making the link between the social, political, economic, environmental and existential dimensions of human life and implores us to envision alternative ways of organising the institutions and relations between them, then Thunberg has brought all these dimensions to the surface as part of a public debate and the need for dialogue. She has alerted us to the fact that we do not need to take for granted existing practice that involves delegating responsibility for solving our problems to the very same people who are currently causing them. This is summed up succinctly in her statement to the United Nations' Climate Change Summit in September 2019:

> We are in the beginning of mass extinction, and all you can talk about is money and fairy tales of eternal economic growth.... We will not let you get away with this. Right here, right now is where we draw the line. The world is waking up. And change is coming, whether you like it or not.
>
> (National Public Radio, 2019)

By questioning the merits of perpetual economic growth and its incompatibility with the long-term health of our planet, Thunberg has disrupted our view of something that politicians and economists have been selling to us for more than half a century (Good, 2019). Crucially, she has shown that our opportunities for the kinds of willed transformation of society that Williams (1978) and Levitas (1990) suggest is a feature of utopianism are rapidly diminishing: a future of plenty and unlimited consumption will not be an option. Instead, needs and wants will be severely restricted and limited by the need for environmental protection and security.

that by January 2019, 30 per cent of global emissions were produced by democratic states run by populist nationalist leaders. Also, evidence produced by the Climate Accountability Institute (Savage, 2019) shows that a mere twenty of the largest oil companies produced 30 per cent of global greenhouse gases between 1965 and 2017. Moreover, these companies and governments were fully aware of the potential damage to the environment and human health; yet they made no attempt to change their policies of promoting fossil fuel usage and even tried to persuade the public that global warming and climate change were not occurring (Savage, 2019).

And yet, when activists such as Thunberg criticise governments and corporations for their conduct and policies they are vilified by these hegemonic forces of global business and politics as extremists and dreamers. Thunberg was dismissed with what Nelson and Vertigan (2019) refer to as a barrage of misogyny and male rage. The forces of patriarchy baulked at the nerve of a young woman who dared to challenge 'malestream' wisdom on the environment, orthodox economic policy and political leadership. The charge was led by the US President Donald Trump and the Australian Prime Minister Scott Morrison, and joined by the likes of the British journalists and broadcasters Jeremy Clarkson (Bagwell, 2019) and Piers Morgan (#Sky_Australia_News, 2019), who variously described her as mentally ill, hysterical, damaged and a spoilt child in need of a spanking (Nelson and Vertigan, 2019). Once again, we are confronted by a perverse logic. In this case a group of spoilt, rich, middle-aged white men who believe it is acceptable to verbally abuse a young woman who is clearly justified in challenging their 'fairy tales' about the benefits of endless and limitless economic growth.

These responses to Greta Thunberg demonstrate the barriers to counterhegemonic voices that are raised in relation to the looming environmental crisis and are replicated in relation to other issues such as poverty, wealth and income inequality, gender discrimination and racism, but which reinforces all the more the need to apply the utopian method as well as critical pedagogy in articulating the desire to create a better world. From the #MeToo movement fighting for justice for women victims of sexual abuse and rape (Sunstein, 2019) to the protests by citizens of Hong Kong demanding democratic rights (Kaeding, 2019), the increase in activism around the world illustrates the growing desire by citizens for change, for something better.

In particular, the activities of Greta Thunberg are part of a worldwide environmental movement led by children and young people from Latin America to Asia to engage in debates and protests as well as judicial activism (Scott, 2018). Unlike the adults in power who have a clear interest in the prevailing global economic and political system, these young activists have a vision of the future which includes a world that is safe for them to live in.

This domination of white male perspectives on the environment is also reflected in a similar orientation to utopian studies. Utopianism and its origins are intimately linked to colonialism and the dreams of the colonial settlers (Hardy, 2012), and this suggests that there is an urgent need to re-evaluate the foundational principles and concepts of utopianism itself.

Utopia, colonialism and postcolonialism

Utopianism and intentional utopian communities are closely associated with colonialism and the realisation of the utopian dreams of the colonial settlers. It is for this reason Sargent (2010: 50) claims that 'Colonies are important to utopianism'. Moreover, he points out that colonies have collectively produced more utopian literature and are places where a greater number of intentional communities

Case study 2.2: Blaming the poor

The often heated and confusing debate about the environment has been dominated by Western, and in particular wealthy white men, who tend to control the key sources of information, be it business, the media or education. They are able to set the agenda and to promote their interests in a highly effective manner using the tools of a supposedly rational and objective science. Ultimately the voices of a few thousands of these men speak louder and command more credibility than those of the billions of the world's poorest people. As a result, such influential individuals have managed to deflect responsibility for many of the world's problems away from themselves and towards the poor. In particular, they have been successful in linking environmental problems such as climate change to the activities and population growth of the poorest regions of the world. George Monbiot (2016: 103) cites James Lovelock, the renowned proponent of the earth systems theory known as Gaia, who presents the standard position on the relationship between population growth and climate change:

> Those who fail to see that population growth and climate change are two sides of the same coin are either ignorant or hiding from the truth. These two huge environmental problems are inseparable and to discuss one while ignoring the other is irrational.

Unfortunately, it is rare that we hear the evidence that challenges the position that conveniently lays the blame for climate change at the door of the poorest and weakest citizens on the planet. However, in 2009 research by the development scientist David Satterthwaite reveals that there is in fact a very weak relationship between population growth and climate change. Indeed, if we examine the evidence Satterthwaite collected between 1988 and 2005, there seems to have been an inverse relationship between population growth and carbon dioxide emissions. In regions such as sub-Saharan Africa where population growth has been one of the highest, producing 18.5 per cent of the global population, the region only produced 2.4 per cent of the increase in carbon dioxide. However, although North America produced only 4 per cent of this global population growth, it created 14 per cent of the extra carbon dioxide (Satterthwaite, 2009).

According to the study, compared with affluent Western nations, the people of the poorest sixth of the world's population, who mainly live in the Global South, are so poor that they produce barely any carbon dioxide at all, and in some parts of the world where the poor are engaged in waste processing and recycling for a living, they are carbon-negative. What this evidence shows is that it is not the poor that are the problem but it is the affluent, and the more prosperous they become the more they consume and the more carbon dioxide they produce. The more evidence we collect about the consumption patterns and lifestyles of the rich, the more we find Satterthwaite's claims being confirmed. In a study of the lifestyles of ten celebrities using evidence from their social media releases during 2017, Gossling (2019) found that in terms of air travel alone, individual celebrities such as Paris Hilton are responsible for ten thousand times more carbon dioxide emissions than the average person. Such is our blind obsession with the lives and activities of the superfluously wealthy, that when the billionaire Roman Abramovich boasts that he spends most of his time in a plane, instead of responding with disapproval and the demand for a tax on excessive flying, the most common reaction tends to be one of admiration (Monbiot, 2016).

have been created than in the countries from which the settlers came. Of arguably equal if not greater significance to utopianism however is the collective impact of (mainly) Western colonialism and utopian settler communities on these colonies and former colonies. It is therefore necessary, according to Hardy (2012), for utopian studies to ensure that the growing body of work being produced by Indigenous peoples on settler colonialism be given equal consideration to that of settler utopianism.

The establishment of settler colonies in what we now call Australia, New Zealand, North and South America and Africa during the sixteenth to the nineteenth centuries was usually accompanied by the destruction not only of the lives of many of the Indigenous peoples but also of what Peter Berger (1973) calls their 'plausibility structures', that is, their cultures and the systems of beliefs which make up their 'universe of meaning'. In some cases, such destruction was intentional and designed to eliminate the religions and beliefs of peoples seen as uncivilised or pagan. Art, literature, religious and historical artefacts, land and places of worship were pillaged and often destroyed, and with them the worlds of the Indigenous peoples who became homeless, not just physically but in terms of identity. This means that not only do we know much less about the cultures of the original inhabitants of these colonies than the settlers, but that these Indigenous people often know little about themselves and who they are.

> Thus, for example, the religious world of pre-Columbian Peru was objectively and subjectively real as long as its plausibility structure, namely pre-Columbian Inca society, remained intact…. Conversely, when the conquering Spaniards destroyed this plausibility structure the reality of the world based on it began to disintegrate with terrifying rapidity.
> (Berger, 1973: 54)

So, despite the existence of highly developed cultures and civilisations that the new settlers encountered, we often know very little about them and 'their myths and dreams of the good life' (Sargent, 2010: 52). What we do know is that their worlds became places of oppression, destruction, disease and misery, and much of the literature and ideas produced by Indigenous people in such colonies in response to their oppression are dystopian in nature, though some offer hope and the restoration of life before European settlement. This can be seen in the Ghost Dance of the Indigenous Americans of the Great Plains, which was a messianic movement that arose during the 1870s to the 1890s as a response the oppression experienced by these Indigenous peoples and the destruction of their traditional ways of life. It promised a utopian future that would bring back from the dead their brothers and sisters killed by white people, as well as the restoration of buffalo to their hunting grounds and the expulsion of the white settlers from their lands (Wishart, 2011).

The need for Indigenous voices

Many Indigenous peoples around the world who have been and continue to be the victims of settler colonialism are determined to revive and keep alive their cultural heritage and, with the emergence of postcolonial theory, we are beginning to learn and understand more about the cultural, scientific, social and spiritual lives of these peoples. Postcolonial theory 'may be defined as that branch of contemporary theory that investigates, and develops propositions about, the cultural and political impact of European conquest upon colonised societies, and the nature of those societies' responses' (Ashcroft, 2012: 1). However, as Ashcroft points out, it is probably more accurate to refer to this as 'post-invasion theory' in that many societies that were once colonies and have now achieved independence from the *metropole* (the colonial powers of France, Britain, Germany and the US) (Connell, 1997: 1522) still contain the remnants of their Indigenous populations that continue to experience the consequences of colonial rule. Within these surviving Indigenous communities, there is a growing body of literature relating to non-Western utopianism; however, it is a field that has so far received little attention in mainstream utopian studies (Ashcroft, 2012). This needs to be redressed, as the emerging debates created by postcolonial scholarship are an essential part of a re-evaluation of the foundations of modern utopianism which are based on predominantly Western, or what is increasingly referred to as 'Northern' (Connell, 1997), perspectives and epistemologies. Postcolonial theory can be seen as part of a wider desire by those seeking a more inclusive academic and educational approach that will help to decolonise the curriculum (Heleta, 2016; Dvolu-Gatsheni, 2017).

Indeed, it is the uncritical adherence to the existing Northern academic tradition that helps to perpetuate a process whereby non-Indigenous intellectuals 'contribute to the ongoing displacement and subjugation of Indigenous peoples' (Hardy, 2012: 124). For example, the very concept of utopia as 'no place' is a Western idea that erases the existence of Indigenous peoples who have been expected to assimilate into the ways of the supposedly superior colonists. Postcolonial theory gives voice to Indigenous peoples dealing with the effects of colonial domination. One of the barriers to developing an authentic Indigenous voice, however, is the dominance of the Northern intellectual tradition over academic, literary, scientific and artistic ideas, systems and structures. In the field of academia, it is still white, mainly male Northern intellectuals/researchers whose ideas and epistemologies take precedence over all others (Connell, 1997, 2007; Dvolu-Gatsheni, 2017). In most of the postcolonial societies in Africa, the Middle East, Asia and North and South America, sometimes called the Global South (Connell, 1997, 2007), there is an ongoing struggle to achieve an intellectual break from Western/Northern ways of thinking, or what the Iranian philosopher Jalal Al-e Ahmad (1982) writing in the 1960s calls *Gharbzadeghi*. This relates to the way cultures that have experienced colonisation or, as in the case of Iran, neocolonialism, come to see themselves through the lens of the colonial rulers rather than in ways they themselves have control over or determine. *Gharbzadeghi* has been variously translated as 'Oxidation', 'plagued by the West' and 'Westoxication' and applies a medical metaphor to suggest how the minds of Indigenous people have been 'contaminated' or 'poisoned' by contact with the West. Referring specifically to the gradual domination of Iran by Western powers such as Britain and the US during the past three hundred years, Al-e Ahmad (1982), in his book entitled *Gharbzadeghi*, claims that Iranians had fallen under the spell of secular Western ideas and so-called modern practices. In particular, Al-e Ahmad claimed that there was an increasing desire by Iranians to gain the approval of Western diplomats, intellectuals and business people who had created their own understanding of Islam and Iranian culture. These Western orientalists' ideas came to dominate not only those of Westerners but also those of the Iranians themselves. They became 'westoxicated', losing all understanding or sense of who they were or of their own culture. For Al-e Ahmad, the way to cure this cultural and psychological 'illness' is by a return to Islam which he saw as the only effective defense against colonialism. He believed that a reformed and forward-thinking *ulama* (Muslim clerical intelligentsia) in alliance with a progressive secularist intelligentsia could administer the cure. Indeed, it was just such an alliance that actually occurred which helped to bring about the Iranian Revolution in 1979. Whatever one thinks about developments in Iran since the revolution, there is no doubting that it is Iranians who are deciding their destiny and not Western/Northern 'experts'.

What seems to emerge from this brief analysis of the links between utopianism and colonialism, particularly settler colonialism as well as neo-colonialism, is the need for a process of internal disruption within utopian studies itself in order to identify taken-for-granted assumptions as well as the position of mainly white Western/Northern academics who have tended to dominate the foundational principles of the subject as well as its focal concerns. As Hardy (2012: 133) suggests, 'This sustained, critical and constructive, de-stabilization of the concept and historical effects of utopia is a healthy endeavor, one that may facilitate the relevance of utopia and utopian studies for a rapidly globalizing world'. Moreover, there is justified belief that the work of Indigenous writers, as well as that of peoples of non-settler colonial societies, need to be given a more central place in mainstream utopian studies literature (Wolfe, 1999). This is essential if we are to prevent a reliance on non-Indigenous academics and intellectuals to speak on behalf of Indigenous peoples and thereby contribute to their continued subjugation. The issue will be examined further in Chapter 5 regarding the debates about decolonising the curriculum.

Conclusion

In this chapter, we have examined the importance and need, not only to dream of a better world but also that a better world is possible. Although utopianism reached a low point in the wake of the dystopias of the twentieth century, utopian literature and theorising have experienced new levels of interest and productivity, to a point where it seems that we are witnessing a new spirit of utopianism which is showing ways to a better future whilst at the same time being alert to the dangers of rigid blueprints promoted by populist demagogues. It is only by imagining and proposing alternatives to an existing system and ways of living that humanity can be inspired to act. Such hope and desire, however, need to be educated and nurtured. In the next chapter, we will examine ways in which this new spirit of utopia can be harnessed together with critical pedagogy so that our children can be educated to create a better future.

Points for reflection and consideration in this chapter

This chapter has covered a wide range of issues relating to the current global crisis of neoliberalism and the need to seek a different and more just world. The education of hope through the belief in a sense of possibility has been proposed as a way forward which sees education, in its widest sense, as a key means of stimulating the utopian spirit and a desire for change.

- Do you ever consider alternatives to the present social and economic system? If so, do you believe that utopian thinking is a useful approach?
- Can education play a role in stimulating and promoting the desire for an alternative world?
- How effectively do you think Abensour deals with the dialectic of emancipation?
- Why might utopian theory be inadequate in its present form as a means of educating hope?

References

Abensour, M. (1999) 'William Morris: The politics of romance', in M. Blechman (ed.), *Revolutionary Romanticism*. San Francisco, CA: City Lights Books, pp. 125–161.

Adorno, T. and Horkheimer, M. (1972) *Dialectic of the Enlightenment*. London: Verso.

Al-e Ahmad, J. [1962] (1982) (trans. John Green and Ahmad Alizadeh) *Gharbzadeghi* (Westsruckness). Lexington, KY: Mazda.
Allison, M.A. (2018) 'Building a bridge to nowhere: Morris, the education of desire, and the party of Utopia'. *Utopian Studies*. Vol. 29, No. 1, pp. 45–66.
Amsler, S. (2008) 'Pedagogy against "Disutopia": From *conscientization* to the education of desire', in H. Dahms (ed.), *No Social Science without Critical Theory*. Bingley: Emerald Group, pp. 291–325.
Ashcroft, B. (2012) 'Introduction: Spaces of Utopia', in L. Tower Sargent, B., Ashcroft, B. and C. Kesler. (eds.), *Postcolonial Utopianism*. Porto: Universidade do Porto. Faculdade de Letras. Biblioteca Digital, pp. 1–17.
Bagwell, M. (2019) 'Jeremy Clarkson Brands Greta Thunberg a "Spoilt Brat" and Tells Her To "Go Back To School"'. *Huffington Post*, 29 September 2019.
Berger, P. (1973) *The Social Reality of Religion*. Harmondsworth: Penguin University Books.
Bloch, E. (1961) *Natural Law and Human Dignity*. Cambridge, MA: MIT Press.
Bloch, E. (1986) *The Principle of Hope*. London: Basil Blackwell.
Bookchin, M. (1991) *The Ecology of Freedom: The Emergence and Dissolution of Hierarchy* (revised edition). Montreal: Black Rose Books.
Brincat, S. (2009) 'Reclaiming the Utopian imaginary in IR theory'. *Review of International Studies*. Vol. 35, pp. 581–609.
Connell, R. (1997) 'Why is classical theory classical?' *American Journal of Sociology*. Vol. 102, No. 6, pp. 1511–1557.
Connell, R. (2007) *Southern Theory*. Cambridge: Polity Press.
Dahrendorf, R. (1990) *Reflections on the Revolution in Europe*. London: Chatto and Windus.
Davenport, C. and Pierre-Lewis, K. (2018) 'U.S. climate report warns of damaged environment and shrinking economy'. *The New York Times*. 23 November. Available at: https://www.nytimes.com/2018/11/23/climate/us-climate-report.html (Accessed 21 March 2019).
Dibley, A. (2018) 'Why the rise of populist nationalist leaders rewrites global climate talks'. *The Conversation*. Online. Available at: https://theconversation.com/why-the-rise-of-populist-nationalist-leaders-rewrites-global-climate-talks-107870 (Accessed 3 November 2019).
Freire, P. (1997) *Pedagogy of the Oppressed*. London: Penguin.
Freire, P. (2001) *Pedagogy of Freedom: Ethics, Democracy and Civic Courage*. New York: Rowman and Littlefield Publishers.
Garfinkel, H. (1967) *Studies in Ethnomethodology*. Englewood Cliffs, NJ: Prentice-Hall.
Garton Ash, T. (1990) *We the People: The Revolution of '89*. London: Granta Books/Penguin.
Giroux, H. (2017) 'Rallying cry: Youth must stand up to defend democracy'. *The Conversation*. Online. Available at: https://theconversation.com/rallying-cry-youth-must-stand-up-to-defend-democracy-81003 (Accessed 5 November 2019).
Good, J.E. (2019) 'Greta Thunberg's radical climate change fairy tale is exactly the story we need'. *The Conversation*. Online. Available at: https://theconversation.com/greta-thunbergs-radical-climate-change-fairy-tale-is-exactly-the-story-we-need-124252 (Accessed 29 October 2019).
Gossling, S. (2019) 'These celebrities cause 10,000 times more carbon emissions from flying than the average person'. *The Conversation*. Online. Available at: https://theconversation.com/these-celebrities-cause-10-000-times-more-carbon-emissions-from-flying-than-the-average-person-123886 (Accessed 2 November 2019).
Gray, J. (2007) *Black Mass: Apocalyptic Religion and the Death of Utopia*. London: Allen Lane.
Hall, S. and Jacques, M. (eds) (1989) *New Times: The Changing Face of Politics in the 1990s*. London: Lawrence and Wishart.
Hamilton, A.C. (ed.) (1990) *The Spencer Encyclopedia*. Toronto: University of Toronto Press.
Hardy, K. (2012) 'Unsettling Hope: Settler-Colonialism and Utopianism', in L. Tower Sargent, B., Ashcroft, B. and C. Kesler. (eds.), *Postcolonial Utopianism*. Porto: Universidade do Porto. Faculdade de Letras. Biblioteca Digital, pp 123–136. Available at: http://ler.letras.up.pt/site/default.aspx?qry=id05id174&sum=sim (Accessed on 12 April 2020).
Havel, V. (1984) 'Politics of Conscience', English translation by Erazim Kohac and Roger Scruton in *The Salisbury Review*, No. 2 (Jan 1985).
Havel, V. (1985) 'An Anatomy of Reticence'. Online. Available at: http://www.vaclavhavel.cz/showtrans.php?-cat=eseje&val=4_aj_eseje.html&typ=HTML (Accessed 15 July 2017).
Hayek von, F. (1944) *The Road to Serfdom*. London: Routledge and Kegan Paul.
Heleta, S. (2016) 'Decolonisation: Academics must change what they teach, and how'. *The Conversation*. Online. Available at: https://theconversation.com/decolonisation-academics-must-change-what-they-teach-and-how-68080 (Accessed 5 April 2019).

Henderson, E. (2016) 'Switzerland will be the first country in the world to vote on having a national wage of £1,700 a month'. *The Independent*. 30th January.
Hobsbawm, E. (1978) 'The forward March of labour halted'. *Marxism Today*. September.
Hobsbawm, E. (1990) 'Goodbye to all that'. *Marxism Today*. October.
Jameson, F. (2004) 'The politics of utopia'. *New Left Review*, Vol. 25, pp. 35–54.
Jameson. F. (2005) *Archaeologies of the Future: The Desire Called Utopia and Other Science Fictions*. London: Verso.
Johnson, B. (2013) 'Boris Johnson: 3rd Margaret Thatcher Lecture (FULL)'. Available online at: www.youtube.com/watch?v=Dzlgrnr1ZB0 (Accessed 14 January 2019).
Kaeding, M.P. (2019) '"We die together": Hong Kong protests are being driven by a fearless young generation'. *The Conversation*. Online. Available at: https://theconversation.com/we-die-together-hong-kong-protests-are-being-driven-by-a-fearless-young-generation-121994 (Accessed 5 November 2019).
Kumar, K. (1992) 'The Revolutions of 1989: Socialism, Capitalism, and Democracy'. *Theory and Society*. Vol. 21, No. 3, pp. 309–356.
Le Guin, U.K. (1974) *The Dispossessed: An Ambiguous Utopia*. New York: Harper and Row.
Levin, K., Cashore, B., Bernstein, S. and Auld, G. (2012) 'Overcoming the tragedy of super wicked problems: constraining our future selves to ameliorate global climate change'. *Policy Sciences*, Vol. 45, No. 2, pp. 123–152.
Levitas, R. (1990) *The Concept of Utopia*. Oxford: Peter Lang.
Levitas, R. (2013) *Utopia as Method: The Imaginary Constitution of Society*. Basingstoke: Palgrave Macmillan.
Marcuse, H. (1955) *Eros and Civilization*. New York: Vintage Books.
Marcuse, H. (1968) *One Dimensional Man*. London: Sphere Books.
Marcuse, H. (1970) *Five Lectures*. London: Allen Lane.
Monbiot, G. (2016) *How Did We Get into this Mess? Politics, Equality, Nature*. London: Verso.
Morris, W. (1891) *News from Nowhere, or An Epoch of Rest, being some Chapters from A Utopian Romance*. London: Longmans, Green and Co. Available at: http://www.gutenberg.org/files/3261/3261-h/3261-h.htm (Accessed 5 November 2019).
Morris, W. and Bax, E.B. (1893) *Socialism: Its Growth and Outcome*. London: Swan Sonnenschein.
Nadir, C. (2010) 'Utopian Studies, Environmental Literature, and the Legacy of an Idea: Educating Desire in Miguel Abensour and Ursula K. Le Guin'. *Utopian Studies*. Vol. 21, No. 1, pp. 24–56.
National Geographic. (2019) 'The Effects of Global Warming'. Available at: https://www.nationalgeographic.com/environment/global-warming/global-warming-effects/ (Accessed 26 March 2019).
National Public Radio. (2019) *Transcript: Greta Thunberg's Speech at the U.N. Climate Action Summit*. 23 September 2019. Available at: https://www.npr.org/2019/09/23/763452863/transcript-greta-thunbergs-speech-at-the-u-n-climate-action-summit?t=1572628154033 (Accessed 29 October 2019).
Ndvolu-Gatsheni, S. (2017) 'Decolonising research methodology must include undoing its dirty history'. *The Conversation*. Available online at: https://theconversation.com/ decolonising-research-methodology-must-include-undoing-its-dirty-history-83912 (Accessed 21 April 2019).
Nelson, C. and Vertigan, M. (2019) 'Misogyny, male rage and the words men use to describe Greta Thunberg'. *The Conversation*. Available at: https://theconversation.com/misogyny-male-rage-and-the-words-men-use-to-describe-greta-thunberg-124347 (Accessed 3 November 2019).
Paynter, E. (2019) 'Europe's refugee crisis explains why border walls don't stop migration'. *The Conversation*. Online. Available at: https://theconversation.com/europes-refugee-crisis-explains-why-border-walls-dont-stop-migration-110414 (Accessed 29 October 2019).
Popper, K. [1945] (1962) *The Open Society and Its Enemies* (Vol. 1). London: Routledge and Kegan Paul.
Ricoeur, P. (1986) *Lecturson Ideology and Utopia*. New York: Columbia University Press.
Sargent, L.T. (2010) *Utopianism: A Very Short Introduction*. Oxford: Oxford University Press.
Satterthwaite, D. (2009) 'The implications of population growth and urbanisation for climate change'. *Environment and Urbanisation*. Vol. 21. No. 2, pp. 545–567.
Savage, K. (2019) 'New research tying 20 companies to one-third of global emissions aids liability argument'. *Climate Liability News*. Online. Available at: https://www.climateliabilitynews.org/2019/10/09/global-emissions-carbon-majors-richard-heede/ (Accessed 3 November 2019).
Scott, K. (2018) 'Can "climate kids" take on governments and win?' *CNN*. 25 July. Available at: https://edition.cnn.com/2018/07/24/health/youth-climate-march/index.html (Accessed 31 March 2019).
Shklar, J.N. (1957) *After Utopia*. Princeton, NJ: Princeton University Press.
#Sky_Australia_News. (2019) 'Piers Morgan mocks Greta Thunberg'. *YouTube* Available at: https://www.youtube.com/watch?v=gfcfxlQtq7M (Accessed 3 November 2019).

Sodha, S. (2017) 'Is Finland's basic universal income a solution to automation, fewer jobs and lower wages?' *The Guardian*. 19th February. Available at: https://theconversation.com/society/2107/feb/19/basic-income-finland-low-wages-fewer-jobs (Accessed 10 June 2020).

Stedman Jones, G. (1990) 'Faith in history: A Cambridge Sermon'. *History Workshop Journal*. Issue 30 (Autumn), p. 63.

Sunstein, C. (2019) 'Why social movements like #MeToo seem to come out of nowhere'. *The Conversation*. Online. Available at: https://theconversation.com/why-social-movements-like-metoo-seem-to-come-out-of-nowhere-113985 (Accessed 5 November 2019).

Taylor-Collins, E. (2018) 'Nearly 60% of young children are social justice activists – a future full of Elin Erssons'. *The Conversation*. Available at: https://theconversation.com/nearly-60-of-young-children-are-social-justice-activists-a-future-full-of-elin-erssons-100634 (Accessed 1 November 2019).

Ted-Ed. (2013) *How economic inequality harms societies – Richard Wilkinson*. Available at: https://www.youtube.com/watch?time_continue=61&v=Ndh58GGCTQo (Accessed 8 February 2019).

The Guardian. (2019) 'The climate doesn't need awards': Greta Thunberg declines environmental prize'. 29 October 2019. Available at: https://www.theguardian.com/environment/2019/oct/29/greta-thunberg-declines-award-climate-crisis (Accessed 1 November 2019).

UNHRC. (2019) Visit to the United Kingdom of Great Britain and Northern Ireland: Report of the Special Rapporteur on extreme poverty and human rights. Available at: https://undocs.org/A/HRC/41/39/Add.1 (Accessed 2 May 2019).

Webb, D. (2009) 'Where's the vision? The concept of utopia in contemporary educational theory'. *Oxford Review of Education*. Vol. 35, No. 6, pp. 743–760.

Weber, M. (1903–1917, 1949) *The Methodology of the Social Sciences*, E. Shils and H. Finch (eds). New York: Free Press.

Wilkinson, R. and Pickett, K. (2009) *The Spirit Level: Why More Equal Societies Almost Always Do Better*. London: Penguin.

Wilkinson, R. and Pickett, K. (2018) *The Inner Level: How More Equal Societies Reduce Stress, Restore Sanity and Improve Everyone's Well-Being*. London: Allen Lane.

Williams, R. (1978) 'Utopia and Science Fiction'. *Science Fiction Studies*. Vol. 5, No. 16, Part 3. November 1978. Available at: https://www.depauw.edu/sfs/backissues/16/williams16art.htm (Accessed 26 November 2019).

Willmetts, S. (2017) 'What are the Orwellian dystopias of the 21st century?' *The Conversation*. Available at: https://theconversation.com/what-are-the-orwellian-dystopias-of-the-21st-century-72135 (Accessed 29 October 2019).

Wishart, D.J. (ed.) (2011) *Encyclopedia of the Great Plains*. University of Nebraska. Available at: http://plainshumanities.unl.edu/encyclopedia/doc/egp.rel.023 (Accessed 3 December 2019).

Wolfe, P. (1999) *Settler Colonialism and the Transformation of Anthropology: The Politics and Poetics of an Ethnographic Event*. New York: Cassell.

Youth Strike 4 Climate (2019) 'UK Strike – #YouthStrike4Climate'. Available at: https://ukscn.org/ys4c (Accessed 1 April 2019).

Zero Hour (2019) 'Getting to the roots of climate change'. Available at: http://thisiszerohour.org/ (Accessed 27 March 2019).

3 Alternative ways of being and educating

Introduction

In the previous chapter, there was an examination of the importance of imagining alternative ways of being and living as well as how, whether as a result of human nature or as a socially created phenomenon, the desire for a better way of being is a feature that is common throughout history and in all cultures. In this chapter, there will be a focus more specifically on how our social, welfare and education systems can be imagined differently to become a crucial part of a socialisation process in which children and students from all social backgrounds are valued equally and are encouraged to become reflective learners able to think critically about the current condition of the world as well as to imagine how to make it a better place for all. The need to involve children from their earliest years is crucial lest they become so used to the way we currently live and see it as normal and 'natural'. This naturalisation of a world in which the excessive wealth of a few is celebrated whilst poverty still persists – even in the most economically advanced democracies (UNHRC, 2019), where, despite the evidence to the contrary (Social Mobility Commission, 2016; Montacute, 2018), children are led to believe that they can achieve their dreams through hard work and ability, where children are taught the merits of selfishness, individualism and competition when, in fact, greater cooperation and collaboration are needed (Alexander, 2009; Robinson, 2010), where the idea of achievement and being an 'educated person' are increasingly measured by regular testing and our growing obsession with what Nikolas Rose (1999: 214) refers to as 'the power of the single number', and where knowledge is commodified and controlled by the wealthy and powerful for profit (Maisuria, 2014; McCowen, 2016) rather than for the benefit of humanity. All of these are making a mockery of education as a public good.

The context of education and welfare in a neoliberal world

Such has been the influence of the neoliberal narrative that education has become just another element in the gradual but effective conversion of public goods into private assets, creating new sources of profit for the wealthy. These policies and myths can be viewed as part of an increasingly oppressive regime of control, surveillance and subjugation of welfare and education by politicians to what is treated as merely a technical process for the creation of societies made up of consumer-citizens (Ford et al., 2015), rather than of reflective and creative human beings who are able to challenge existing ideas and practices. Indeed, although education continues to be viewed as an entitlement, it is one that has come to be envisaged in increasingly narrow and limited ways both in terms of what education is for and how it is to be delivered and experienced. This is a result of the increasing grip states are now exercising over previously publicly owned assets and institutions – schools, social housing, care homes, natural resources, transport systems, public spaces, playing fields, parks, libraries and other public services – that once added social, health and educational benefits to ordinary people's lives are now being sold off without public say through the implementation of neoliberal policies (Olssen and Peters, 2005; Christophers, 2019). As Harvey (2007: 23) states:

> Neoliberalism has, in short, become hegemonic as a mode of discourse and has pervasive effects on ways of thought and political-economic practices to the point where it has become incorporated into the commonsense way we interpret, live in, and understand the world.

The form this takes varies from country to country, but the US and the UK are two nations at the forefront of these reforms (Harvey, 2007). In cases such as Iraq, however, a new state based on neoliberal free market fundamentalism was imposed by force. In 2003, in the aftermath of the second Iraq war, the Coalition Provisional Authority led by the US announced a number of commands among which were the 'full privatisation of all public enterprises' including public services, 'full ownership rights by foreign firms of Iraqi US businesses, full repatriation of foreign profits' and 'the opening of Iraqi banks to foreign control' (Harvey, 2007: 25). However, what is clear is that there is a strong centripetal force pulling societies into the neoliberal orbit driven by spurious claims of protecting political freedom and individual liberty in terms of choice to participate in free markets and ownership of property against arbitrary state intervention. There is, in other words, apparently no alternative (TINA) (Berlinski, 2011). The consequences, however, have been increasing levels of poverty and inequality and, in the case of Iraq, social and political collapse.

The impact of neoliberal austerity

This can be seen in the countries such as the UK – England, Wales, Scotland and Northern Ireland – where public services such as education, health, welfare, youth services and social care for those with disabilities and the elderly are each being hollowed out by the state to reduce government spending, and thereby the tax burden on the wealthy, through the provision of minimal services whilst at the same time creating opportunities for private organisations to profit from the process through the creation of a quasi-market in education and the public services.

The betrayal of such citizens is palpable (UNHRC, 2019), particularly in relation to the most vulnerable including the sick, those with disabilities, children and young people who are powerless against the ideological onslaught of politicians and their corporate funders who dominate the political agenda through their control of the culture industry, including traditional and social media, as well as the political and electoral systems (Chakrabortty, 2016; Neate, 2019). The consequences for such groups have been severe as these austerity measures have taken place against a background of increasing levels of poverty in the UK, and a growth in the wealth of an economic elite (Piketty, 2014; Savage et al., 2015). Evidence suggests that poverty has been growing in the UK after a period of decline under New Labour (1997–2010) (Wright and Anderson, 2018; Corlett,

2019) and is likely to increase further over the next five years (2019–2024) if current policies continue (Corlett, 2019).

Further evidence suggests that such policies are already adversely affecting children from poorer backgrounds in terms of their growth, their education, their experience of childhood and their life chances generally. Wilkinson (2019) uses the term 'bodies remember', to emphasise the permanent effects of deprivation on children's physical development. A study by Goldacre et al. (2014) reports that in poorer parts of the UK hospital admissions for rickets have reached a fifty-year high, and Hancock et al. (2015) found that in such deprived areas children are on average one centimetre smaller than children in more affluent ones. In the 2015 budget, huge cuts in benefits were announced, one of which limited claims to two children per family, meaning that larger families are losing around £2,800 a child per year. These cuts together with an increasingly harsh benefits system and the punitive sanctions which stop benefits for minor infringements are resulting in a dehumanising system that lacks compassion for those at the bottom of society who are frequently in no position to support or defend themselves.

A 'disgrace', a 'calamity' and a 'disaster'

The effects of the British government's policies have not escaped the attention of international human rights organisations such as the United Nations Human Rights Commission (UNHRC). In a preliminary statement on his fact-finding trip to the UK in 2017, Philip Alston, the UN's Special Rapporteur on Extreme Poverty and Human Rights, points to Britain's great wealth as a global trading and economic power and to its welfare state that had once been the envy of the world. However, what he found during his visit to all parts of the UK led him to conclude that he had witnessed 'not just a disgrace, but a calamity and an economic disaster all rolled into one' (Alston, 2018: 1) and, moreover, that the UK was probably in breach of its human rights obligations (UNHRC, 2019: 8). Noting the effects of the benefits system and the cuts in benefits, Alston seems all too aware of their consequences for poorer families and their increasing dependence on food banks. Indeed, of the 4.5 million children living in poverty in the UK in 2016–2017 (Social Metrics Commission, 2018) 10 per cent were experiencing *extreme food insecurity* meaning that they were frequently hungry as a result of having to go without food (Pereira et al., 2017). The European average for extreme food insecurity is 4 per cent. The British government dismissed Alston's report as 'barely believable' and 'a completely inaccurate picture of our approach to tackling poverty' (Booth, 2019). Amber Rudd, Secretary of State for Work and Pensions, stated that she intended to make a formal complaint to the UNHRC, accusing Alston of bias and inadequate research.

There was a similar response by the government to the findings of a report by the international human rights group Human Rights Watch, released a few months before Alston's in May 2019. In the report entitled *Nothing Left in the Cupboards* (HRW, 2019), which focused specifically on the plight of poor children and families in three areas of England with high levels of deprivation – Oxford, Cambridgeshire and Hull – it is claimed that the austerity policies being followed by the government and its implementation of Universal Credit were 'exacerbating poverty' (HRW, 2019: 6). The study, based on interviews with school leaders, staff in food banks, charity workers, families affected by food poverty, as well as reviews of official government statistics, provides a picture of these areas which former head teacher Geoff Barton describes as a 'national shame' (Marsh, 2019). Schools and families report that they are having to increasingly turn to food banks as children are arriving at school hungry and unable to concentrate on their studies. The Trussell Trust alone, the UK's largest food bank charity, reported a more than 5,000 per cent increase in the distribution of food parcels between 2008 and 2018. The government once again dismissed the report as misleading and not a representative picture of what was happening in the country (Marsh, 2019). However, this is another shameful denial in the face of the overwhelming evidence revealing a government in neglect of its responsibilities and ignoring the rights of its poorest, youngest and most vulnerable citizens.

Education, testing and the well-being of learners in a neoliberal context

The growing influence of neoliberalism means that schools are becoming increasingly subjected to oppressive welfare policies and performance-driven regimes that are blighting children's lives. This, combined with growing levels of childhood poverty, means that children in England and the US, two of the countries most affected by the impact of neoliberal policies, are some of the least happy compared to children from other affluent countries and are also less likely to believe that their lives have meaning (OECD, 2019; Twenge, 2019). In a system where high-stakes testing tends to take up an increasing proportion of schools' resources, time and focus and where school success is measured primarily in terms of a 'single number', there is a reasonable assumption that children's welfare and mental well-being are adversely affected (Andrews et al., 2014).

The pressures on nations around the world to develop education systems geared primarily for a race to the top of international league tables is acting to distort the nature and purpose of education. One of the most prominent sources of such pressure is the Programme for International Student Assessment (PISA) introduced in 2000, initially in the most developed countries, but is slowly incorporating poorer, less developed ones. PISA is a branch of the Organisation for Economic Co-operation and Development (OECD) which has pretty much appointed itself as the world's arbiter of good educational practice and performance by setting up the system of triennial testing of pupils around the world and locating each country in a list on which the 'clever' kids (nations) are at the top and the 'dunces' are at the bottom. What is highly significant is that the OECD specialises in (and prioritises) economic development rather than pedagogy, and its director, Dr Andreas Schleicher (OECD, 2019), is a data analyst and statistician specialising in testing rather than being a pedagogue; therefore, its focus is on children as sources of economic capital for nations rather than as future citizens for whom the role of worker or employee is merely one of many.

This can be seen in the nature of the tests and the OECD's educational philosophy which is based very much on what Paulo Freire (1996) would refer to as the 'banking system' of education. The process involves testing the *skills* and *knowledge* in science, mathematics and reading of half-a-million fifteen-year-olds from 72 countries under strict time conditions (PISA, 2018). And it is here that the problems lie, for the PISA tests symbolise much of what is wrong with a growing number of education systems. In particular, it has been pointed out by many educationalists (Andrews et al., 2014) that because of the snowballing effect of nations' desires for their education systems to provide indicators of the 'quality' and potential employability of their young people in a global market, it is seen as essential to be able to participate in a regular process of comparison and assessment against other states. PISA results are therefore increasingly seen as a key indicator of a nation's standing in a globalising economy and represent a sign of success or failure of their governments, educators and, of course, their children. Most participants in the PISA process wait with great trepidation for the results to be published, fearing any potential drop in their standing in the table, thereby adding to the already high levels of stress in schools that threaten the well-being of teachers and pupils (Andrews et al., 2014).

One of the consequences has been the emergence of perverse incentives for nations to ensure that they are seen to be heading in the right direction up the PISA league table by any means possible. There is evidence of jurisdictions, pupils and teachers cheating the system, including in the assessments (Niyozov and Hughes, 2019). Moreover, many countries are altering their education systems and local practices, and thereby narrowing their curricula, to focus primarily on cognitive skills and knowledge development at the expense of other less quantifiable, or even non-quantifiable skills and qualities, for no other reason than to be in a better position to improve their PISA rankings (Andrews et al., 2014).

The problems associated with the PISA system are well-known to the national governments that participate in its testing programme. These include the persistent bias in sampling of schools (Sands, 2017; Jerrim, 2019), the dubious validity of a few numbers to sum up a nation's educational system (Birrell, 2014) and that much of the difference in scores of schools within OECD countries such as the UK can be explained by socioeconomic disadvantage so that, rather than looking at school-related factors such as teaching, levels of resources or the levels of school funding, what we are actually seeing is the effects of inequality and deprivation (Masci et al., 2018). Moreover, the limited range of criteria covered in the tests using a combination of multiple-choice and open-answer format (PISA, 2018) provide very limited information with which to measure what is considered to be an educated young person. Yet increasing numbers of nations persist in subjecting their children to these as well as to other regular high-stakes testing systems. They seem to be sucked into the flawed logic of training children to pass tests as the path to personal and economic success, as though they have no alternative.

Added to this is the growing influence of private multinational companies such as Pearson International in the PISA process, through their involvement in identifying supposed deficits and weaknesses in the education systems of individual member-states. Such companies are making vast profits out of the resulting 'PISA shock' (Strauss, 2015) experienced by these 'failing' states, offering services and advice about how to improve or restore their position in the PISA league table. The consequences can only be a continued entrenchment of the banking system of education in which, in order to do well, young people are taught to anticipate responses to increasingly standardised questions rather than to develop their own creative skills in art, music, aesthetics, morality, ethics as well as independent thinking, caring for and empathising with others, and problem-solving by working collaboratively.

Domination by Western academic and cultural values

The group thinking perpetuated by PISA is based on Western cultural, social and economic values in which individuals and nations compete against each other, rather than learning through dialogue and collaboration. Testing becomes the focus and the ability to pass tests on a narrow range of content-oriented skills and knowledge, rather than a wider range of skills and competencies such as creativity, empathy and the ability to work effectively with others (Robinson, 2010). We have a good deal of evidence that goes back a long way (Klineberg, 1928; Dorling, 2011) to show that cultural practices have a great influence on the way children are expected to learn, play and to solve problems. A comparison of the results of intelligence tests administered to Indigenous American Yakima, Black American and white American children in the 1920s revealed that compared to the white American children, the other two groups performed less well (Klineberg, 1928). A superficial and simple reading of these findings might lead one to believe that white children are more able or intelligent than the two other groups. However, Klineberg (1928) found that when certain variables were altered, such as increasing the amount of time the children had, or allowing the children to work together, the Black and Indigenous children performed as well as the white children. In some cultures, problem-solving is considered a collaborative activity, and to expect children to do so on their own is anathema. Among the Inuit of the Canadian Arctic, for instance, this is known as the principle of *piliriqatigiingniq* (Anielski, 2007: 128). This is why these children may find such tests problematic. In this respect, it would seem that PISA tests, based as they are on hegemonic Western values of competitive individualism, lack validity in terms of their foundational principles. It is probably no coincidence that First Nation Canadians attending state-funded schools have not, thus far, been included in the Canadian PISA data (Nyozov and Hughes, 2019). The fact that Indigenous schools in Canada are reported to be 'chronically underfunded' and such communities experience high levels of deprivation suggest that the inclusion of these schools would have a significant negative impact on Canada's PISA standing (Nyozov and Hughes, 2019). The consequence is that educational inequalities between marginalised groups and the rest of the Canadian population are concealed.

In defence of PISA

However, in the heated debate about the relative merits of the PISA programme, Sahlberg and Hargreaves (Strauss, 2015), whilst agreeing with many of the criticisms of PISA cited above, argue that in the two decades of its existence we should not lose sight of its many positive achievements and that these should be highlighted and promoted further in the interest of improving equity and the testing process. In particular, they suggest were it not for PISA, the leading proponents of neoliberal policies such as the UK and the US would not be exposed as the poor performers that they are.

In the case of Sweden, which had once been a high performer in the PISA tests, there was a dramatic collapse in its PISA assessment results in 2012, following the introduction of free schools that were run by for-profit companies, once again exposing the myth of the market as a solution to all our problems. This led to a widespread public debate in Sweden over the role of its free schools programme in the country's poor results. Moreover, Sahlberg and Hargreaves (Strauss, 2015) believe that were it not for the PISA programme we would not have witnessed the consistently high-scoring education systems of Canada and Finland, with the latter held up as the model of progressive education which values its teachers and provides them with the training and professional autonomy to develop curricula based on the specific needs of their students.

However, Sahlberg's and Hargreaves's position can be seen as somewhat inconsistent, for, after questioning the reliability of PISA data and the validity of the PISA programme for 'narrowing' children's learning and for being over-reliant on standardised tests, they then proceed to use the PISA data to assess the relative merits of various countries' education systems. As Birrell (2014) states, 'We can't have it both ways. If our weak results have "scant validity", so do our good ones'. They are also inconsistent in their acceptance of how reliable the PISA data are. Their uncritical acknowledgement of Canada's repeatedly high performance, despite its non-inclusion of Indigenous pupils from its PISA data (Nyozov and Hughes, 2019) on the one hand, and their dismissal of many of the high-performing Asian countries on the grounds of their questionable methods on the other, is a case in point.

The key issue here is not to defend a faulty system on the grounds that it has the potential benefits of exposing unfounded neoliberal claims and policies, or that the OECD is an 'advocate' of equity in education (OECD, 2011), which is something most governments would support in principle, but to advocate for the wholesale reform, if not abolition, of a system that is unaccountable to anyone and has the potential to irreparably damage schools and students and education systems around the world (Andrews et al., 2014). It is already the case that all OECD countries and an increasing number of non-member countries, which in future will include those in Africa (Andrews et al., 2014), have or are in the process of altering their educations systems to align them more closely with the PISA testing regime, thus leading to a potential spread in the narrowing of curricula around the world and the learning experience, as well as of constant testing and rote learning. The consequences for non-Western cultural and educational practices are likely to be considerable. For-profit organisations are already setting up collaborative schemes with schools in Africa in anticipation of the introduction of PISA testing there (Andrews et al., 2014). The notion that most governments and indeed their citizens will respond in a measured and rational manner to the evidence in the way Sweden has done is somewhat optimistic when we see the strength of the ideological commitment to neoliberalism by global economic powers and standards setters such as the US and China. In countries such as Britain and the US, where neoliberalism has become so entrenched it is almost akin to a religion, ideology takes precedence over the evidence, no matter how strong the evidence. This can be seen in the way a number of right-wing governments have responded to reports of the negative consequences of privatisation and marketisation within their public sectors, in the form of increasing social inequality and rising levels of poverty.

Ignoring the evidence

Instead of responding to the evidence in ways that are sensitive to the needs of children and other vulnerable groups, the UK government has, in the words of Alston (UNHCR, 2019:20) 'doubled down' on its policies and implemented even greater levels of austerity by cutting benefits, imposing harsher penalties and further stigmatising the poor. Rather than accepting the evidence produced by independent experts suggesting that existing policies are lacking in care and compassion, and are in fact damaging the physical and educational development of young people, what we are witnessing is the creation of a regime that is constantly raising our threshold of tolerance for policies which are causing harm to those considered to be less valued members of society and to a position that could be said to accept such outcomes as a necessary part of a process of rejuvenating the nation's social and economic vigour. This is not an implausible assumption given the views of Dominic Cummings, the UK Prime Minister Boris Johnson's former senior policy adviser, which can only be described as advocating eugenics. This is evident in Cummings's suggestion that the NHS should be funded to allow people, or more specifically 'the rich', to be able to select genetic traits such as high intelligence for their offspring (Read, 2020).

This is mirrored in the government's response to the consequences of its performance and assessment-driven education policy. In a system where high-stakes testing tends to take up most schools' resources, time and focus, and where school success is measured primarily in terms of examination performance, there is a reasonable assumption that children's welfare and mental well-being are being adversely affected. As Ford (cited in Severs, 2017) states,

> I think we should not underestimate the influence of the school, which can be highly positive but also for some children highly negative. It is no doubt very painful for teachers to realise that the structures of the school may not be good for the mental health of pupils.

Findings produced by international organisations (UNICEF, 2007, 2013; OECD, 2019) and national ones (The Children's Society, 2017) consistently report of a decline in the sense of children's well-being in the UK since 2010. The latest PISA results for 2018 found 8.7 per cent of fifteen-year-olds in the UK reported being sad all the time compared with the OECD average of 6.9 per cent. The reasons for this are complex and varied; however, Len Barton, general secretary of the Association of School and College Leaders, suggests that it 'is clear that many young people feel under great pressure in a society in which the stakes often seem very high to them in terms of achieving their goals' and that we 'must do more to understand the complex factors which affect wellbeing' (Civinini, 2019). It is perhaps no coincidence that the English and Welsh education systems are two of the most significantly affected by performance-driven reforms in which regular inspection and testing are key features. In a review of the evidence in the UK entitled *The Mismanagement of Learning*, the National Union of Teachers (2016) suggests that the education systems in England and Wales are becoming so obsessed with the testing of pupils that the stress this causes is affecting both teachers' and their pupils' well-being.

However, rather than considering these increasing pressures as well as the growing levels of child poverty as needing further investigation in terms of their effects on children and their experience of childhood, the UK government has instead placed the onus on children and young people to 'toughen up' and show more resilience. The Education Secretary Damian Hinds claims that the government's policy is effectively 'equipping young people for adulthood in a changing world' and 'encouraging young people to gain resilience and skills…' (Parton, 2019).

Resilience is a seemingly benign term used by policymakers suggesting a supportive and rational response to our increasingly stressful and precarious lives. However, what it actually represents is an attempt to shift responsibility for the negative consequences of policies such as the state's withdrawal from its welfare role and the collapse of public services, as well as the imposition of harsh and punitive new benefits regimes on the population. As White (2013) suggests, it enables the government to 'reframe the debate' and steer it in a direction that deflects criticism and culpability away from itself and towards others. In this case, there is an expectation placed on those at the receiving end of such dramatic and often traumatic changes to their lives, such as cuts to their benefits or the closure of services, to adapt to their new situation and to respond in a positive and constructive manner by upskilling, working harder, spending more wisely and being less reliant on the state. Regarding the increasing stress experienced by children resulting from regular testing, the negative feedback from teachers, and the consequences of failure, the advice to them has been to develop the skills and qualities known as 'academic resilience'. This is described as the ability to cope with and respond positively to the persistent challenges that children are now experiencing at school, such as 'chronic underachievement' (Kendrick, 2019) and/or the effects of poverty on their educational progress (Ebersohn, 2017). Clearly, all children need to learn how to cope with the effects of stress and failure; it is part of growing up. However, what Martin and Marsh (2008) suggest is that because of the increasing levels of such experiences, children need to increase their academic resilience through an ability to cope with such setbacks more or less on a daily basis. They refer to this as *academic buoyancy*. So, an improved ability to deal with regular or daily setbacks can, in theory, develop a child's overall academic resilience. Kendrick (2019) rather optimistically states that:

> Buoyant children and youth recognise that the daily setbacks associated with school are temporary and non-threatening. A failing grade does not endanger long-term success and even final year end tests can be re-done. Critical feedback in school is a necessary part of learning, not the end of the world.

The evidence, however, does not support this assertion. Poorer children's educational achievement and ability to cope with adversity are clearly affected by such things as their family's living conditions, family resources, income and general family climate. This is borne out by the PISA data as well as the wealth of research carried out on countries in the OECD (Wilkinson and Pickett, 2009, 2018). An increase in academic resilience on its own is unlikely to compensate for the effects of material disadvantage and the lack of social and cultural capital possessed by children from deprived communities, as well as minority ethnic groups who may experience the added stresses caused by racism.

It could be argued that the advocates of such things as improving academic resilience and working within existing national and international structures such as PISA for the reform and improvement of education systems as a means of achieving greater equity in education are merely being realistic. However, this flies in the face of the evidence which is conveniently ignored by many experts, policymakers, politicians and the very wealthy who are unlikely to want to implement the kinds of measures needed to create a more equitable society (Neate, 2019). Clearly, improving education systems as a general principle is a position that few if any would gainsay; however, as Volante and Jerrim (2018) state, 'education is important but not enough to change inequities around the world'. Education systems reflect their societies – their dominant cultures, values and the wider economic and class inequalities that prevail; hence, greater equity in education would need to be underpinned and accompanied by 'the redistribution of financial resources, and on minimizing educational disparities between rich and poor' (Jerrim and Macmillan, 2015: Conclusion).

Imagining a different pedagogy

If, as Savage et al. (2015: 215) remind us, 'equality of opportunity can only be made real when it is associated with equality in general', then what role can education play in this process? It is clearly possible for education to promote social justice in relation to ethnicity, gender, disability, age and resource allocation; however, education needs to be a moral enterprise and not merely a route to employment and a servant to the economy. Education should never be subordinated to the desire for profit because the outcome of such an unequal relationship will inevitably result in a society losing its moral grounding. Above all, education should be about transformation of the student and the teacher, and the creation of a better world for all, not just the few. This would involve a change in the relationship between teachers and the state, between teachers and students, as well as between students and the state.

relating to working collaboratively, decision-making, problem-solving and creativity, if their learning culture is one primarily of responding to instruction and orders.

In terms of their current status and treatment by those in power in Western societies, such as the UK, children and young people occupy a very ambiguous position. Despite the state's official role as 'supreme parent' (Fitz, no date) and its obligations to its children with regard to their protection, safeguarding and education, there are some serious concerns over how these are carried out. The evidence presented so far regarding the growing levels of child poverty, the persistent and growing inequality in educational progress between children from poorer and those from more affluent backgrounds, as well as the comparatively poor levels of well-being amongst young people in the UK and the US (Wilkinson and Pickett, 2009, 2018), suggests that government rhetoric clearly does not correspond to the reality and the everyday lives of these children and their families. It is increasingly the case that in many so-called advanced democratic societies, children's rights and protection against such conditions as poverty and poor living conditions are not guaranteed. Both the US and the UK present themselves to the world as 'civilised' democracies that respect and protect the welfare of their citizens, and yet the US refuses to ratify the United Nations Declaration on the Rights of the Child (1989) and both the US and the UK received damning reports from the Special Rapporteur on extreme poverty and human rights in 2017 (UNHRC, 2017) and 2019 (UNHRC, 2019), respectively, for their extreme levels of child poverty. Alston (UNHCR 2019: 8) goes so far as to suggest that the UK government's policies in relation to these issues are 'a clear violation of the country's human rights obligations'.

The vulnerability of children and young people

Lansdown (1994) and Oakley (1994) suggest that children share a similar status to women in that both groups can be seen as weak in relation to patriarchal power. They both occupy positions of 'structural vulnerability' in terms of their continuing high level of dependence on men. The infantilisation of women alongside children through patriarchal ideology has meant that both groups have been deprived of the right to make decisions for themselves and have depended on men to speak for them. This lack of 'voice' has been instrumental in their oppression. Although women globally and in the UK still suffer from considerable inequalities in terms of their weak economic position (Office for National Statistics, 2018; Healey and Ahmed, 2019), their lack of equal representation in politics (Annesley, 2016) and in terms of being poorly served by the legal system (Fawcett Society, 2018; McCarthy-Jones, 2018), over the past century they have developed political and social movements that have successfully won them important rights. They also have a language and concepts through which *feminism* has been able to articulate women's position and their demands for equity and justice.

Conclusion

All this suggests that there also need to be dramatic changes to young people's and children's rights and the way they are implemented. It should include the extension of their *political rights*, such as the right to vote at age sixteen, as well as an increasing say in their education, including the curriculum. Moreover, young people should have much stronger *legal rights* that protect them from arbitrary government policies that lead to the increase in financial hardship for them and their families. There are no reasons why affluent states such as the UK should have children living in poverty (Alston, 2018) and extreme food insecurity (Marsh, 2019). However, if children are to be able to engage in dialogue and decisions relating to them and other issues of social, political and environmental significance, they need to be able to articulate their ideas effectively. Through the teaching of philosophy in schools, children would be able to develop the language that enables them to think and discuss ideas regarding fundamental concepts such as equality, fairness, justice and tolerance, in ways that are appropriate to their level of understanding, thereby creating a community of enquiry (CoE) (Lipman, 2003). For Dawid (2006), this would include helping to create responsible and socially aware citizens prepared for such important democratic acts as voting and engaging in activities that would help to transform the world. For critical pedagogy, inspiration for this comes from Dewey whose *pragmatism* is about students testing ideas in real-life situations to solve problems in the community and not merely confining their learning to the classroom. Through identifying and tackling such things as injustice, young people will be in a better position to defend and protect themselves against those who seek to abuse or exploit them (Verharen, 2002).

Moreover, this praxis should be reinforced with the right of young people to vote, thereby ensuring that political leaders will be mindful of their obligations towards them. In the UK, there have been some developments in Scotland, where politicians have enabled sixteen- and seventeen-year-olds to vote in Scottish parliamentary elections and also gave them a say in the Scottish independence referendum of 2014. Also, Welsh sixteen-year-olds now have the right to vote for their local AM (Assembly Member) in the Welsh Assembly (Electoral Reform Society, 2017). However, the British government still refuses to give them the vote in Westminster Parliamentary elections (Hossein-Pour, 2019), and, recently, in 2016, the government denied them the opportunity to play a part in the momentous decision that will affect them more than any other group in the electorate, namely Britain's continuing membership of the European Union, asserting that 'full citizenship rights including voting should be gained at adulthood' (Hossein-Pour, 2019) and that young people lack 'sufficient maturity and responsibility' (Stephenson, 2019).

In terms of the curriculum, young people should be consulted regarding its content and delivery, and it should reflect the diverse cultures and experiences of children in Britain, rather than there being one version of the world dominated by a single Western patriarchal ideology. This issue and the need to decolonise the curriculum will be examined in Chapter 5.

Points for reflection and consideration in this chapter

This chapter has examined the effects of neoliberal governments' policies on the welfare and education of their citizens. From the systems of welfare, education and testing, the harmful consequences are evident and yet governments such as those in the US and the UK seem to ignore the evidence and persist in their punitive strategies.

- Critics of government austerity policy believe the consequences have been a 'disgrace'. What are the possible alternative perspectives on the issue?
- Is testing children on a regular basis the best way to find out how 'educated' they are?
- Traditionalists such as Michael Gove and Melanie Phillips believe that children need to be taught in a controlled and safe environment of the classroom. Moreover, they cannot be

trusted to make important decisions about their learning, as they are not mature enough to know what is best for them. Do you agree?

References

Alexander, R. (ed.) (2009) *Children, Their World, Their Education: Final Report and Recommendations of the Cambridge Primary Review*. London: Routledge.

Alston, P. (2018) *Statement on visit to the United Kingdom, by Professor Philip Alston, United Nations special rapporteur on extreme poverty and human rights, London*. 16 November. Available at: www.ohchr.org/en/NewsEvents/Pages/DisplayNews. aspx?NewsID=23881&LangID=E (Accessed 2 December 2018).

Andrews, P. +80 (2014) 'OECD and Pisa tests are damaging education worldwide – academics'. *The Guardian*, 6 May. Available at: https://www.theguardian.com/education/2014/may/06/oecd-pisa-tests-damaging-education-academics (Accessed 5 December 2019).

Anielski, M. (2007) *The Economics of Happiness: Building Genuine Wealth*. Gabriola Island, BC: New Society Publishers.

Annesley, C. (2016) 'Getting more women into ministerial jobs is not that hard – Here's how to do it'. *The Conversation*. Available at: https://theconversation.com/getting-more-women-into-ministerial-jobs-is-not-that-hard-heres-how-to-do-it-55897 (Accessed 5 March 2020).

Berlinski, C. (2011) *There Is No Alternative: Why Margaret Thatcher Matters*. New York: Basic Books.

Birrell, G. (2014) 'PISA education rankings are a problem that can't be solved'. *The Conversation*. Available at: https://theconversation.com/pisa-education-rankings-are-a-problem-that-cant-be-solved-24933 (Accessed 28 February 2020).

Booth, R. (2019) 'Amber Rudd to lodge complaint over UN's austerity report'. *The Guardian*, 22 May. Available at: www.theguardian.com/politics/2019/ may/22/amber-rudd-to-lodge-complaint-over-un-austerity-report (Accessed 2 June 2019).

Chakrabortty, A. (2016) 'The super-rich blackmail us with threats to leave the UK. We should call their bluff'. *The Guardian*. Available at: https://www.theguardian.com/commentisfree/2016/may/17/super-rich-leave-uk-london-media-housing-market (Accessed 9 March 2020).

Christophers, B. (2019) 'Ending austerity: stop councils selling off public assets'. *The Conversation*. Available at: https://theconversation.com/ending-austerity-stop-councils-selling-off-public-assets-113858 (Accessed 5 March 2020).

Civinini, C. (2019) 'Pisa: UK teenagers "less happy than in other countries"'. *TES*, 3 December 2019. Available at: https://www.tes.com/news/pisa-uk-teenagers-less-happy-other-countries (Accessed 2 March 2020).

Coles, T. (2014a) *Never Mind the Inspectors: Here's Punk Learning*. Carmarthen: Crown House Publisher.

Coles, T. (2014b) 'Critical pedagogy: schools must equip students to challenge the status quo'. *Teacher Network, The Guardian*, February. Available at: www.theguardian.com/teacher-network/teacher-blog/2014/feb/25/critical-pedagogyschools-students-challenge (Accessed 5 March 2014).

Corlett, A. (2019) *The Living Standards Outlook 2019*. Available at: www. resolutionfoundation.org/publications/the-living-standards-outlook-2019/ (Accessed 30 May 2019).

Crouch, D. (2018) 'The Swedish 15-year-old who's cutting class to fight the climate crisis'. *The Guardian*. Available at: https://www.theguardian.com/science/2018/sep/01/swedish-15-year-old-cutting-class-to-fight-the-climate-crisis (Accessed 6 March 2020).

Dawid, J. (2006) 'Communities of enquiry with younger children'. LT Scotland Early Years and Citizenship Conference, July. Available at: www.docstoc. com/docs/26387812/Communities-of-Enquiry---Early-Years-Conference-notes (Accessed 15 January 2015).

Dorling, D. (2011) *Injustice: Why Social Inequalities Persist*. Bristol: The Policy Press.

Ebersohn, L. (2017) 'Why resilience matters for schools trying to thrive in tough situations'. *The Conversation*. Available at: https://theconversation.com/why-resilience-matters-for-schools-trying-to-thrive-in-tough-situations-78207 (Accessed 2 March 2020).

Electoral Reform Society. (2017) Votes at 16 'Scottish and Welsh 16 and 17-year-olds can vote while their peers across the border are still disenfranchised'. Available at: https://www.electoral-reform.org.uk/campaigns/votes-at-16/ (Accessed 11 March 2020).

Faulkner, K. (2010) 'Children will learn poetry and monarchs of England by heart under Tory plans.' *The Mail Online*. 6 March. Available at: https://www.dailymail.co.uk/news/article-1255899/Children-learn-poetry-monarchs-England-heart-Tory-plans.html (Accessed 20 April 2020).

Fawcett Society. (2018) 'Legal system "failing" women and in need of reform, says Fawcett in landmark sex discrimination law review'. Available at: https://www.fawcettsociety.org.uk/news/legal-system-failing-women-need-reform-says-fawcett-landmark-sex-discrimination-law-review (Accessed 5 March 2020).

Fitz, J. (no date) *'Welfare, the Family and the Child' Unit 12 in Society Education and the State*. Milton Keynes: The Open University.

Ford, D. R., Portfilio, B. and Goldstein, R.A. (2015) 'The News Media, Education, and the Subversion of the Neoliberal Social Imaginary'. *Critical Education*. Vol. 6. No. 5, pp. 1–24.

Freire, P. (1970) *Cultural Action for Freedom*. Cambridge, MA: Harvard Educational Review.

Freire, P. (1996) *Pedagogy of the Oppressed*. London: Penguin.

Goldacre, M., Hall, N. and Yates, D. (2014) 'Hospitalisation for children with rickets in England: a historical perspective'. *The Lancet*. Vol. 383, No. 9917, pp. 597–598.

Hancock, C., Bettiol, S. and Smith, L. (2015) 'Socioeconomic variation in height: Analysis of National Child Measurement Programme data for England'. *British Medical Journal*. Vol. 101, No. 5. Available at: https://adc.bmj.com/content/101/5/422.long (Accessed 6 June 2020).

Harvey, D. (2007) 'Neoliberalism as a creative destruction'. *Annals of the American Academy of Political and Social Science*. Vol. 610, pp. 22–44.

Healey, G. and Ahmed, M. (2019) 'Gender pay gap hasn't been fixed by transparency – Fines may force companies to act'. *The Conversation*. Available at: https://theconversation.com/gender-pay-gap-hasnt-been-fixed-by-transparency-fines-may-force-companies-to-act-112540 (Accessed 5 March 2020).

Hirsch, E.D. (1987) *Cultural Literacy: What Every American Needs to Know*. Boston, MA: Houghton Mifflin Company.

Hossein-Pour, A. (2019) 'Boris Johnson rejects plan for teenagers and EU nationals to vote in December election'. *Politics Home*. 29 October. Available at: https://www.politicshome.com/news/uk/politics/news/107638/boris-johnson-rejects-plan-teenagers-and-eu-nationals-vote-december (Accessed 6 March 2020).

Human Rights Watch. (2019) *Nothing Left in the Cupboards: Austerity, Welfare Cuts, and the Right to Food in the UK*. May 2019. Available at: www.hrw.org/report/2019/05/20/nothing-left-cupboards/austerity-welfare-cuts-and-right-food-uk (Accessed 25 April 2020).

Jerrim, J. (2019) 'Is England's PISA 2018 data reliable?' *IOE London* Blog 3 December. Available at: https://ioelondonblog.wordpress.com/2019/12/03/is-englands-pisa-2018-data-reliable/ (Accessed 18 February 2020).

Jerrim, J. and Macmillan, L. (2015) 'Income inequality, intergenerational mobility, and the Great Gatsby curve: Is education the key?' *Social Forces*. Vol. 94, No. 2, pp. 505–533.

Kendrick, A.H. (2019) 'To help students overcome setbacks, they need to develop "academic buoyancy"'. *The Conversation*. Available at: https://theconversation.com/to-help-students-overcome-setbacks-they-need-to-develop-academic-buoyancy-113469 (Accessed 2 March 2020).

Klineberg, O. (1928) 'An experimental study of speed and other factors in "racial" differences'. *Archives of Psychology*, Vol. 15, No. 93, pp. 1–111.

Lansdown, G. (1994) 'Children's rights', in B. Mayall (ed.), *Children's Childhoods Observed and Experienced*. London: Routledge, pp. 33–44.

Lipman, M. (2003) *Thinking in Education*. Cambridge: Cambridge University Press.

Maisuria, A. (2014) 'The neo-liberalisation policy agenda and its consequences for education in England: a focus on resistance now and possibilities for the future'. *Policy Futures in Education*. Vol. 12, No. 2, pp. 286–295.

Masci, C., Johnes, G. and Agasisti, T. (2018) 'Student and school performance across countries: A machine learning approach'. *European Journal of Operational Research*, Vol. 69, No. 3, pp. 1072–1085.

Marsh, S. (2019) '"A national shame": Headteachers voice anger about pupils' hunger'. *The Guardian*, 20 May. Available at: www.theguardian.com/education/2019/may/20/a-national-shame-headteachers-voice-anger-about-pupils-hunger (Accessed 7 June 2019).

Martin, A.J. and Marsh, H.W. (2008) 'Academic buoyancy: Towards an understanding of students' everyday academic resilience'. *Journal of School Psychology*. Vol. 6, No. 1, pp. 53–83.

McCarthy-Jones, S. (2018) 'Survivors of sexual violence are let down by the criminal justice system – here's what should happen next'. *The Conversation*. Available at: https://theconversation.com/survivors-of-sexual-violence-are-let-down-by-the-criminal-justice-system-heres-what-should-happen-next-94138 (Accessed 7 March 2020).

McCowen, T. (2016) 'Universities and the post-2015 development agenda: An analytical framework'. *Higher Education*. Vol. 72, pp. 505–532. Available at: https://link.springer.com/article/10.1007/s10734-016-0035-7 (Accessed 21 September 2019).

Montacute, R. (2018) *Access to Advantage: The Influence of Schools and Place on Admissions to Top Universities*. London: The Sutton Trust.

National Union of Teachers. (2016) *The Mismeasurement of Learning: How Tests Are Damaging Children and Primary Education*. London: NUT.

Neate, R. (2019) 'Super-rich prepare to leave UK "within minutes" if Labour wins election'. *The Guardian*. Available at: https://www.theguardian.com/news/2019/nov/02/super-rich-leave-uk-labour-election-win-jeremy-corbyn-wealth-taxes (Accessed 10 March 2020).

Niyozov, S. and Hughes, W. (2019) 'Problems with PISA: Why Canadians should be skeptical of the global test'. *The Conversation*. Available at: https://theconversation.com/problems-with-pisa-why-canadians-should-be-skeptical-of-the-global-test-118096 (Accessed 20 February 2020).

Oakley, A. (1994) 'Women and children first and last: Parallels and differences between children's and women's studies', in B. Mayall (ed.), *Children's Childhoods Observed and Experienced*. London: Routledge.

OECD. (2011) *Equity and Quality in Education – Supporting Disadvantaged Students and Schools*. Available at: http://www.oecd.org/education/school/equityandqualityineducation-supportingdisadvantagedstudentsandschools.htm (Accessed 26 February 2020).

OECD. (2019) *Programme for International Student Assessment (PISA) Results from PISA 2018*. Available at: https://www.oecd.org/pisa/publications/PISA2018_CN_GBR.pdf (Accessed 21 January 2020).

OECD. (2020) *OECD Countries 2020*. Available at: http://worldpopulationreview.com/countries/oecd-countries/ (Accessed 14 February 2020).

Office for National Statistics. (2018) *Gender Pay Gap in the UK: 2018*. Available at: https://www.ons.gov.uk/employmentandlabourmarket/peopleinwork/earningsandworkinghours/bulletins/genderpaygapintheuk/2018 (Accessed 7 March 2020).

Olssen, M. and Peters, M. (2005) 'Neoliberalism, higher education and the knowledge economy: from the free market to knowledge capitalism'. *Journal of Education Policy*. Vol. 20, No. 3, pp. 313–345.

Parton, D. (2019) 'Government must "create childhood strategy", charity urges'. *Children and Young People Now*. 9 July 2019. Available at: https://www.cypnow.co.uk/news/article/government-must-create-childhood-strategy-charity-urges (Accessed 2 March 2020).

Pereira, A., Handa, S. and Holmqvist, G. (2017) *Prevalence and Correlates of Food Insecurity among Children across the Globe*. Florence: UNICEF.

Phillips, M. (1996) *All Must Have Prizes*. London: Little, Brown & Company.

Piketty, T. (2014) (trans A. Goldhammer) *Capital in the Twenty-First Century*. Cambridge, MA: The Belknap Press.

Programme for International Student Assessment (PISA). (2018) 'PISA 2018: Released field trial new reading items'. Available at: www.oecd.org/pisa/test/PISA2018-Released-New-REA-Items.pdf (Accessed 8 February 2019).

Read, J. (2020) 'Dominic Cummings suggested NHS could fund selection of genetic traits in babies'. *The New European*. Available at: https://www.theneweuropean.co.uk/top-stories/dominic-cummings-blog-on-genetics-1-6523494 (Accessed 2 March 2020).

Robinson, K. (2010) *Changing Education Paradigms. TED Talks: RSA Anime*. Available at: https://www.ted.com/talks/ken_robinson_changing_education_paradigms (Accessed on 23 December 2019).

Rose, N. (1999) *Powers of Freedom: Reframing Political Thought*. Cambridge: Cambridge University Press.

Rudduck, J. and Flutter, J. (2004) *How to Improve Your School*. London: Continuum.

Sands, G. (2017) 'Are the PISA education results rigged?' *Forbes*. Available at: www.forbes.com/sites/realspin/2017/01/04/are-the-pisa-education-results-rigged/?sh=5e02902b1561 (Accessed 15 February 2019).

Savage, M., Cunningham, N., Devine, F., Friedman, S., Laurison, D., McKenzie, L., Miles, A., Snee, H. and Wakeling, P. (2015) *Social Class in the 21st Century*. London: Pelican.

Severs, J. (2017) 'The Truth about mental health in schools'. *TES* 30 January 2019. https://www.tes.com/news/truth-about-mental-health-schools (Accessed 12 March 2020).

Social Metrics Commission (2018) *A New Measure of Poverty for the UK*. September. London: Legatum Institute.

Social Mobility Commission. (2016) *Social Mobility and Higher Education*. Available at: https://assets.publishing.service.gov.uk/government/uploads/system/uploads/attachment_data/file/545821/Higher_Education_factsheet.pdf (Accessed 23 December 2018).

Stephenson, B. (2019) 'Should the voting age be lowered to 16?' *The Independent*, 23 May. Available at: https://www.independent.co.uk/news/uk/politics/should-the-voting-age-be-lowered-to-16-a8882731.html (Accessed 11 March 2020).

Strauss, V. (2015) 'The tower of PISA is badly leaning. An argument for why it should be saved'. *Washington Post*. 24 March. Available at: https://www.washingtonpost.com/news/answer-sheet/wp/2015/03/24/the-tower-of-pisa-is-badly-leaning-an-argument-for-why-it-should-be-saved/ (Accessed 26 February 2020).

Taylor, M., Lavelle, S., Walker, A., Noor, P. and Henley, J. (2019) 'School pupils call for radical climate action in UK-wide strike'. *The Guardian*, 15 February. Available at: www.theguardian.com/environment/2019/feb/15/uk-climate-changestrike-school-pupils-children-environment-protest (Accessed 20 March 2019).

The Guardian. (2014) 'Michael Gove urges "traditional" punishments for school misbehaviour', 2 February. Available at: https://www.theguardian.com/education/2014/feb/02/michael-gove-traditional-punishments-school-misbehaviour (Accessed 2 March 2020).

The Washington Post (2015) 'The Tower of PISA is badly leaning'. 24 March. Available at: https://www.washingtonpost.com/news/answer-sheet/wp/2015/03/24/the-tower-of-pisa-is-badly-leaning-an-argument-for-why-it-should-be-saved/ (Accessed 25 April 2019).

Thunberg, G. (2018) 'Climate strike'. Available at: www.youtube.com/channel/ UCQbz6u1CyABskXzDhav-3vxw (Accessed 27 March 2020).

Twenge, J. (2019) 'The mental health crisis among America's youth is real – and staggering'. *The Conversation*. Available at: https://theconversation.com/the-mental-health-crisis-among-americas-youth-is-real-and-staggering-113239 (Accessed 5 March 2020).

UNHRC. (2017) Statement on Visit to the USA, by Professor Philip Alston, United Nations Special Rapporteur on extreme poverty and human rights. Available at: https://www.ohchr.org/EN/NewsEvents/Pages/DisplayNews.aspx?NewsID=22533 (Accessed 3 March 2020).

UNHRC. (2019) *Visit to the United Kingdom of Great Britain and Northern Ireland: Report of the Special Rapporteur on Extreme Poverty and Human Rights*. Available at: https://undocs.org/pdf?symbol=en/A/HRC/41/39/Add.1 (Accessed 18 July 2019).

UNICEF. (2007) *Child Poverty in Perspective: An Overview of Child Well-Being in Rich Countries*. Florence: UNICEF.

UNICEF. (2013) *Child Well-Being in Rich Countries: A Comparative Overview*. Florence: UNICEF.

Verharen, C.C. (2002) 'Philosophy's role in Afrocentric education'. *Journal of Black Studies*. Vol. 32, No. 3, pp. 295–321.

Volante, L. and Jerrim, J. (2018) 'Education does not equal social mobility'. *The Conversation*. Available at: https://theconversation.com/education-doesnot-always-equal-social-mobility-106386 (Accessed 7 February 2019).

White, I. (2013) 'Governments shirk their responsibilities in the name of "resilience"'. *The Conversation*. Available at: https://theconversation.com/governments-shirk-their-responsibilities-in-the-name-of-resilience-15117 (Accessed 2 March 2020).

Wilkinson, I. (2019) 'Food poverty: Agony of hunger the norm for many children in the UK'. *The Conversation*. Available at: https://theconversation.com/food-poverty-agony-of-hunger-the-norm-for-many-children-in-the-uk-116216 (Accessed 16 February 2020).

Wilkinson, R. and Pickett, K. (2009) *The Spirit Level: Why More Equal Societies Almost Always Do Better*. London: Penguin.

Wilkinson, R. and Pickett, K. (2018) *The Inner Level: How More Equal Societies Reduce Stress, Restore Sanity and Improve Everyone's Well-being*. London: Allen Lane.

Wright, D. and Anderson, H. (2018) 'Unacceptable rises in child poverty as more working parents left unable to make ends meet'. Joseph Rowntree Foundation Home/Press. Available at: www.jrf.org.uk/press/rises-child-poverty-moreparents-left-unable-make-ends-meet (Accessed 25 April 2020).

4 Austerity in a time of spectacular wealth

Introduction

In March 2019, *Forbes*, the journal of the wealthy, reported that for the second year in a decade there had been a decline in the number of billionaires as well as a drop in their overall wealth by $400 billion (*Forbes*, 2019). The consequences of poor stock market performance and other 'economic forces' had been the cause of this decline in their 'fortunes'. Despite this, however, Hwang (2018) points out that the wealthiest and highest paid are flourishing and the gap between them and the poorest and lowest paid is getting ever wider (World Inequality Report, 2018). We live, once again, in a time of growing extremes globally, in terms of the gap between the poorest and lowest paid, and the richest and highest paid.

The ethics of excessive wealth

It is significant that in the rare debates about wealth and income inequality in countries such as Britain and the US the ethical and moral position of the very wealthy, including their often-excessive lifestyles, their disproportionate consumption of the world's resources and their relatively large carbon footprint (see Chapter 2), are rarely seriously discussed in the mainstream media in comparison to the so-called underclass (Jones, 2011; Savage et al., 2015), who are subjected to regular accusations of moral weakness and are stigmatised as being welfare 'scroungers' and therefore undeserving of support. If anything, the super-rich are treated as a class apart separated from the rest of us by favourable legal, political, fiscal and taxation rules and a celebrity aura that together create a social and cultural taboo against raising such matters for fear of offending them, or worse. In the 2019 general election when Clive Lewis, Labour's shadow Treasury minister, suggested that billionaires 'shouldn't exist. It's a travesty that there are people on this planet living on less than a dollar a day' (Neate, 2019), his comments were met with outrage. Legal and public relations representatives of the very wealthy issued statements claiming that, should a Labour government be elected and impose higher taxes on them, or tackle such practices as their tax avoidance and evasion with more enthusiasm than Conservative governments ever have, they would leave the country (Neate, 2019). British billionaire Peter Hargreaves, a founder of the stockbrokers Hargreaves Landsdown, who has an estimated wealth of £3bn (Neate, 2019) suggested that he and his fellow billionaires were 'petrified' by what a Labour government would do to the 'wealth creators' of the country suggesting that: 'if 50 of us [the biggest taxpayers] got on a plane and left, that would put a big hole in the chancellor's budget' (Neate, 2019). This, indeed, is what many of them threatened to do.

By claiming to be the 'wealth creators' as well as the ones on whom the country relies to pay the taxes that help to keep public services operating (Johnson, 2013), this small but highly influential group of very wealthy individuals have managed to create a narrative that not only justifies such excessive amounts of wealth but also underplays, if not denies, the contribution of ordinary workers and employees to the creation of a nation's wealth as well as welfare. As the economist Jim Stanford (2015: 68) states, 'Just about anything we need or want in our lives requires human effort to produce it … almost nothing comes without work'. So, none of the wealth acquired by these billionaires would exist had it not been the case that many workers toiled, often on low wages, on their behalf. And this raises a simple question of how hard the owners of such businesses work. Most of the very wealthy boast about their industry, inventiveness and dedication to their product or service. Bearing in mind that a growing proportion of the wealthy, and not necessarily the super-rich, are rentiers (Piketty, 2014), that is, individuals who own enough in the way of business assets that already exist, often through inheritance, such as corporate shares and real estate, that they do not have to work at all should they choose not to on account of the returns on their capital (Piketty, 2014; Stanford, 2015; Bregman, 2017). Bregman (2017) describes this group of capitalists as 'parasitic', living on the profits of business and industry without actually working, producing or creating anything themselves, while often benefitting from favourable tax systems around the world (Harrington, 2018).

Although there are reports of some billionaires in the UK and the US actually suggesting that they should be paying more in taxes (Coudriet, 2019), there seems to be little in the way of them renouncing the right to *be* a billionaire and to own or earn such vast sums that it would be virtually impossible for any individual to spend it in any meaningful way during their lifetime. It is, indeed, very difficult to comprehend the nature and scale of such large numbers given that most of us rarely deal with sums above tens of thousands of pounds, dollars or euros. When we enter the realm of hundreds of millions and billions, many find it difficult to relate to numbers at this range (Landy et al., 2013). However, a few cursory calculations reveal some stark facts. If, for example, we take the amount accumulated by Bill Gates between 1987 and 2016, which was $120bn, it can be estimated that over this thirty-year period his average yearly income would have been $4bn (Hwang, 2018). Or, assuming you are a highly 'successful' individual earning $200m per year over ten years, you would be earning an average of $6 per second or approximately $21,000 per hour. If we place someone's earnings in a 'per hour' value, one which most of us have experience of, it is possible to gain a much clearer picture of how the average worker compares. We may even have a debate about whether anyone is worth such an hourly rate and whether it is morally justifiable to allow individuals to control such huge resources when globally and within nations poverty persists, even in the most affluent societies (UNHRC, 2017, 2019). In a capitalist global economy, the general consensus among the wealthy is that not only do they deserve what they earn or possess but that their right to unlimited accumulation of the world's limited resources and assets is inalienable and based on the principle that there should be minimal restrictions and regulations in a free market. Moreover, any attempts by governments or international organisations to interfere with this freedom in any way is seen as likely to distort the 'efficiency' of the market and act as a brake on innovation and enterprise.

Unlimited wealth without responsibility

As we have already seen, this neoclassical approach to economic activity places no moral or ethical obligation on economic actors to seek or create social or public good. It is merely something one should be free to do, rather than be forced to do by the state. Indeed, governments that are committed to neoliberal economic policies promote philanthropy and charity as the best way of supporting those in need rather than through the state, and if the state is to provide welfare it should be basic, minimal and designed to encourage individuals to view employment of any kind as the preferred option. This was in fact one of the themes of Boris Johnson's 2013 Margaret Thatcher Lecture in which he accused those who advocate imposing higher taxes on the very wealthy as suffering from the politics of envy and urged them instead to celebrate these individuals for being the *Stakhanovites* of the tax system in terms of the record levels of taxation they contribute to the state that is used to support our education and welfare systems. They should in his view be hailed as heroes rather than punished for what some may see as their greed and avarice. To illustrate his point, he invokes Margaret Thatcher's interpretation of the parable of the Good Samaritan in Luke's Gospel, Chapter 10: 'He would not have been of much use to the chap who fell amongst thieves if he had not been rich enough to help' (Johnson, 2013). Not only does Thatcher, and indeed Johnson, provide what could be described as a somewhat distorted reading of the teachings of Jesus Christ (see Matthew 19–24 and Luke 18–25, King James Version); it is also a clearly dissonant message to one that parents, teachers and religious leaders are expected to teach children, such as the values of fairness and sharing (Irvine, 2017; Northern Ireland Curriculum, 2020). For Johnson, it is those who accumulate great wealth that offer the hope of salvation and a better life for us all here on earth, not the greater sharing and distribution of such wealth through progressive systems of taxation. However, he does urge the wealthy to recapture the culture of philanthropy that once existed in Britain in the nineteenth century and which, allegedly, currently does so much good in the USA (Osisli and Zarins, 2018), so that they can spread their largesse in the ways they choose to the rest of us.

Managing the poor

The current debate about dealing with the poor in Britain seems to have changed little over the past one hundred and fifty years (Mooney, 1998). During Victorian times, it was dominated not by a belief in the need to reduce poverty but by the idea that state welfare intervention for the poor and charitable giving, if needed, should not be unconditional or long-term. The natural order was seen as one where the poor needed to be controlled and managed in such a way that they did not pose a threat to the ruling classes. For the Charity Organisation Society of Britain (founded 1869) which was made up of the various charitable groups, the purpose of charity is not to give 'indiscriminately' but to instil in the poor working class a sense of self-reliance rather than reliance on the state or charity. 'Indiscriminate' charitable giving was seen as creating a demoralised poor who would become incapable of caring for themselves through work. Mooney (1998) suggests that philanthropy in Victorian times was about the 'remoralization' of the poor as well as imposing control over their personal habits and practices in their families in order to alter their behaviour in line with prevailing ideas of Victorian morality, deference and living within one's means. It was very much a method of control imposed by the middle and upper classes over the working class, but specifically in the private world of the family. This is why the process was both gendered and class-based in that female philanthropists were seen as being most suited to the task of monitoring, advising and supporting the poor by entering their domestic world (Mooney, 1998).

The minimal state

With the growth of inequality in many affluent democratic countries such as the US and Britain as a result of a collapse of the post-war political consensus on welfare between 1945 and 1979 and the impact of neoliberal policies from the 1970s onwards (Boronski and Hassan, 2020; Goldin and Muggah, 2020), there has been a renewed debate about the role of the state and the consequences of high levels of unemployment and the growing precariousness of employment due to the increasing restrictions on trades unions' activity and workers' rights and large-scale privatisations by many Western democracies (Harvey, 2007). Right-wing think tanks such as the Institute for Economic Affairs (Lister, 1996) raise similar concerns to those of the Victorian period about the emergence of a 'culture of dependency' within a working class that was deemed to have lost any incentive to seek work due to the 'handout culture' of state welfare (Marsland, 1996). The American sociologist Charles Murray (1996) visited Britain in the mid-1990s and painted a picture of a country seemingly under threat from a degenerate underclass, rather than of a society in which the poor were being demonised and scapegoated by politicians and the right-wing press for the rising levels of urban decay, crime, family breakdown, educational failure and other social disorders caused by the withdrawal of the state from its responsibility to care for its citizens. In one of the most vituperative assessments of the welfare system in the UK, the British social scientist David Marsland (1996) claims that the Welfare State is not the symbol of a civilised society but a 'philosophically incoherent' concept that is a drain on national resources which saps the economic energy and enterprise of the nation through excessive taxation and expenditure on hopeless causes such as poverty, which he claims is a myth perpetrated by socialists, university academics and the poverty lobby.

Higher education has come in for particular criticism. Marsland (1996) and other critics of the welfare state such as Peter Saunders (2010, 2012) have attacked their fellow university academics, claiming that social science departments of most universities are dominated by left-wing sociologists who, they claim, promote a false view of society as being riven with inequality caused by social disadvantage rather than by natural differences in ability and intelligence and thereby legitimating a belief in the need for a 'bloated' welfare state (Marsland, 1996). It could be argued that these attacks on policy and welfare researchers have played a key role in promoting the current scepticism many right-wing populist and conservative politicians show for the ideas and findings of 'experts', particularly research evidence that challenges the prevailing ideology of neoliberalism. Mrs Thatcher was particularly suspicious of sociologists claiming that sociology was neither a proper subject for study nor a science, seeing it instead as an ideology that gave credibility to Soviet communism. She also challenged the notion of *society* as a relevant intellectual and policy concept, insisting that governments only need to think in terms of 'individual men and women' and 'families' who should, as far as possible, take responsibility for looking after themselves and then their neighbours (Keay, 1987).

These views of welfare from Victorian times through to the 1980s and 1990s link seamlessly to those in more recent years which have led to a continued assault on the welfare state by both

Labour and Conservative-led governments. However, in the neoliberal age, as recommended by Marsland (1996), Murray (1996) and others, the state plays a significant role in engaging the services of private business in the process of imposing a regime of surveillance and remoralisation on benefits claimants and the poor, which culminated in the introduction of the system of Universal Credit in the UK. The moralising rhetoric of Victorian times, though, is still strong as we can see from the comments of Iain Duncan Smith, the architect of the system of Universal Credit, who once commented to a claimant: 'This is not an easy life any more chum. I think you're a slacker' (Toynbee, 2018). We are witnessing the continued withdrawal of the state from the welfare of its citizens, particularly the poor and vulnerable, the increasing use of private companies to administer social and welfare services for a profit, as well as forcing these groups to rely increasingly on charitable organisations and philanthropy to fill the growing cracks in the system which can only lead to greater levels of injustice and inequalities in terms of wealth and income (Dorling, 2011; Savage et al., 2015). The evidence presented by global policy analysts (Wilkinson and Pickett, 2009, 2018; Jerrim and Macmillan, 2015; Volante and Jerrim, 2018) suggests that in more unequal societies it is the wealthy who benefit most, as measured in terms of such criteria as health, life expectancy, social mobility and education. In more equal societies, on the other hand, everyone benefits. However, it would seem that it is the former type of society that Conservative governments wish to create.

The welfare state: a civilised state

An alternative view is that the welfare state and progressive taxation are the signs of a civilised society. Rather than being philosophically incoherent and a corrupting force, as Marsland claims, it helps to create a society in which the weak, those with disabilities and the vulnerable can be valued and protected from the excesses of the few. It is a place where everyone is more likely to be supported and cared for in times of need, regardless of their means and how much they have paid into the system. Moreover, a welfare state is a crucial long-term investment in a society's children and its future security in the event of long-term national crises such as war, natural disasters or, indeed, global pandemics. Marsland (1996) however sees this as an extravagant waste as he claims the number of those who are unable to look after themselves and their families is likely to be very small. In such cases:

> the state should remain responsible. This does not require the massive machinery of the welfare state. Modest help organised through the tax system and by means of small-scale organisations at local level, making maximum use of voluntary agencies, would be sufficient.
> (Marsland, 1996)

We have seen how charitable as well as philanthropic organisations are now playing an increasingly dominant role in filling the gap in welfare left by the state. Philanthropic organisations globally have been donating ever-increasing sums to worthy causes, and the wealthy donors have been lauded as heroes with their often high-profile projects that claim to be dedicated to such ideals as increasing access to education, promoting human rights or ridding the world of disease (Hay and Muller, 2014). In the case of the COVID-19 virus pandemic, Vogel and Kurak (2020) report very positively about the record levels of philanthropic funding of projects to tackle the pandemic which reached $1bn across the world by early March 2020 (Vogel and Kurak). Vogel and Kurak also emphasise the ability of wealthy 'enterprising families' who own companies that fund philanthropic causes, to act more quickly and effectively in crisis situations than the state or other types of business, such as those controlled by shareholders.

The rise of 'philanthrocapitalism'

However, whereas many charities such as the Trussell Trust are associated with ideas of 'compassion', human 'dignity', and 'justice' (Trussel Trust, 2021), with no motive to give, other than there being a perceived need caused by the absence of state provision, and an ultimate desire to make their own existence unnecessary (Trussel Trust, 2021), philanthropic foundations are usually run by persons or groups with a particular agenda and 'the active promotion of causes' (Deane,1996, cited by Mooney, 1998). These have been exposed by Hay and Muller (2014), who claim we are entering a 'golden age of philanthropy'. They point out that since the late 1990s a growing number of the very rich have been donating ever-increasing amounts of their wealth to a range of causes, be it health programmes (Bill and Melinda Gates Foundation, 2010), housing, education and medical research (Chan Zuckerberg Initiative) or alleviating poverty (Brian Armstrong's GiveCrypto.org). Evidence for the US, for example, shows that although individuals are giving less, down by 1.1 per cent in 2018, giving by foundations and philanthropic organisations run by the very wealthy is at record levels, up by 7.3 per cent for the same period (Giving USA, 2019). Indeed, so popular has giving to good causes become among the super-rich that signing up to The Giving Pledge (The Giving Pledge, 2020) has become almost a certificate of compassionate humanitarianism. The initiative was started in 2010 by Warren Buffet, billionaire CEO of Berkshire Hathaway, and Bill Gates, head of Microsoft, to encourage billionaires to pledge the majority of their wealth to charity. The pledge entails no legal contracts or specified causes, merely a 'moral' commitment to use one's private wealth for public good (The Giving Pledge, 2020). The causes are therefore self-selected and, it would seem, arbitrary rather than being based on a coordinated programme or a clear philosophy of what constitutes a good cause.

Reading the testimonies and homilies on The Giving Pledge website, one gets the impression that these super-rich pledgers are donating the majority of their wealth in a selfless manner with no motive other than that of pure altruism, just as any 'ordinary' person might do. However, if we look beyond the public relations material and news releases of the website, it is possible to discern why, in principle, this organisation and the growth of 'super-philanthropy' (Hay and Muller, 2014) is highly problematic, and if we also examine the evidence, it is possible to understand the underlying motives and benefits some of these billionaires derive from such ostentatious acts of giving. What they reveal is that there appear to be grounds for concern about what Hay and Muller (2014) describe as the growth of 'philanthrocapitalism'.

Looked at in terms of principle alone, philanthropic relationships often place the recipient and 'benefactor' in an asymmetric relationship whereby the latter is seen as the superior party, morally as well as financially and the former owes deference and gratitude to the latter in order to secure the relationship: continued support for the recipient may be dependent upon potentially arbitrary requirements or rules imposed by the benefactor. This is due to the fact that philanthropists often have their own personal or ideological agenda or, possibly, a moral crusade that may be at odds with the interests of recipients or specific groups in the community. While the role of such organisations in the US is currently much greater than many other Western democracies (Hay and Muller, 2014), particularly due to the general absence of state support in many aspects of people's lives in that country, in Britain there also exists a wide range of philanthropic groups, some of which promote causes and fund projects based on fundamentalist Christian and extreme right-wing ideologies. This growth has been facilitated primarily by prising open the state education systems in countries such as the US and Britain and the attempt to create quasi-markets in education. In Britain, the Scottish multimillionaire founder of the Stagecoach group, Brian Souter, is a Christian fundamentalist and promoter of socially conservative causes who privately funded a referendum to retain Section 28 of the Local Government Act (1986), introduced under the Conservatives in 1987. Section 28 of the act banning the 'promotion' of homosexual relationships by local authorities in schools was repealed in 2003, but Souter, who campaigned strongly against its decriminalisation, spent £1m to fund a private referendum on the issue (Topham, 2019). In an increasingly laissez fair global economy, wealthy philanthropists are able to use their wealth to promote causes that may be highly controversial or even objectionable. In some jurisdictions, they may have free rein to promote any causes they choose. It could be argued that a caring and humanising welfare society should not be subject to the whims of personally motivated and unaccountable individuals who have the power to greatly affect people's lives. It should instead be guided by principles of human rights and welfare needs that take account of each individual's and group's social, cultural and political rights as citizens, rather than those defined by someone whose only qualification is that of being a 'very wealthy person'.

The threat posed by philanthrocapitalism

In terms of the evidence relating to the activities of the super-rich, it would seem that they have found a means of making their excessive wealth more respectable as well as presenting themselves as the savours of humanity, often through heroic donations of vast sums to worthy causes such as education, health and housing (Bloom and Rhodes, 2018a). This can certainly be one way of interpreting the record donations by the super-rich during the COVID-19 pandemic (Vogel and Kurak, 2020). What seems to be occurring, according to Hay and Muller (2014), is a paradigm shift in terms of the reconfiguration of charitable giving from one that is a simple act of giving, with the intention of addressing a specific issue or problem, to one that is now subject to market principles: in other words, there is now expected to be some form of payback to the donor, just as one might expect a profit to be made on one's capital investment in the market. Hence the term 'philanthrocapitalism'. In the neoliberal world, every possible interaction and encounter is becoming monetised and allocated value. This, as we have seen, now includes public goods such as health and education (Ford et al., 2015). Moreover, as with the more conventional business ventures that successful entrepreneurs engage in, they now also expect to take control of their charitable investments. So, rather than merely giving to a cause and leaving it to others to execute the charitable act itself, in the Golden Age of Philanthropy decisions on a macro level are increasingly being made by the super-rich donor, thereby ensuring that their particular charitable investment target is met in the most tax-efficient manner (Hay and Muller, 2014), as well as coinciding with specific ideological, moral and economic principles.

This approach often involves a desire to influence or change public policy, so there is usually a high level of engagement with policymakers through political fundraising events and party donations (Syal, 2020). And this is clearly paying off, as CEOs of big corporations are engaging increasingly in activities that are prising open new ways of making a profit by providing services such as social housing, healthcare, education, prison services and administering welfare (Bloom and Rhodes, 2019). As Bloom and Rhodes (2019) suggest, the CEOs of many of the biggest corporations are now quasi-politicians developing policies and delivering service on behalf of government, both local and national.

The impact on education

This is particularly evident in the field of education which has become increasingly deregulated and accessible to non-educational agents in many countries such as the US and Britain where major philanthropic foundations, founded and funded by super-rich donors, are setting up their own schools or investing billions of dollars in university research programmes (Dodgeson, 2018; Reich, 2018). It could be argued that such generous giving by very wealthy individuals to education is highly welcome at a time of government cuts in their education budgets. Indeed, as Robert Reich (Reich, cited by Inside Philanthropy, 2019) points out, such giving has been presented as 'a voluntary expression of liberty that we should celebrate, not scrutinize'. However, it is precisely because such huge sums are involved and there is a decline in regulation and democratic accountability regarding what causes are sponsored and by whom such funds are invested, that there is all the more need to scrutinise this philanthropic giving in such fields as education (Reich, 2018). If, as suggested, education represents a sacred relationship of trust between children, young people and those who fund and educate them, the motives and ideologies of these philanthropists are highly relevant. Furthermore, it is reasonable to ask whether those who have been fortunate enough to amass huge wealth and now claim to be giving back to society are actually making a difference to levels of inequality in society generally and in education in particular.

The evidence regarding all of these issues, however, is not encouraging. With regard to addressing growing inequality, research by Hay and Muller (2014) and Reich (Reich, cited by Inside Philanthropy, 2018) reveals that charitable giving by big donors 'does not predominantly benefit the poor' and, moreover, such wealthy donors in the US who benefit significantly from tax deductions for charitable giving, give least to the poor. The tax benefit costs the US treasury $50 billion a year (Reich, in De Witte, 2018), and yet 'the higher up the income ladder, the less likely donors are to direct their giving to the poor' (Reich, cited by Inside Philanthropy, 2019).

Growing evidence against philanthrocapitalism

In recent years, however, the super-rich chief executive officers (CEOs) find themselves having to defend their positions on a number of fronts, first in relation to their ever-increasing wealth and other forms of compensation in comparison to the average or lowest paid employees, particularly those who toil for them in often terrible conditions and low wages in their factories and workshops around the world (Burke, 2015; McVeigh, 2017). Second, with regard to the evident ineffectiveness of philanthropy in relation to the trickle-down theory of wealth distribution which they have been espousing for decades (Jericho, 2018). Around the world, governments guided by this and other neoliberal doctrines have been cutting company taxes as well as those of their bosses, claiming that this will stimulate investment and higher wages. However, as Joseph Stiglitz, a

Case study 4.1: Philanthrocapitalism, the religious right and the assault on state education

In terms of the declining regulation over who is able to donate and the lack of openness and accountability of wealthy foundations, there do indeed seem to be reasons for concern (Reich, 2018). Foundations and institutions representing Christian fundamentalism and extreme right-wing views that seek to reduce and even shut down state education systems are increasingly influential in countries such as the US (Gehring, 2016). The case of the Koch brothers is particularly troubling. Fred Koch, who founded Koch industries, one of the biggest donors to right-wing causes and education in the US, was an opponent of desegregation in the US and a founder-member of the John Birch Society (JBS) known for its extreme right-wing views and activities (Towler, 2018). In the 1960s, the JBS sought to impeach Chief Justice Earl Warren who, in 1954, issued the US Supreme Court's unanimous decision to desegregate public schools in *Brown v Board of Education*. Fred Koch's sons, Charles and David, are also JBS members. They are also known to contribute to extreme right-wing causes as well as those relating to climate change denial. Koch Industries was identified as one of 140 foundations that were discovered to have channelled $558 million into one hundred organisations set up specifically to deny climate change (Brulle, 2013).

There is, according to Cervone (2017), also a strong and seemingly growing relationship between the religious right and neoliberal foundations in the US, such as those funded by the Koch brothers, which are not only undermining public education in many rural states but are also threatening the belief in education as an experience which involves the free, open and unrestricted investigation of ideas and beliefs by young people. Cervone's research reveals that the growing influence of Christian fundamentalism in rural America means that increasing numbers of local citizens are losing trust in public schools and the so-called liberal educational elite who are often seen as atheistic and intent on wanting to impose what are believed to be dangerous un-Christian ideas, such as the theory of evolution, on their children. These fundamentalist Christians have also been successful in local politics, taking advantage of increasing political apathy. The result is that they are having an increasing influence on the curriculum which often means restrictions on the kinds of ideas that are taught in rural schools. Neoliberal organisations and foundations have capitalised on the anger of local Christians by taking over public schools and offering a curriculum that meets with their approval, and then selling these schools back for a profit. The consequences of this, according to Corvone (2017), have been disastrous not only for democracy but also for the right of children to a curriculum that encourages open and free dialogue and helps to bring about new and innovative ways of thinking and practice which are essential for the next generation if they are to tackle the persisting economic and political crises and to save humanity from impending environmental disaster.

former head of the World Bank and Nobel Prize-winning economist states, 'I don't think there's any validity in it' (Jericho, 2018), and he is well supported by the evidence (IMF, 2015; Tcherneva, 2017). He states that there is very little economic data to show that increases in company profits are leading to higher wages for workers (Jericho, 2018). Moreover, the gap between the highest earners in corporations and their workers is growing ever wider. In the UK, top business executives now earn 133 times more than the average worker (Makortoff, 2019) and in the US the figure is around 300 (Tuttle, 2020).

A shift in opinions about the super-rich

There are signs that ordinary citizens/workers are beginning to see through the myth of trickle-down. Well over half of British people believe that 'the rich are not paying enough tax and their tax should be increased' (YouGov, 2020). Surveys in the US also suggest that there is an increasing belief that the wealthy should pay more. Several years ago, a wealth tax in the US would not even have been contemplated (Reisz, 2020). This has been particularly evident since the passage of the President Trump's Tax Cuts and Jobs Act of 2017 from which America's highest earners benefitted greatly (Tuttle, 2020). Indeed, as a result of this act, in 2018 for the first time in American history, billionaires paid a lower rate of tax (23 per cent) than the lowest paid half of American households (24.2 per cent) (Kelly, 2019). Hence, the very public and dramatic statements by the super-rich declaring their huge pledges to charitable causes: they wish to show that they are 'giving back' to society through charitable giving. But once again the evidence does not support their claims (Bloom and Rhodes, 2018b):

> Neither the philanthropy of the super-rich nor socially directed corporate programmes have any real effect on combating this trend. . . . Instead, vast fortunes in the hands of the few, whether earned through inheritance, commerce or crime, continue to grow at the expense of the poor.

The continuing threat of neoliberalism

However, in the minimal state that neoliberal governments are aspiring to achieve, a combination of charity, philanthropy and basic state welfare provision administered for the state by for-profit organisations is still the direction of travel. But the progress of neoliberalisation, as Harvey (2007) points out, varies in terms of geographical location and the political culture of the countries concerned. Those in which trades unions are still an integral part of industrial relations, such as some of the Scandinavian countries, and Germany which has managed to become the industrial powerhouse of Europe, have been able to develop progressive welfare and health systems (Harvey, 2007). However, in Britain which has been a pioneer of neoliberal thinking and practice since the election of Margaret Thatcher in 1979, the process is much more advanced.

The consequences of further neoliberalisation

It is clear from much of the evidence that a feature of the increasing influence of neoliberalism is the rise in global inequality (World Inequality Report, 2018). Moreover, privatisation, deregulation and liberalisation have led to the collapse of many welfare systems and the emergence of the 'hollow state' (Haeder, 2010) in the form of declining levels and standards of provision for citizens in such areas as health, education, housing and benefits, with services increasingly delivered by for-profit companies. The impact of these developments has meant a deterioration in the quality of life as well as greater hardship, particularly for the most vulnerable (Wilkinson and Pickett, 2009, 2018). Moreover, this declining role of the state in many societies, in terms of investment and planning for future crises, exposes their populations to potentially great harm as we have seen in relation to the COVID-19 pandemic. The effects of neoliberalism on the lives of workers and their rights in less developed countries (LDCs) is magnified that much more in those that lack any welfare provision and have poor working conditions (Burke, 2015; McVeigh, 2017).

A new age of 'hypercapitalism'

Thomas Piketty (2020) suggests that we have entered a time of 'hypercapitalism' in which, following the line of argument in his earlier book *Capital in the 21st Century*, inequality has grown since the decline of the 'golden age of social democracy' when there was a political consensus during the immediate post-war period. This took the form of an agreement in many social democracies on the need for a welfare state and the importance of investing in public education, the health of the nation, the equity of progressive taxation and pension reform: some of the key elements of a humane and ethically driven society. However, with the collapse of the consensus from around 1980, resulting from the growing influence of neoliberalism in the form of Thatcherism in Britain and Reaganomics in the US, there was an assault on these welfare states and their equalising effects resulting from a free education for all, progressive taxation, free healthcare and other investments in the common good (Boronski and Hassan, 2020). The temporary civilising and humanising period of welfare democracy gave way once again to the ideas of neoclassical economics. A consequence of this, according to Piketty (2020), is a return to growing inequality because neoclassical economics is the ideology of inequality: it provides a doctrinal justification for growing wealth inequality which is incompatible with social democracy and social justice. As Piketty (2020) suggests, it does not have to be this way. The evidence that he and his team have collected for the World Inequality Database (no date) set up in 2015 and which was used in the writing of *Ideology and Capitalism* (Piketty, 2020) shows that there is a 'long-term trend towards equality' (Piketty, in Reisz, 2020). In his wide-ranging analysis of historical data on cultures from around the world, he claims that a common theme is the search for equitable ways of distributing resources, but there is always the threat of regressive ideologies taking control: history is made up of a series of 'inequality regimes' (Piketty, 2020) hindering the progress of social justice.

His claims are not made on the basis of any economic doctrine but on the basis of the patterns gleaned from long-term historical data (Piketty, 2014). What this reveals is that over time growth (g) in the economy slows down and is outstripped by returns on capital (r). Because over a lifetime average annual returns on inherited wealth will always be greater than wealth gained from a lifetime of labour, 'the risk of divergence in the distribution of wealth is very high' (Piketty, 2014: 25), and when levels of wealth become extreme then, according to Piketty (2014: 26), they become 'incompatible with principles of social justice fundamental to modern democratic societies'.

Piketty's economic analysis demonstrates a moral and ethical perspective rarely found in mainstream economics. He views current levels of inequality as unacceptable and in need of government intervention through progressive taxation, equal education budgets for every citizen, co-management in which employees are involved in company decision-making and curbs on property accumulation. However, it seems that at present electorates have been reluctant to vote for such policies as can be seen from the general elections in the US in 2016, France in 2017, and the UK in 2015, 2017 and 2019 which have tended to return conservative or populist right-wing governments (Merelli, 2019). There would seem to be an increasing willingness to place their faith in nationalist leaders who have been able to scapegoat foreigners, migrants and so-called educated elites for their problems rather than change the economic system that has so clearly failed.

The need for a critical economics

A key obstacle to the much-needed change in the economics education and thinking that pervades much of the world now is the pre-eminence of neoclassical economics. It provides a set of principles that guide the economic actions of governments and businesses and constitutes, ironically, almost a monopoly in terms of ways of thinking about the economy (Reed, 2018; Piketty, 2020). The grip that neoclassical economics has over our thinking about acts of wealth creation and distribution can be seen in the universities, many of which are now also run on competitive quasi-market principles (Olssen and Peters, 2005; Maisuria, 2014), and where most economics undergraduates are taught a narrow curriculum that presents economics as a unified body of ideas (International Student Initiative for Pluralism in Economics, 2014). Recognition for what is purported to be the highest achievements in the fields of research and original thinking in economics takes the form of a Nobel Prize, which is also dominated by laureates of the neoclassical school (Cahill, 2011), and the top-rated economics journals publish almost exclusively the research findings and theoretical musings of academics of the same persuasion (Thompson, 1997; Elliot, 2017). Moreover, in government, right-wing politicians impose policies of austerity on their most vulnerable citizens whilst simultaneously carrying out tax cuts for the already well-off and super-rich and continue to promote the false hopes of trickle-down theory, proclaiming: 'We are all in this together'. They deregulate the financial sector, open up state welfare provision to private business and generally encourage individual greed over community well-being on the basis of a perverse and failed doctrine that has long promised but failed to 'produce prosperity and lead to maximum happiness' for all (Werner, 2005: 3).

The marginalisation of alternative or heterodox economic thinking and the consequences of this for global economic progress and justice are something that educators and students are beginning to address (Inman, 2014a, 2014b; Piketty, 2014; Reed, 2018). Provoked to action by the financial crash of 2008, which, according to most neoclassical economists, could not have been predicted (Keen, 2017), disillusioned young people and students around the world are seeking to develop a new and *critical economics* as they realise that 'Until we ditch the old textbook, we'll never face up to the challenges of the modern world – or move beyond neoliberalism' (Reed, 2018).

Mainstream economics is still stuck in a metaphysical world of a benevolent invisible hand in which rational actors in pursuit of their individual self-interests operate in conditions of perfect competition resulting in aggregate outcomes that benefit society as a whole (Lavoie, 2014). The consequences have been that neoclassical economists are not good at predicting events such as the financial crash of 2008. August institutions such as the Bank of England, the International Monetary Fund (IMF) or the Organisation of Economic Co-operation and Development (OECD) with

Austerity in a time of spectacular wealth 69

Case study 4.2: The development of 'critical economics'

However, there is cause for optimism that a change in economic thinking is coming. Once again, as in the issue of the climate crisis, young people are leading the way and campaigning for a change in the university economics curriculum. Groups of university undergraduates from around the world are engaged in dialogue with their universities as well as each other in an attempt to redefine the problems of economics (The Post-Crash Economics Society, 2014; Coreecon, 2017; Rethinking Economics, 2020). They are moving it from one based on that of greed and self-interest to notions of 'fairness' (Post-Crash Society, 2014), tackling local as well as global issues such as poverty and growing levels of inequality (Coreecon, 2017). Under their slogan 'Escaping from imaginary worlds', The Core Project launched in 2015 has carried out a survey of economics undergraduates around the world about to embark on their economics studies on what they thought 'were most pressing issue economists today should be addressing' (Coreecon, 2017). From the data collected they found that there are common themes that emerge out of the word clouds they created (Coreecon, 2017). Students from as far apart as the University of Los Andes in Colombia, the University of Arkansas in the United States, the University of La Reunion in the Indian Ocean, and University College London seem most concerned not by market stability, profit maximisation and economic growth but by inequality, sustainable growth and the environment. Moreover, there was evidence of students' concern for local issues that affect their communities such as corruption, unemployment, debt, healthcare and poverty.

The movement is in its early stages and often battling the power of vested interests, university authorities as well as their lecturers (Inman, 2014a, 2014b). Nevertheless, these students show a higher level of awareness as well as concern regarding the most pressing issues that currently face humanity than many of their supposedly wiser and more learned professors. They are also alert to the need for economists to work in collaboration with other disciplines in the behavioural and social sciences in order to understand the 'real world' (International Student Initiative for Pluralism in Economics, 2014). At the fundamental levels of thinking and empirical knowledge, neoclassical economics is so flawed it is difficult to imagine how so many talented intellectuals have been able to propound such ideas within the academy for so long without challenge. Thompson (1997: 293) refers to this as 'ignorance squared'; the actual promotion of ignorance within the profession as well as in their students, which is part of their hegemonic control of the discipline. Assumptions about human nature, the rejection of the importance of social and historical context, the claim that morality and economics are separate realms, as well as a belief in the existence of benign endogenous forces controlling the free market, are made on the basis of no supporting evidence, and, as we have seen, there is a refusal to accept the relevance of evidence that refutes most features of the neoclassical approach. In terms of their assumptions regarding human behaviour and the notion of *homo economicus*, for example, the assertion that human actors always behave rationally and are able to take account of all relevant information in an economic transaction, as propounded in the standard model (Marshall 2013[1890]), is far too simplistic and needs to be much more informed by the insights and evidence of psychology and the other behavioural sciences (Hodgson, 2012; Hanley, 2016; Ruiz-Villaverde, 2019). Despite attempts by neoclassical economists to update and modify the standard theory, 'practically all economic models taught in universities start from this assumption of full rationality. In addition, many research models, such as in game theory, also start from the same assumption' (Ruiz-Villaverde, 2019: 19). It is not easy to transcend this approach, for what is considered 'rational' or valid knowledge depends on culture, time and the power of those who dominate knowledge transmission (Boronski, 1987). Economists need to use the insights and evidence from psychologists, sociologists and historians regarding what factors influence human behaviour in cultures as well as from past events. In the words of the students who drew up the Initiative for Pluralism in Economics (2014):

> Economics is a social science; **complex economic phenomena can seldom be understood if presented in a vacuum** [Emphasis added], removed from their sociological, political, and historical contexts. **To properly discuss economic policy, students should understand the broader social impacts and moral implications of economic decisions.** [Emphasis added]

You might like to find out more about what Rethinking Economics, The Post-Crash Economics Society and Coreecon have to say on the issue of an alternative economics. Their websites can be found in the reference list at the end of the chapter.

all their highly skilled economists trained in the neoclassical method had no idea what was coming (Bosco, 2011; Samuelson, 2014; Elliot and Treanor, 2015). However, heterodox thinkers such as Ann Pettifor (2017) and Steve Keen (2009), who take levels of debt seriously and looked at the relevant data at the time as well as the historical records, claimed that the evidence pointing to a crash was there and 'is incontrovertible' (Keen, 2017). But Ben Bernanke (2004), head of the US central bank and a supposed expert on past financial crashes, did not even think such data that should have alerted him to the problem was relevant: 'economists turn a blind eye to this data because it doesn't suit their preferred model of how banks operate' (Keen, 2017). Although central banks have now been taking the lessons of the 2008 financial crisis more seriously, most mainstream academic economists are in denial, still claiming that the 2008 crash could not have been predicted (Keen, 2017).

What the evidence and the historical record demonstrate is that the adherence to the doctrine of neoclassical economics in the form of government policy, university curricula and economic thinking generally is having a detrimental effect on our ability to predict problems in the future and limiting our ability to think creatively about developing a more equitable and environmentally sustainable economy.

Conclusion

There are many factors that contribute to this situation; however, Thompson (1997) uses Gramsci's concept of hegemony (1971) to argue that the system of control exercised by the organic intellectuals of the economics profession is such that the ignorance they perpetuate and reproduce is seen as normal and inevitable by successive generations of students and ordinary citizens. By presenting the doctrine of neoliberalism as the only way of seeing economic relations, which comes to be accepted as something normal and eternal that can't be changed, economists contribute to the domination of society by the ruling political and economic classes. They act as mediators between the realms of culture, in this case education, and production (the economy) creating ideas and a worldview that subordinate groups come to accept as legitimate. This reproduction of ignorance-squared makes a mockery of the university as a place for dialogue and open-mindedness in the pursuit of wisdom and truth. However, with the next generation of young people developing alternative ways of thinking, there is hope that they will create a new economics and will also be able to work in collaboration with philosophers, sociologists, historians and policymakers to more effectively challenge conventional views of the needs of humanity and the planet.

Points for reflection and consideration in this chapter

- What are your views on the arguments used by the super-rich to justify their wealth and the huge gap in wealth between the richest and poorest?
- You might like to reflect on the claim by billionaires such as Bill Gates of Microsoft and George Bezos of Amazon that they actually earned all their wealth.
- Do you think that philanthropy is the way governments should deal with the health, welfare, educational and housing needs of their citizens?
- Should economics and economics education have ethical and moral foundations?

References

Bernanke, B.S. (2004) *Essays on the Great Depression*. Princeton, NJ: Princeton University Press.
Bill and Melinda Gates Foundation. (2010) *Global Health Program*. Washington, DC: Bill and Melinda Gates Foundation.
Bloom, P. and Rhodes, C. (2018) *CEO Society: The Corporate Takeover of Everyday Life*. London: Zed Books.
Boronski, T. (1987) *Sociology in Focus: Knowledge*. Harlow: Longman.
Boronski, T. and Hassan, N. (2020) *Sociology of Education*, 2nd edn. London: Sage.
Bosco. (2011) 'Why didn't the IMF predict the financial crisis?' *FP*. 10 February. Available at: https://foreignpolicy.com/2011/02/10/why-didnt-the-imf-predict-the-financial-crisis/ (Accessed 14 April 2020).
Bregman, R. (2017) 'No, wealth isn't created at the top. It is merely devoured there'. *The Guardian*. Available at: https://www.theguardian.com/commentisfree/2017/mar/30/wealth-banks-google-facebook-society-economy-parasites (Accessed 21 March 2010).
Brulle, R.J. (2013) 'Institutionalizing delay: Foundation funding and the creation of U.S. climate change counter-movement organizations'. *Climatic Change*. Available at: https://drexel.edu/~/media/Files/now/pdfs/Institutionalizing%20Delay%20-%20Climatic%20Change.ashx (Accessed 20 November 2020).
Burke, J. (2015) 'Bangladesh garment workers suffer poor conditions two years after reform vows'. *The Guardian*. Available at: https://www.theguardian.com/world/2015/apr/22/garment-workers-in-bangladesh-still-suffering-two-years-after-factory-collapse (Accessed 8 April 2020).
Cahill, D. (2011) 'Why does neoclassical thinking still dominate economics?' *The Conversation*. Available at: https://theconversation.com/why-does-neoclassical-thinking-still-dominate-economics-3861 (Accessed 10 April 2020).
Cervone, J. A. (2017) 'Fundamentalist Christianity, neoliberal capitalism, and the destruction of rural public education'. *Review of Education Pedagogy and Cultural Studies*. Vol. 39, No. 3, pp. 307–328.
Coreecon. (2017) *Escaping from imaginary worlds*. Available at: https://www.core-econ.org/escaping-from-imaginary-worlds/ (Accessed 26 June 2020).

Coudriet, E. (2019) 'These billionaires want the ultra-wealthy to pay more in taxes'. *Cato at Liberty (Cato Institute)*. Available at: https://www.forbes.com/sites/cartercoudriet/2019/10/15/billionaires-more-taxes-gates-buffett-bloomberg/#1b0ac1737792 (Accessed 20 March 2020).

De Witte, M. (2018) 'Stanford scholar addresses the problems with philanthropy'. *Stanford News*. 3 December. Available at: https://news.stanford.edu/2018/12/03/the-problems-with-philanthropy/ (Accessed 15 December 2020).

Dodgeson, M. (2018) 'How philanthropy could change higher education funding'. *The Conversation*. 28 February. Available at: https://theconversation.com/how-philanthropy-could-change-higher-education-funding-92260 (Accessed 25 November 2020).

Dorling, D. (2011) *Injustice: Why Social Inequalities Persist*. Bristol: The Policy Press.

Elliott, L. (2017) 'Heretics welcome! Economics needs a new Reformation'. *The Guardian*. 17 December. Available at: https://www.theguardian.com/business/2017/dec/17/heretics-welcome-economics-needs-a-new-reformation (Accessed 25 April 2020).

Elliott, L. and Treanor, J. (2015) 'The minutes that reveal how the Bank of England handled the financial crisis'. *The Guardian.* 7 January. Available at: https://www.theguardian.com/business/2015/jan/07/bank-of-england-minutes-financial-crisis-bank-bailouts (Accessed 14 April 2020).

Forbes (2019) 'Billionaires: The richest people in the world'. *Forbes*, 5 March. Available at: https://www.forbes.com/billionaires/#6c9ec90d251c (Accessed 18 March 2020).

Ford, D., Porfilio, B. and Goldstein, R. (2015) 'The news media, education, and the subversion of the neoliberal social imaginary'. *Critical Education*. Vol. 6, No. 7, pp. 1–24.

Gehring, J. (2016) 'Koch Brothers' latest target: Pope Francis'. *The American Prospect.* 13 October. Available at: https://prospect.org/culture/koch-brothers-latest-target-pope-francis/ (Accessed 20 November 2020).

Giving USA. (2019) *Giving USA 2019: Americans gave $427.71 Billion to Charity in 2018 Amid Complex Year for Charitable Giving*. Chicago, IL: Giving USA Foundation.

Goldin, I. and Muggah, R. (2020) 'Viral Inequality'. *Project Syndicate.* 27 March 2020. Available at: https://www.project-syndicate.org/onpoint/viral-inequality-by-ian-goldin-and-robert-muggah-2020-03? (Accessed 29 March 2020).

Gramsci, A. (1971) *Selections from Prison Notebooks*. London: Lawrence and Wishart.

Haeder, S. (2010) *Hollow State, Hollow Community? Healthcare Privatization in Fresno County California*. Master's Thesis, California State University, Fresno. Available at: https://repository.library.fresnostate.edu/bitstream/handle/10211.3/118949/SimonHAEDER.pdf?sequence=1 (Accessed 20 May 2020).

Hanley, N. (2016) 'Is economists' view of people as rational still credible?' *The Conversation*. Available at: https://theconversation.com/is-economists-view-of-people-as-rational-still-credible-64338 (Accessed 16 May 2020).

Harrington, B. (2018) 'The bad behavior of the richest: what I learned from wealth managers'. *The Guardian*. 19 October. Available at: https://www.theguardian.com/us-news/2018/oct/19/billionaires-wealth-richest-income-inequality (Accessed 21 March 2020).

Harvey, D. (2007) 'Political and economic dimensions of free trade'. *Annals of the American Academy of Political and Social Science.* Vol. 610, pp. 22–44.

Hay, I. and Muller, S. (2014) 'Questioning generosity in the golden age of philanthropy: Towards critical geographies of super-philanthropy'. *Progress in Human Geography*. Vol. 38 No.5, pp. 635–653.

Hodgson, G. (2012) 'On the limits of rational choice theory'. *Economic Thought*. Vol. 1, pp. 94–108.

Hwang, A. (2018) 'The world on a billionaire's budget'. *The Conversation*. Available at: https://theconversation.com/the-world-on-a-billionaires-budget-88355 (Accessed 26 March 2020).

IMF. (2015) *Causes and Consequences of Income Inequality: A Global Perspective. IMF Discussion Note*. Available at: https://www.imf.org/external/pubs/ft/sdn/2015/sdn1513.pdf (Accessed 8 April 2020).

Inman, P. (2014a) 'Economics students call for shakeup of the way their subject is taught'. *The Guardian*. 4 May. Available at: https://www.theguardian.com/education/2014/may/04/economics-students-overhaul-subject-teaching (Accessed 10 April 2020).

Inman, P. (2014b) 'Manchester University move to scrap banking crash module angers students'. *The Guardian*. 2 April. Available at: https://www.theguardian.com/education/2014/apr/02/manchester-university-decision-scrap-banking-crash-module-angers-students (Accessed 5 March 2020).

Inside Philanthropy. (2019) 'Impossible to justify: A political scientist's take on American Philanthropy'. Available at: https://www.insidephilanthropy.com/home/2019/1/7/impossible-to-justify-a-political-scientist-takes-on-american-philanthropy (Accessed 12 December 2020).

International Student Initiative for Pluralism in Economics. (2014) *Open Letter*. Available at: http://www.isipe.net/open-letter/ (Accessed 12 April 2020).

Irvine, S. (2017) '5 tips for teaching your toddler how to share'. *Parents Today*. 3 January. Available at: https://www.todaysparent.com/toddler/toddler-behaviour/teach-your-child-how-to-share/ (Accessed 20 November 2020).

Jericho. (2018) 'Joseph Stiglitz: 2018 Sydney Peace prize winner on tax cuts and Trump'. *The Guardian*. 20 April. Available at: https://www.theguardian.com/business/2018/apr/21/joseph-stiglitz-2018-sydney-peace-prize-winner-on-tax-cuts-and-trump (Accessed 7 April 2020).

Jerrim, J. and Macmillan, L. (2015) 'Income inequality, intergenerational mobility, and the Great Gatsby curve: Is education the key?' *Social Forces*, Vol. 94, No. 2, pp. 505–533.

Johnson, B. (2013) 'Boris Johnson: 3rd Margaret Thatcher Lecture (FULL)'. Available online at: www.youtube.com/watch?v=Dzlgrnr1ZB0 (Accessed 15 December 2017).

Jones, O. (2011) *Chavs: The Demonization of the Working Class*. London: Verso.

Keay, D. (1987) 'Interview for Woman's Own ("no such thing as society")'. *Woman's Own*. 23 September. Source: Thatcher Archive. Available at: https://www.margaretthatcher.org/document/106689 (Accessed 30 March 2020).

Keen, S. (2009) 'The dynamics of the monetary circuit', in J.-F. Ponsot and S. Rossi (eds.), *The Political Economy of Monetary Circuits: Tradition and Change*. London: Palgrave, pp. 161–187.

Keen, S. (2017) 'I predicted the last financial crisis – now soaring global debt levels pose risk of another'. *The Conversation*. Available at: https://theconversation.com/i-predicted-the-last-financial-crisis-now-soaring-global-debt-levels-pose-risk-of-another-84136 (Accessed 10 April 2020).

Kelly, J. (2019) 'For the first time in history, U.S. Billionaires paid a lower tax rate than the working class: What should we do about it?' *Forbes*. 11 October 2019. Available at: https://www.forbes.com/sites/jackkelly/2019/10/11/for-the-first-time-in-history-us-billionaires-paid-a-lower-tax-rates-than-the-working-class-what-we-should-do-about-it/#77e1aafb1fce. (Accessed 5 April 2020).

Landy, D., Silbert, N. and Goldin, A. (2013) 'Estimating Large Numbers'. *Cognitive Science*. Vol. 37, No. 5, pp. 775–799.

Lavoie, M. (2014) *Post-Keynesian Economics: New Foundations*. Cheltenham: Edward Elgar Publishing.

Lister, R. (ed.) (1996) *Charles Murray and the Underclass: The Developing Debate*. London: IEA.

Maisuria, A. (2014) 'The neoliberalisation policy agenda and its consequences for education in England: A focus on resistance now and possibilities for the future'. *Policy Futures in Education*. Vol. 12, No. 2, pp. 286–295.

Makortoff, K. (2019) 'UK CEOs make more in first three days of 2019 than worker's annual salary'. *The Guardian*. 4 January. Available at: https://www.theguardian.com/business/2019/jan/04/uk-ceos-make-more-in-first-three-days-of-2019-than-workers-annual-salary (Accessed 6 April 2020).

Marshall, A. (2013)[1890] *The Principles of Economics*. London: Palgrave.

Marsland, D. (1996) 'From cradle to grave mistake'. *THE* 17 May. Available at: https://www.timeshighereducation.com/news/from-cradle-to-grave-mistake/93669.article?storycode=93669 (Accessed 26 March 2020).

McVeigh, K. (2017) 'Cambodian female workers in Nike, Asics and Puma factories suffer mass faintings'. *The Guardian*. 25 June. Available at: https://www.theguardian.com/business/2017/jun/25/female-cambodian-garment-workers-mass-fainting (Accessed 8 April 2020).

Merelli, A. (2019) 'Turn Right: The state of global right-wing populism in 2019'. *Quartz*. 30 December. Available at: https://qz.com/1774201/the-global-state-of-right-wing-populism-in-2019/ (Accessed 10 April 2020).

Mooney, G. (1998) '"Remoralising" the Poor?: Gender, Class and Philanthropy in Victorian Britain', in G. Lewis (ed.), *Forming Nation, Framing Welfare*. London: Routledge, pp. 55–104.

Murray, C. (1996) 'The emerging British underclass', in R. Lister (ed.), *Charles Murray and the Underclass: The Developing Debate*. London: IEA, pp. 24–53.

Neate, R. (2019) 'Super-rich prepare to leave UK "within minutes" if Labour wins election'. *The Guardian*. 2 November. Available at: https://www.theguardian.com/news/2019/nov/02/super-rich-leave-uk-labour-election-win-jeremy-corbyn-wealth-taxes (Accessed 19 March 2020).

Northern Ireland National Curriculum. (2020) *Personal Development and Mutual Understanding: Key Stage 2, Year 7 Strand 2: Mutual Understanding in the Local and Wider Community Unit 6: Who Cares?* Available at: http://www.nicurriculum.org.uk/docs/key_stages_1_and_2/areas_of_learning/pdmu/livinglearning together/year7/yr7_unit6.pdf (Accessed 21 November 2020).

Olssen, M. and Peters, M. (2005) 'Neoliberalism, higher education and the knowledge economy: From the free market to knowledge capitalism'. *Journal of Education Policy*. Vol. 20, No. 3, pp. 313–345.

Osisli, U. and Zarins, S. (2018) 'Fewer Americans are giving money to charity but total donations are at record levels anyway'. *The Conversation*. Available at: https://theconversation.com/fewer-americans-are-giving-money-to-charity-but-total-donations-are-at-record-levels-anyway-98291 (Accessed 25 March 2020).

Pettifor, A. (2017) 'I was one of the only economists who predicted the financial crash of 2008 – in 2017 we need to make urgent changes'. *The Independent*. 6 January. Available at: https://www.independent.co.uk/voices/brexit-economy-economists-predict-financial-crash-recession-2008-michael-fish-austerity-cant-solve-a7513416.html (Accessed 14 April 2020).

Piketty, T. (2014) *Capital in the 21st Century*. Transl. Arthur Goldhammer. Cambridge: Harvard University Press.

Piketty, T. (2020) *Capital and Ideology*. Transl. Arthur Goldhammer. Cambridge: Harvard University Press.

Reed, H. (2018) 'Rip it up and start again: The case for a new economics'. *Prospect Magazine*. 13 April. Available at: https://www.prospectmagazine.co.uk/magazine/the-case-for-a-new-economics (Accessed 10 April 2020).

Reich, R. (2018) *Just Giving: Why Philanthropy Is Failing Democracy and How It Can Do Better*. Princeton, NJ: Princeton University Press.

Reisz. (2020) 'Thomas Piketty: "Economists are no different from other social scientists"'. *THE* 27 February. Available at: https://www.timeshighereducation.com/features/thomas-piketty-economists-are-no-different-other-social-scientists?utm_source=THE+Website+Users&utm_campaign=60dee3ccb9-EMAIL_CAMPAIGN_2020_02_27_03_58&utm_medium=email&utm_term=0_daa7e51487-60dee3ccb9-75198909 (Accessed 9 April 2020).

Rethinking Economics. (2020) 'Why rethink economics'? Available at: http://www.rethinkeconomics.org/get-involved/why-rethink-economics/ (Accessed 3 June 2020).

Rhodes, C. and Bloom, P. (2018) 'The trouble with charitable billionaires'. *The Guardian*. 24 May. Available at: https://www.theguardian.com/news/2018/may/24/the-trouble-with-charitable-billionaires-philanthrocapitalism (Accessed 5 April 2020).

Ruiz-Villaverde, J. (2019). 'Editor's Introduction: The Growing Failure of the Neoclassical Paradigm' *American Journal of Economics and Sociology*. Vol. 78. No.1, pp. 13–34.

Samuelson, R. (2014) 'Why we didn't see the GFC: OECD admits failures'. *The Sydney Morning Herald*, 19 February. Available at: https://www.smh.com.au/business/markets/why-we-didnt-see-the-gfc-oecd-admits-failures-20140219-330go.html (Accessed 14 April 2020).

Saunders, P. (2010) *Social Mobility Myths*. London: Civitas.

Saunders, P. (2012) *Social Mobility Delusions: Why So Much of What Politicians Say about Social Mobility in Britain is Wrong, Misleading or Unreliable*. London: Civitas.

Savage, M., Cunningham, N., Devine, F., Friedman, S., Laurison, D., McKenzie, L., Miles, A., Snee, H. and Wakeling, P. (2015) *Social Class in the 21st Century*. London: Pelican.

Stanford, J. (2015) *Economics for Everyone: A Short Guide to the Economics of Capitalism*, 2nd edn. London: Pluto Press.

Syal, R. (2020) 'Banned City trader an organiser of Tories' Black and White ball'. *The Guardian*. 26 February. Available at: https://www.theguardian.com/politics/2020/feb/26/carphone-warehouse-founder-helped-plan-exclusive-tory-fundraiser (Accessed 25 April 2020).

Tcherneva, P. (2017) 'Inequality update: Who gains when income grows?' *Policy Note, Levy Economics Institute of Bard College*. Available at: http://www.levyinstitute.org/publications/inequality-update-who-gains-when-income-grows (Accessed 6 April 2020).

The Giving Pledge. (2020) *A Commitment to Philanthropy*. Available at: https://givingpledge.org/ (Accessed 2 April 2020).

The Post-crash Economics Society. (2014) *Economics, Education and Unlearning: Economics Education at the University of Manchester*. Manchester: Post-Crash Economics Society at the University of Manchester

Thompson, H. (1997) 'Ignorance and Ideological Hegemony: A Critique of Neoclassical Economics'. *The Journal of Interdisciplinary Economics*. Vol. 8, pp. 291–305.

Topham, G. (2019) 'Stagecoach chairman Sir Brian Souter to step down'. *The Guardian*. 11 December. Available at: https://www.theguardian.com/business/2019/dec/11/sir-brian-souter-stagecoach-chairman-to-step-down (Accessed 5 April 2020).

Towler, C. (2018) 'The John Birch Society is still influencing American politics, 60 years after its founding'. *The Conversation*. Available at: https://theconversation.com/the-john-birch-society-is-still-influencing-american-politics-60-years-after-its-founding-107925 (Accessed 19 December 2020).

Toynbee, P. (2018) 'It's official: universal credit is a colossal, costly, hellish catastrophe'. *The Guardian*. 15 June. Available at: www.theguardian.com/commentisfree/2018/jun/15/universal-credit-colossal-catastrophe-national-audit-office. (Accessed on 15 May 2019).

Trussel Trust (2021) 'Vision and Values'. *The Trussel Trust: Stop UK Hunger*. Available at: https://www.trusselltrust.org/about/mission-and-values/ (Accessed 21 April 2020).

Tuttle, B. (2020) 'Most Americans want the rich to pay higher taxes, according to every poll everywhere'. *Money*. 20 January. Available at: https://money.com/wealth-tax-rich-tax-rates-2020-presidential-election/ (Accessed 5 April 2020).

UNHRC. (2017) *Statement on visit to the USA, by Professor Philip Alston, United Nations Special rapporteur on extreme poverty and human rights*. Available at: https://www.ohchr.org/EN/NewsEvents/Pages/DisplayNews.aspx?NewsID=22533 (Accessed 3 March 2020).

UNHRC. (2019) *Visit to the United Kingdom of Great Britain and Northern Ireland: Report of the Special Rapporteur on extreme poverty and human rights*. Available at: https://undocs.org/pdf?symbol=en/A/HRC/41/39/Add.1 (Accessed 18 July 2019).

Vogel, P. and Kurak, M. (2020) 'Coronavirus has sparked an unprecedented level of philanthropy'. *The Conversation*. Available at: https://theconversation.com/coronavirus-has-sparked-an-unprecedented-level-of-philanthropy-134858 (Accessed on 20 May 2020).

Volante, L. and Jerrim, J. (2018) 'Education does not equal social mobility'. *The Conversation*. Available at: https://theconversation.com/education-doesnot-always-equal-social-mobility-106386 (Accessed 7 February 2019).

Werner, R.A. (2005). *New Paradigm in Macroeconomics*. London: Palgrave

Wilkinson, R. and Pickett, K. (2009) *The Spirit Level: Why More Equal Societies Almost Always Do Better*. London: Penguin.

Wilkinson, R. and Pickett, K. (2018) *The Inner Level: How More Equal Societies Reduce Stress, Restore Sanity and Improve Everyone's Well-being*. London: Allen Lane.

World Inequality Database. (no date) *World Inequality Database*. Available at: https://wid.world/ (Accessed 5 March 2020).

World Inequality Report. (2018) *World Inequality Report: Executive Summary*. Available at: https://wir2018.wid.world/files/download/wir2018-summary-english.pdf (Accessed 20 March 2020).

YouGov. (2020) 'Are taxes on the rich too high or low in Britain?' *Tracker*. Available at: https://yougov.co.uk/topics/politics/trackers/are-taxes-on-the-rich-too-high-or-low-in-britain (Accessed 11 April 2020).

5 Decolonising the curriculum and society

Introduction

At the height of the victory celebrations of the 'Leave' campaign in the UK in relation to the European Union (EU) Referendum held on 23 June 2016, Grant Shapps, a senior member of the governing Conservative Party, stated:

> we must resolve to make ourselves the world's greatest trading nation. As an island, we need to rediscover that swashbuckling spirit of the 19th Century when we practically owned the concept of free-trade.
>
> (Shapps, 2016)

Shapps's comments might seem innocuous enough to a general public nurtured on a diet of pride in Britain's past and the perpetual commemoration and celebration of Empire through institutions such as the monarchy, the Commonwealth, national culture, the education system and the mass media. Notions of Empire and Britain's imperial past are given continued respectability in the form of the national honours system in which the Queen, as head of the United Kingdom *and* the Commonwealth, awards titles and recognition in the name of Empire (Encyclopaedia Britannica, 2020; Gov.UK, 2020). Indeed, the sentiments of Shapps and the Conservative Party seem to be shared by much of the wider population if we look at opinion polls on the subject. In 2014, a YouGov (Dahlgreen, 2014) poll reported that 59 per cent of the British public agreed that the British Empire was 'something to be proud of', though in a more recent YouGov poll (Smith, 2020) this had fallen to 32 per cent. Nevertheless, Britons generally have a tolerant if not a positive view of Empire, and they are not alone in such attitudes. In the 2020 YouGov (Smith, 2020) survey which also included respondents from European countries that once had colonies (Britain, France, Italy, Spain, Belgium, Japan, the Netherlands and Germany), 27 per cent of Britons, 26 per cent of Dutch and 21 per cent of Belgian respondents stated that they would still like to have their former empires. In Britain, this 27 per cent rose to 40 per cent of 'Leave' voters in the 2016 Brexit Referendum as well as of those who voted Conservative in the 2017 UK general election. The dominant view on empire among all eight countries, though, was one of tolerant indifference, despite evidence of the terrible impact of colonialism on the former colonies (Mukerjee, 2010; Olusoga, 2016; Tharoor, 2017a). Only 17 per cent of British respondents in the 2020 YouGov survey thought that Britain's former colonies were 'worse off' due to colonisation. This view is not surprising given that, in the UK at least, many of the opinions we hold as a nation on this issue are based on a poor grasp of history, and this means, as David Olusoga (2016) points out, most of us know too little about British history to make a sound judgement about the Empire. Even at degree level, the experience of university teachers of colonial history, such as Deana Heath (2017), is that 'Many of the undergraduates who greet me know virtually nothing about any of the subjects I teach'. Such ignorance is a result of an education system that does not teach the nation's past in a reflective and open manner but instead presents it as a period in which, according the historian Niall Ferguson (2002), on balance the world gained more than it lost during this period. This balance sheet approach helps to perpetuate a national myth in which, despite the terrible things perpetrated by those who built and ran the Empire, Britain is presented ultimately as a benevolent and civilising force that helped to create the 'modern world' with the 'gifts' of liberal capitalism, parliamentary democracy, systems of civil administration, systems of accounting and, 'perhaps the most important export of the last 300 years' – the English language (Ferguson, 2002: 366). Ferguson names this positive and modernising force of the British Empire 'Anglobalisation' and claims that we are all still benefitting from its effects.

The enduring power and nostalgia of Empire

The British government has attempted to harness this nostalgia for the Empire in its campaign to leave the EU and to 'make Britain great again' (Faulconbridge and MacLellan, 2019). In an invocation of the glory of Empire during which Britain exercised almost unassailed domination over other nations in terms of trade and military might, the Conservative government set up an initiative to rename the Commonwealth 'Empire 2.0' (Coates, 2017; Schultz, 2017), with the intention of using it and its established network of political and economic ties with the former colonies to launch Britain's post-Brexit free trade policy. There was a clear expectation that these former colonies would welcome Britain back with favourable and easy trade terms despite having 'betrayed' them when it joined the Common Market in 1973 (Boffey, 2018). Both the title and the expectations upon which this initiative was based could be said to show a naivety and insensitivity that demonstrates what Brian Kwoba refers to as Britain's imperial 'blind spot' (Rawlinson, 2016). Indeed, so engrained is the ideology of Empire and the belief among the Conservative leadership that this view is shared by other nations of the Commonwealth, that no one thought to ask what the former colonies made of its proposed new role or what they thought of its proposed title (Schultz, 2017).

The 'other' view of empire

However, whereas the British tend to know very little about the experiences of the victims of British colonial rule, and this is one of the strongest arguments for the decolonisation of society as well as the curriculum, in ancient civilisations such as India and China the humiliations and violence visited on these places by the British are still strong in the minds of their citizens and political leaders. In India, all children are aware of the difference between the Bengal famines of 1770 and 1943, during the latter in which it is estimated that three million people died. This is believed to have been partly, if not primarily, the result of Winston Churchill's policy in the colony which was driven by his hatred of the Indian people (Mukerjee, 2010; Tharoor, 2017a). It is not uncommon for Indians to compare Winston Churchill to Hitler in terms of the cruelty he inflicted on their people (Tharoor, 2017; Oppenheim, 2018; Anderlini, 2020). In China, the leadership is also acutely aware of the humiliation inflicted on the country during the first opium war of 1840 in which Britain, with a force of ten thousand troops, defeated a huge army of the Qing Empire. This led to China paying reparations and ceding the island of Hong Kong to Britain (*South China Morning Post*, 2017):

> That page of Chinese history was one of humiliation and sorrow. It was not until the Communist Party of China led the Chinese people to victory in a … struggle for national independence and liberation … that the Chinese people truly stood up and blazed a … path of socialism with distinctive Chinese features.
>
> (Xi Jinping cited in *South China Morning Post*, 2017)

Both China and India, the two most populous countries in the world that now account for about a third of the global economy in terms of purchasing power, are more or less guaranteed economic superpower status within the next few decades (Anderlini, 2020). Moreover, as two nations created in direct opposition to British and Western imperialism, it is unlikely that they will allow Britain to dictate any post-Brexit trade terms: Britain is no longer in a position to impose its economic will on other countries as it used to in the 'swashbuckling spirit of the 19th Century'. This was made very clear by former Minister of State for India and author of *Inglorious Empire* Shashi Tharoor (2017a) who, in a radio interview (Tharoor, 2017b) on the British government's Empire 2.0 initiative, claimed that it would 'go down like a lead balloon' in India. He pointed to the myth that Britain was a benign force in his country during the period of empire, bringing with it the railways, bureaucracy and the legal system, claiming that these 'were brought in to enhance British control, and make British profits', and not for the benefit of Indians (Tharoor, 2017b). Moreover, when Britain arrived in the seventeenth century, India was one of the richest countries on earth with a thriving textile industry producing cottons, muslin and calicoes that were exported to markets around the world and which Britain destroyed by imposing its own terms of trade by force. Punitive tariffs on Indian exports and the lifting of tariffs on British imports to India devastated her economy. According to Tharoor, Britain did not practice free trade in India: 'They were giving themselves a captive market in India of millions of people to buy the products of the dark satanic mills that Dickens wrote about, of Britain'. Tharoor concludes by saying: 'So obviously those are not terms of trade that we recall with any happiness, and we certainly would like to clarify that those Empire terms are not on offer today' (Tharoor, 2017b).

A tradition of blame and xenophobia

It does seem somewhat ironic, however, that Jacob Reece-Mogg, one of the nationalist cheer leaders of the Conservative Party, should describe Britain's transitional membership of the EU between 2019 and 2020 as akin to that of *vassal* status; that is, one of a medieval servant, or one who owes allegiance to and takes orders from a superior with few if any rights (Poole, 2018), given that this was the status of the so-called citizens of the Empire through much of the three hundred years of British colonial rule. However, Reece-Mogg's somewhat inappropriate comparison conveniently helped to divert attention once more away from the problems at home caused by a decade of austerity, by shifting the focus again to the threat of foreign domination. As with other populist governments, strongly nationalist Conservative leaders in Britain have a penchant for blaming those from outside the nation's borders for being 'the problem', with migrants allegedly putting a strain on housing, welfare, the health service and education system (Prince, 2010; BBC, 2019), and where EU leaders and unelected EU bureaucrats are accused of meddling with Britain's ancient constitution and rights. One of the most infamous and shameful of such xenophobic episodes is the 'rivers of blood' speech made in 1968 by Enoch Powell (Thames TV, 2014), a member of the Conservative shadow cabinet at the time, who used his considerable oratorical skills to criticise the levels of immigration to the UK from the Commonwealth, making reference the Roman poet Virgil to warn the nation of what he saw as the threat this posed to British values, politics and culture. Although Powell's rhetoric was viewed as too extreme for the Conservative leadership at the time, particularly for Edward Heath, the Conservative Party leader, who removed Powell from the shadow cabinet, nevertheless, the speech was seen by some to have played a part in the Conservative general election victory of 1970 (Studlar, 1976), suggesting that such talk does have an effect. More recently, Conservative politicians, since the defeat of Labour in 2010, have become more emboldened in voicing such views, particularly since the declaration by David Cameron in 2011 that 'multiculturalism is dead' (Cameron, 2011). Before he became prime minister in 2019, Boris Johnson had been particularly busy in his xenophobic musings on the EU, African people (Johnson, 2002) and Asians for *The Telegraph* newspaper (Johnson, 2018), though these were usually concealed behind a façade of public school humour and banter, but are no less mischievous in intent and potentially dangerous in their consequences (Press Gazette, 2019). In his *Telegraph* article of 5 August 2018 entitled 'Denmark has got it wrong. Yes, the burka is oppressive and ridiculous – but that's still no reason to ban it', he discusses the issue of banning the wearing of full-face veils. Whilst giving with one hand, by not advocating a ban, Johnson nevertheless takes with the other by suggesting that Muslim women who choose to wear them look simultaneously like 'letterboxes' and 'bank robbers', thereby revealing contempt for these women and their cultures. Tell Mama (2018), the organisation that monitors anti-Muslim incidents in the UK, reported 'a near four-fold increase (375 per cent) in anti-Muslim incidents in the week following Johnson's article' (Press Gazette, 2019) when compared with the week before. Johnson has been no less mischievous in his comments about the EU (Rankin and Waterson, 2019) and Africans (Johnson, 2002). It is hardly surprising that this relentless mockery, casual racism and the irresponsible construction of half-truths about these issues have had a significant effect and resulted in the rising popularity of policies such as seeking to leave the EU and imposing restrictions on immigration (Rankin and Waterson, 2019). In his final piece for *The Telegraph* as its EU correspondent, Johnson (1994) lists the ways in which British sovereignty was allegedly being handed over to Brussels and concluded presciently with the words: 'I foresee trouble ahead' (Johnson, 1994).

Once again, Anderson's (2006) concept of the imagined community comes to mind here, where politicians invoke a putative common national interest and destiny, to fend off a perceived external or foreign threat. This can be seen also in other countries with populist leaders such as President Trump, who blames Mexico and other Latin American countries for exporting their problems such as criminals, drugs traffickers and the unemployed to the US in order to deflect blame from the high levels poverty and crime, low wages and overburdened public services resulting from the US's own inadequate welfare, health, social and justice systems (Lach, 2020). This was also clearly the case when Trump saw an opportunity to scapegoat the Chinese and the World Health Organisation

(WHO) for the rapid spread of the COVID-19 virus in the US in order to take attention away from criticisms of his leadership during the pandemic and the hopelessly inadequate US healthcare system (Shear and McNeil, 2020).

Keeping the myth alive

Such scapegoating of foreigners and the portrayal of a nation's past as essentially heroic and ultimately blameless are reflected in many official national histories and indicate clearly a position of UK governments of the past and certainly that of Conservative governments since 2010. Britain's history is now presented as the story of an island people following their manifest destiny of glory and greatness, led by national 'saints' such as Nelson and Churchill. This indeed is what Michael Gove had proposed for a new National History Curriculum for England before the general election in 2010, when he stated that what most parents wanted was 'a traditional education, with children sitting in rows, learning the kings and queens of England' (Faulkner, 2010), adding that 'lessons should celebrate rather than denigrate Britain's role through the ages, including the Empire' and, moreover, that 'Guilt about Britain's past is misplaced', claiming it as a 'trashing of our past' (Faulkner, 2010). It should be pointed out here that Scotland has its own education system and that is why Gove was referring to the English History National Curriculum.

As part of the coalition government, Gove announced a complete review of the English history curriculum in 2011. He restated his intention to return to a more traditional approach to history teaching. The first draft was a history curriculum inspired by the work of Niall Ferguson (2002), who takes a linear narrative approach and, as we have seen, presents a balance sheet assessment of Britain's role in the world, concluding that overall, despite the fact that Britain did not always 'live up to its own ideals' (Ferguson, 2002: 366), it has done more good than harm in the world. Children were to be taught historical 'facts' in a chronological manner and tested regularly on them with a focus on British values and perspectives. Any historian with an understanding of the complexity of historical analysis and method should be very critical of such an approach (Historical Association, 2013). As the Parekh Report (The Runnymede Trust, 2000) advises, we should be cautious of accepting one 'official' version of history. So concerned were some historians and teachers at the overt bias of Gove's proposed curriculum and its 'jingoistic' tone that one hundred of them signed an open letter (Garner, 2013) stating they believed that to teach it would be in breach of the Education Act of 2002, which requires the curriculum to be 'balanced and broadly based'.

This approach to the English school history curriculum also caused concern among many minority ethnic groups for its lack of diversity and voice of the peoples of the Commonwealth. It was described by some as an attempt to whitewash the crimes of Britain's colonial past and to silence the voices of its victims (Mishra, 2011). Mr Gove, perhaps due to the threat of legal action, agreed to review his proposals. The subsequent and final version of the history curriculum recognises the need for children to learn more than just facts and that the facts do not speak for themselves. Gove accepted the need to provide more opportunities for the views of minority ethnic groups to be heard, as well as more coverage of the contributions that women have made to the modern world (The Historical Association, 2013). Nevertheless, this final version is still lacking in opportunities to examine the impact of colonialism on Indigenous populations or of its continuing effects (Heath, 2017). There is also still an emphasis on British values which 'omits the contribution of Black British history in favour of a dominant white, Eurocentric curriculum that fails to reflect our multi ethnic and broadly diverse society' (Arday, 2020). This, Edwards claims, can only alienate Black, Asian and other ethnic groups who may feel marginalised by such coverage (Edwards, 2013).

The exceptionalism of Britain

Such a situation seems to persist because, as Schultz (2017) points out, Britain just like the US suffers from a view of itself and its role in the world as being exceptional. This *exceptionalism* is aptly defined by Tunzelmann (2019) as 'the idea that Britain is inherently different from, and superior to, other nations and empires', and once again reveals Britain's imperial blind spot. Its negotiating stance on a post-Brexit agreement with the EU is one in which it seems to expect all parties to concede to its demands, making threats to implement a no-deal Brexit if they don't, despite the potential harm this could cause to the country's citizens, the economy and relations with other states (Goodman et al., 2019). In terms of its relationship with the Commonwealth, it seems that Britain's political establishment is still reluctant to see the other member-states as its equals and, as with the EU, has an aversion to foreign powers 'dictating' to Britain how to run its affairs, having once been the world's most powerful nation. As Tunzelmann (2019) concludes, Brexit has exposed the problems of Britain's political culture that seems averse to criticism and of the need to reflect seriously about the necessity for change in a nation that still thinks like an imperial power.

The growing demands for decolonisation of the curriculum

Despite the resistance of Conservative and populist politicians in Britain and other parts of the world, it would seem that there is a growing tide of desire to challenge such versions of history, as well as the wider curricula of schools and universities that are taught in both the former colonies and their *metropoles* – the former colonial powers of the Netherlands, France, Britain, Germany and the US (Connell, 1997: 1522). Once again, it would seem that the initiative to address another of the world's persisting problems is being highlighted and led by young people with the movement to decolonise universities and their curricula. It started in South Africa in 2015 (Behari-Leak, 2015; Hendricks and Leibowitz, 2016) with the successful campaign to remove the statue of Cecil Rhodes from the University of Cape Town campus. Rhodes (South African History Online, 2017) was the British-born prime minister of the Cape Colony during the 1890s and was instrumental in setting up the system of racial segregation in South Africa, so his continued presence, albeit in an inanimate form, has been viewed as an act of symbolic violence against Black students who attended the university. The movement known as #RhodesMustFall triggered campaigns in other parts of the world, most notably in Britain where, in a niche on the façade of the Oriel College Rhodes Building of the University of Oxford, sits another statue of Cecil Rhodes. It is here that as a scholar during the 1870s he developed his theories of race and racial segregation and is therefore highly symbolic of the sorts of ideas that Northern white intellectuals developed about the geographic South. This remains a symbol of Eurocentric ideas, epistemologies and their continuing dominance in the academy in many former colonies.

Academic debate and research on the impact of Northern (Connell, 2007), i.e. Western colonialism, on the economic, cultural, intellectual and artistic development of the former colonies of the British, Spanish, French and Portuguese empires, has a longer history than these recent events might suggest (Hendricks and Leibowitz, 2016). Earlier ideas about the postcolonial condition of countries in Africa, Asia and Latin America tended to focus on their economic development or lack thereof (Alatas, 2003) and blamed the leadership of the former colonies for a lack of 'modern', i.e. Western, ways of thinking and acting. However, within the former colonies alternative perspectives emerged which focused on the continued domination over these ex-colonies by their former colonial masters.

The emergence of dependency theory

Theories of political and economic dependency emerged in Latin America from the work of Raúl Prebisch (1959) and Andre Gunder Frank (1969), who challenged the theories propounded by the dominant Northern neoclassical economists and other social scientists such as W.W. Rostow (1960) who outlined the route to economic growth and development for the newly independent former colonies. For Northern theorists, the lack of economic development, or the 'underdevelopment', of countries in Latin America was a result of factors internal to those countries and a poor adherence to neoclassical economic principles. However, dependency theorists such as Gunder Frank (1969) and Prebisch (1959) instead claimed that the issue of underdevelopment arose not as a result of factors internal to the society but instead due to global economic forces which were believed to influence the economic development of the former colonies in Latin America and resulted in the disparities both between and within economies. The countries of Latin America, they claimed, were locked in a state of underdevelopment due to their dependence on Northern economies.

An analysis of the Northern modernisation theories relating to the postcolonial period after 1945 reveals a number of significant problems in terms of their views of the political and economic relationships between the dominant Northern nations and the newly independent former colonies. First, there was an assumption that the former colonies would 'evolve' from traditional agrarian societies to eventually become 'modern' mass production consumer societies, just as in the geographic North. Second, that in order to modernise, all these newly independent nations needed to do was to adopt the values and practices of the geographic North, including those of the desire to achieve through individual self-interest. In those societies that did not seem to be growing economically, such as India, the problem was deemed to lie within that society – they must be lacking in these competitive capitalistic norms and values. There was no attempt in these Northern theories of modernisation to consider the effects of colonialism on these countries, such as the fact that India had been one of the most flourishing economies in the world when the British arrived there in the seventeenth century, and when the British left three hundred years later it was a political and economic mess. Third, Northern conceptions of progress, modernisation and successful development are always associated with capitalism. Alternative routes to development such as socialism or Indigenous approaches were seen as deviant and to be discouraged, if not prevented by force. Indeed, few regions of the world were left unscathed by these often-brutal acts of neo-imperialism in which the major global powers usually exercised their control indirectly 'via international law, the power of major commercial banks, the threat of military intervention by the superpowers, and covert and clandestine operations by various governments of advanced nations' (Alatas, 2003: 602).

Academic neocolonialism and dependency

A further type of dependency that Alatas (2003) identifies is *academic dependency* which arises from the colonial experience and is one of the key issues that the movement to decolonise the curriculum is seeking to address. Referring primarily to the social sciences, Alatas (2003) suggests that during the age of imperial domination the colonial powers were able to impose their ideas by force through their direct control over the sources and transmission of knowledge within the colonies such as schools and universities. Moreover, as we have seen in Chapter 2, the process of colonial domination often involves the subordination and even destruction of indigenous culture and forms of knowledge which form their 'universe of meaning' (Berger, 1973). During colonialism, Indigenous scholars and intellectuals become socialised and dominated by the ideas and epistemologies of the colonisers, and with the end of colonialism many colonies remain stuck in this mind-set, often seeing their own cultures as inferior to that of their former colonial masters. The consequences can be catastrophic for Indigenous cultural and intellectual development, which the Iranian philosopher Jalal Al-e Ahmad (1982) refers to as *Gharbzadeghi* and Syed Hussain Alatas (1972) calls the 'captive mind'.

Colonialism and the dominance of Northern sociology

This process can be seen in the way the newly emerging social sciences such as sociology became intimately linked with the colonial project. Just as Utopian studies, which has been closely linked to the experiences of the Northern settlers and dominated by the ideas of mainly white Northern academics, needs to be decolonised by drawing on the experiences of Indigenous peoples, their dreams and utopian desires, so too do social sciences such as sociology need to reveal the contribution of non-Northern sociological thinkers to the origins of the discipline and to ensure that they are able to contribute to its future development in their societies.

If any student new to sociology were to carry out a survey of the most popular and mainstream sociology textbooks, journals and lecture programmes from the last century they could be forgiven for assuming that sociology and sociological ways of thinking are almost exclusively the product of Northern intellectuals and researchers, or the 'Western, mind'. In *A Short History of Sociological Thought*, first published in 1984, which is a popular introduction to the subject used by British and English-speaking undergraduate students around the world in the late twentieth century, Alan Swingewood devotes his entire account of the intellectual origins and development of sociology to European and American thinkers. In his authoritative *Capitalism and Modern Social Theory* (Giddens, 1971), Anthony Giddens does the same, stating in the *Introduction*: 'If Renaissance Europe gave rise to a concern with history, it was industrial Europe which provided the conditions for the emergence of sociology' (Giddens, 1971: xi). These texts from the late twentieth century were chosen because, although things are beginning to change, those who were the students then are the teachers of today (Garuba, 2015). They are in many ways still influenced by the sociology curriculum of that time and their early socialisation in the subject and may find the idea of decolonising the sociology curriculum disconcerting perhaps because, in the words of the Puerto Rican Professor of Ethnic Studies Nelson Maldonado-Torres (cited in Hendricks and Leibowitz, 2016), 'It unsettles one's sense of well-being and belonging. It calls identities and the project of enlightenment into question'.

The need for a new approach

There is now a great deal of evidence to show that sociological thinking and sociology as a discipline in the making has a long history stretching back centuries, even though it was not called 'sociology'.

The Arab philosopher Ibn Khaldun [1958] (2005) writing in the fourteenth century CE was effectively writing and thinking sociologically long before August Comte coined the term in 1839. This, indeed, is the claim of some sociologists (Gumplowicz, 1980; Alatas, 2006; Soyer and Gilbert, 2012) who suggest that sociology was born at that time because, they believe, Ibn Khaldun effectively produced the first sociological study ever written. In his epic work the *Muqaddimah* (2005) [1958], originally published in Cairo in 1370 (Lawrence, 2005), Ibn Khaldun claims to have developed a new way of studying and understanding the world that, to his knowledge, had not been proposed before. In his attempt to write comprehensive history of Islam and the social changes it was experiencing at the time, he believed there was a need to complement the 'religious sciences' with an approach based on reason and the use of evidence in order to avoid producing an account that relied merely on tradition and unsubstantiated assertions. In the process Khaldun developed a rational, evidence-based analysis of history and averred that this was a much more reliable method than any other being used at the time. Ibn Khaldun (2005) even suggests that there are social laws in operation and that societies with similar types of social organisation tend to follow similar patterns of development.

Despite this foundational schema representing what we now call sociology, little if any reference is made to Ibn Khaldun by the major figures who developed what has come to be seen as the accepted canon of the origins of modern sociology (Parsons, 1937; Gerth and Mills, 1948; Merton, 1949). Although there has been acknowledgement of Ibn Khaldun as the founder of sociology amongst some earlier social thinkers (Flint, 1884; Gumplowicz, 1928 cited in Enan, 1979), the classical texts on the origins of sociology devote little if any space to the ideas of Ibn Khaldun who developed a clearly sociological approach to the dramatic changes occurring in Islamic societies at the time. Though writing several hundred years before industrialisation it was, nonetheless, sociology (Barnes and Becker, 1938). However, the dominant Northern view of sociology is that it emerged in the newly industrialising countries of Europe (Giddens, 1971; Swingewood, 1984) from the attempt by Northern philosophers and intellectuals (Weber, Durkheim and Marx) to understand the effects of change on societies caused by industrialisation. This, in short, is the official version of how modern sociology was born (Parsons, 1937; Gerth and Mills, 1948; Merton, 1949; Giddens, 1971; Swingewood, 1984).

Academic dependency

A consequence of the notion of the social, cultural and scientific superiority of the North is that metropolitan intellectuals often seem unaware of the writings and knowledge produced by intellectuals from Latin America, Australia, Africa and India. In terms of the epistemological approach of Northern sociology, there is an assumption of universal applicability and relevance in presenting the world and its problems as conceived by the 'centre', by the theories of European and American sociologists (Connell, 2007). Rather than being seen as sources of valid knowledge, the ideas of intellectuals from the South, especially those who write from a 'local' or non-metropolitan perspective, are often ignored. Southern sociology is therefore underdeveloped because it is dependent on Northern epistemologies, methods of research and systems of assessing academic achievement and excellence. In order to be treated seriously and to have any credibility at all, Southern sociologists are expected to adopt the epistemologies of the North, particularly if they wish to participate

Case study 5.1: Bourdieu's Logic of Practice: the absence of indigenous voices

Focusing on Connell's analysis of *The Logic of Practice*, which contains many of Pierre Bourdieu's (1990) ideas and concepts that inform his sociology of education, Connell (2007) points to its universalist intentions to develop a 'logic of practice', which is essentially a sociological method for the study and understanding of social laws that can be applied to *all societies*. For Connell (2007), *The Logic* is a classic example of the continuing practice of metropolitan sociology in which material and information are collected from the colony and the process of theorising is conducted inductively by metropolitan sociologists using the ethnographic data. Induction lends itself more to original theory formation than deduction, as the latter is usually led by prior theoretical assumptions. *The Logic* is the culmination of Bourdieu's early ethnographic research carried out in the 1950s among the Kabyle of Algeria, a French colony at the time, during which there was a particularly brutal war of independence (1954–1962). His fieldwork on kinship relations of the Kabyle yielded data on marriage and inheritance practices and customs. From these data, Bourdieu developed a world of agents (individuals) operating within a set of practices relating to taste, behaviour and thought, or a *habitus*, through which they negotiated the rules and customs of kinship in ways that enabled them to gain maximum advantage. Connell's intention in her analysis is not to provide a critique of Bourdieu's ideas (for this, see Connell, 1983) but to identify the problems that arise from their production. She shows that in developing *The Logic*, Bourdieu makes no attempt to engage in the debate on the anticolonial struggle going on at the time or to include the ideas of Islamic scholars on colonialism and modernisation. Connell (2007) suggests that it is difficult to understand why such material was not considered by Bourdieu. In *The Logic* he only mentions the war of independence once, and that is in the Preface. In the rest of his analysis, time seems to have stood still or, as Connell (2007: 44) states, there is an 'ethnographic time-warp' with the potential effects of the war on Algerian society left unexamined.

During the time that Bourdieu was researching the Kabyle, Frantz Fanon, the famous anticolonial theorist and activist, had been to Kabylia and had, like Bourdieu, conducted ethnographic fieldwork there. Fanon also wrote on the Algerian situation and participated in the revolution (Fanon, 1959, 1970); yet, despite Fanon's great insights into the colonial condition and the transformations taking place in Algeria, none of his work is mentioned in *The Logic*. It seems, as Lane (2000) points out, that although Bourdieu was an anticolonialist, in this omission he was attempting to distance himself from the radical left in France which, he claimed, had created a dangerous view of the revolutionary potential of the Algerian peasantry and emerging proletariat. However, it is also the case that he tended to ignore Indigenous and local intellectuals. Bourdieu was in effect putting his faith in his own theoretical insights above those of others who may have provided relevant contributions to an understanding of the situation in Algeria. The key issue here for Connell (2007) is not that Bourdieu disagreed with Fanon's position or other intellectuals in the field but that he saw these ideas and the anticolonial struggle as having little relevance to the theory he was developing. Colonialism and the anticolonial struggle were, it would seem, merely incidental

> to his intention to develop a universally applicable theory of practice. As Connell (2007: 43) claims, 'the European conceptual framing is self-sufficient. In the centre of this debate ... there are no voices from Africa'.
>
> Connell (2007) suggests that it is unlikely that Bourdieu intended this outcome, but the logic of Northern sociology effectively led him in that direction. Indeed, Bourdieu's anticolonialism is noted by Connell and others such as Ho (2013), who provides an excellent survey of Bourdieu's early writing on colonialism and its effects on colonial culture and identity. Ho (2013) shows how Bourdieu examined colonialism as a system of racial domination (Bourdieu, 1958) based on coercion and violence (Bourdieu, 1958, 1963) which, he claimed, only revolution could bring to an end (Bourdieu, 1958). Ho (2013) goes further suggesting that Bourdieu's early work sits comfortably in the camp of Southern theory, and this is pretty much acknowledged by Connell who nevertheless concludes that the 'possibility for a different structure of knowledge that undoubtedly existed in Bourdieu's earlier work are never realised in the later writings' (Connell, 2007: 44).

internationally in the discipline and be published in high-profile journals (Connell, 2007; Keim, 2011). As Alatas (2003: 603) states:

> the social sciences in intellectually dependent societies are dependent on institutions and ideas of western social science such that research agendas, the definition of problems areas, methods of research and standards of excellence are determined by or borrowed from the West.

Furthermore, Connell's (2007) and Alatas's (2003) research supports claims that there is a global division of labour in the social sciences which started during the colonial encounter. This is where raw material, i.e. data, is provided by the periphery in the form of studies of Indigenous peoples of the geographical South, from which those in the metropolitan North develop the theories with which to understand and interpret them. It is a practice that is believed to continue in the postcolonial world. These aspects of academic dependency can be illustrated by Connell's (2007) analysis of some of the most influential works of Northern sociology of the twentieth century.

Academic neocolonialism

So, rather than the academic imperialism of the colonial period, we are now experiencing academic neocolonialism (Alatas, 2003), in which control over the production, flow and transmission of academic knowledge is exercised by the North through the structures, organisation and curricula of the universities of the now politically independent former colonies. It is these institutions and their entrenched systems that scholars such as Alatas and Connell are attempting to challenge.

However, the responses to Connell's findings and claims are not those one should expect from a community supposedly operating within an ethos of academic open-mindedness and an objective analysis of the evidence; indeed, one might say, in the manner Ibn Khaldun would have recommended more than six hundred years ago. One of Connell's Australian colleagues, the eminent sociologist Randall Collins, dismissed her assertions as no more than a 'sociological guilt trip' (Collins, 1997). Refusing to take the evidence seriously, he could not accept that an academic discipline as noble as sociology could have concealed such a shameful past and suggested that it was not appropriate to judge the past by the standards of the present. He urged his readers instead to consider the progress sociology has made since its inception. This refusal to countenance such claims about sociology and its origins seems to miss the point which is that to maintain any credibility and integrity as a discipline, particularly among a growing number of students from the South, it needs to reassess its 'global intellectual footprint in order to develop a new and more globally inclusive discipline' (Boronski and Hassan, 2020: 44).

Hendricks and Leibowitz (2016) state that, from their experience of the South African context, little has little changed since 1997. However, as Behari-Leak et al. (2015) suggest, there really is no stopping the movement for change, given the growing awareness students are developing of the injustices in which some universities and academic disciplines have been complicit. These include the continued teaching of curricula that lack the voices, ideas and experiences of Indigenous people; huge increases in fees by universities around the world, which disproportionately affect poorer students; the symbolic violence experienced by students in the form of the continued presence on university campuses of symbols and signs of colonial oppression; and the continued interest many academics and academic institutions have in the current situation.

What is a decolonised curriculum?
The end of multiculturalism and a revival of nationalism

The election successes of the Conservative governments in 2010 (coalition), 2015, 2017 and 2019, as we have seen, have led to even greater reaction against those daring to challenge the idea of the greatness of the British Empire. The new English National History Curriculum is more of a celebration of this period, with its critics branded as 'trashing' our past (Faulkner, 2010). Moreover, the ideology of Empire was harnessed by the Conservative government in its Brexit campaign. In a former colonial power such as Britain which bases its national identity on the Monarch and Empire and many of whose elite institutions are still strongly rooted in Britain's colonial past, it would appear that the nation is struggling with the idea of facing the potential damage that a decolonised curriculum could cause to its self-concept, to the continuing legacy of Empire as well as to its international reputation. This is well illustrated by the reaction of one of Britain's elite educational establishments to the #RhodesMust Fall campaign.

Africa and Britain: the academic legacy of Empire

The history of Empire links Africa and Britain in a complex web of relationships and ties that still endure. These very occasionally become openly visible, but in many cases, this happens only by chance. This was clearly demonstrated in the way the campaign to have Cecil Rhodes' statue removed from the campus of the University of Cape Town in 2015 spilled over and reached, literally, the portals of one of Britain's elite universities. As a student at Oriel College Oxford in the 1870s Sir Cecil Rhodes developed many of his ideas of a greater British Empire,

Case study 5.2: Kenya

Despite the progress disciplines such as sociology have made in raising issues of gender, sexuality, race and disability, there is a growing demand by students and academics (Pett, 2015; Le Grange, 2016; Ndvolu-Gatsheni, 2017; SOAS, Students' Union, 2019) to make the curriculum more inclusive and a belief that it is still dominated by white, male, Western/ Northern perspectives. This has led to the growth of a number of academics and student groups in both the former colonies and the metropole asking 'why is my curriculum white?' (Hussain, 2015; Pett, 2015), making calls for the 'decolonisation of the curriculum' and suggesting ways to reform the systems and institutions that perpetuate the academic dependence of Southern academics on those of the global North (Keim, 2011).

The history of attempts at decolonisation of the curriculum teach us many lessons, so, as Garuba (2015) states, we are not starting from 'ground zero'. One of the early landmarks in this history occurred in Kenya when in 1968 at the University of Nairobi, an academic in the English department proposed the expansion of the English curriculum to include works form the wider English-speaking world to the existing list of British writers on the department's syllabus. This was, on the face of it, a reasonable and logical development within a programme to add diversity and richness to an otherwise narrow group of white British authors. However, in a memo, entitled 'On the Abolition of the English Department', to the board of the arts faculty, Ngugi wa Thiong'o (then named James Ngugi) and two other colleagues at the University of Nairobi, objected to the proposal, on the grounds that merely adding non-Western authors to the dominant cultural medium of English did nothing to 'illuminate the spirit animating a people' (Ngugi, 1972: 146). Moreover, they requested the abolition of the English literature department and the study of English literature as the focus of literary studies at the university.

Ngugi and his colleagues objected to the placing of Africa in a position of secondary importance to the study of English language and literature, claiming that 'the content of the literary text and its orientation, its connections to national traditions, were much more important than its language' (Ngugi, 1972: 146). Ngugi found inspiration in his ideas from Black thinkers such Franz Fanon in whose book Black Skin, White Masks [1959](1967), the author writes of the need for Black people to liberate their minds from the damaging psychological effects of colonialism that destroyed their sense of self-worth. A psychology of being unattractive, bad and inferior is instilled in Black colonised people in an unconscious way, according to Fanon. Moreover, they learn that most ideas of culture, philosophy, aesthetics and positive traits are associated with 'whiteness'. This is why the decolonisation of the curriculum is seen as so important to Ngugi and of the need to place African thought at the centre of education for Kenyans. There was eventually a meeting of Kenyan academics in 1969 in which the delegates condemned the domination of Western models over the Kenyan education system. This led ultimately to widescale reforms in which most British literature was removed from the school and university curriculum and replaced with African literature (Young, 2017).

stretching from South Africa in the south of the continent to Egypt in the north (South African History Online, 2017). He believed that the superior race of white Europeans would come to govern those territories of the world that he saw as being occupied by a 'despicable specimen of human being' (South African History Online, 2017). Most of his wealth was acquired through the extraction of the minerals and diamonds of the region using the labour of these 'despicable specimens'. So fond was Rhodes of his *alma mater* that, on hearing of the financial difficulties it was experiencing during a visit to the college in 1899, 'he *offered to leave* it £100,000 in his will' (Oriel College Oxford, 2021) (emphasis added). However, it seems that on his death he actually left most of his six million pounds (equivalent to $960m in 2015) (South African History Online, 2017) to the college. This final amount is not actually stated on the official Oriel College website (June 2020). Nevertheless, whatever the actual amount, some was used in capital expenditure for the construction the Rhodes Building, some spent 'to support the endowment of Fellowships and other college expenses' (Oriel College Oxford, 2021) and the rest to fund Rhodes Scholarships for students from former British colonies – the US and Germany – to study at Oxford.

The links between South Africa and Oxford are therefore still strong though not entirely transparent, but it is evident that the privileged academic institution that is Oxford today was and is at least partly funded by the wealth extracted from Africa by this 'businessman and ... political deal-maker' (Oriel College Oxford, 2021) and which continues to benefit from this legacy through the funding of fellowships and 'other college expenses'. However, whereas most of us in Britain are unaware of who or what Cecil Rhodes was and what he stood for, in South Africa his name and legacy are well-known. As one of the founders of a state based on institutionalised racism, for over eighty years his statue stood prominently on the University of Cape Town (UCT) campus in a continuing act of symbolic violence against not just Black students but, indeed, all members of the university community, the entire country and the continent of Africa. How was it that more than twenty years after the collapse of apartheid the statue was still in its place? This was very much symbolic of the general lack of progress made by Black South Africans since the collapse of the apartheid system (Behari-Leak, 2015; Pett, 2015).

However, things started to change when on 9 March 2015, a student named Chumani Maxwele threw a bucket of human excrement over the statue (Pett, 2015). This act sparked the #RodesMustFall movement which ultimately led to the removal of the statue a month later. Inspired by the success of #RhodesMustFall in South Africa, students from both countries joined together to demand the removal of a statue of Cecil Rhodes in Oriel College Oxford, as well as the decolonisation of the curricula of South African, British and other universities. There has been very little change in the university curriculum in South African universities since the ending of apartheid with most of the reform being focused on such things as governance, mergers, incorporations and quality assurance rather than the legacy of apartheid. As Heleta (2016a) states: 'Two decades after the end of apartheid, the curriculum at South African universities is still largely Eurocentric, rooted in the colonial and apartheid dispossession, looting and humiliation of Africa and its people'. He points to the barriers to change in the form of 'many powerful individuals and interest groups who will do all it takes to contest, resist and water down the change in order to maintain the status quo' (Heleta, 2016a). Moreover, although the number of Black students attending the university has increased, the proportion of white academic staff has not changed (Le Grange, 2016), despite many promises of reform and change made by the government (Heleta, 2016b). Students and staff continue to campaign for the decolonisation of the curriculum, but as Behari-Leak et al. (2017) have found, there is no simple or precise answer to what it actually means.

#RhodesMustFall Oriel College Oxford

Unlike the success of the students at the University of Cape Town to remove their statue of Cecil Rhodes, the goal of #RhodesMustFall to remove the statue of Rhodes from the façade of Oriel's Rhodes building is yet to be realised (July 2020). The university did seem to feel the need to do something as a gesture to those pointing to the offensiveness and inappropriateness of such a memorial. It conducted what is described as extensive consultations with a range of stakeholders including 'students and academics, alumni, heritage bodies, national and student polls and a further petition, as well as over 500 direct written responses to the college' (Rawlinson, 2016). On the basis of the information and evidence collected in this enquiry, the university authorities decided that there was 'overwhelming' support to leave the statue in its place. They also claim that the decision had been reached 'in a spirit of free speech and open debate, with a readiness to listen to divergent views' (Rawlinson, 2016). It is probably safe to suggest that this decision will not put an end to the matter. The events in the US following the killing of George Floyd by a police officer in May 2020, which led to renewed protests and activities against institutional racism around the world, including another attempt by protestors to bring down the statue of Rhodes, have placed Oxford University under renewed pressure, and in late 2020 another committee was set up by Oriel College to address the issue.

A positive outcome of the campaign, however, is that academics and university authorities in South Africa and other countries are being encouraged to rethink their positions on the history of the colonial period. The Oxford historian Timothy Garton-Ash (2016) admits that the campaign has started an important 'debate' about Britain's colonial past and that he has found himself 'wondering whether there was not a little facing up to be done in my own family' (Garton-Ash, 2016). His grandfather was a civil servant in India when it was part of the Empire. Garton-Ash concedes that more could be done at Oxford to represent 'people of colour among both faculty and students' (Garton-Ash, 2016) and suggests more academic research should be conducted on the legacy of colonialism on its victims and their descendants. However, he rejects the demands for the decolonisation of the curriculum and does not believe that the 'obscure' statue of Rhodes in Oriel College constitutes a symbol of oppression to 'most of those who live here' (Garton-Ash, 2016). It could be suggested, however, that Garton-Ash's position is not consistent with his stated belief that the consequences of colonialism and the voices of its victims and descendants need to be heard. Moreover, in Britain legislation such as the Equality Act 2010 protects *minorities* from the 'display of racially offensive material' (Birkbeck University of London, 2019), and Garton-Ash does not present any evidence to support his claim.

Mary Beard, another eminent historian who could also be said to represent an 'establishment' view on this matter, suggests that 'the battle isn't won by taking the statue away and pretending those people didn't exist' (Beard, 2016). However, Beard would appear to be conflating two related but separate issues: first, whether the statue is offensive and an act of continued tribute to a symbol of colonial oppression and, second, implying that the removal of Rhode's statue would remove him from the curriculum and from the national debate. From the evidence it would seem that there certainly is offence, particularly amongst a significant proportion of Oxford's students (Gosling,

2016), but this does not lead us to the conclusion that Rhodes should not be studied or his statue displayed in a more appropriate place. In a decolonised curriculum, colonial figures such as Cecil Rhodes and other prominent figures of the empire are likely to have a place, but in a much more critical way and within a more ethnically and culturally diverse syllabus (Pett, 2015). In a move in this direction, the University of Oxford has set up the Oxford and Colonialism Project (OCP) which was established in 2016 to 'engage critically' with the university's 'colonial legacy', and in 2020 it launched its Oxford and Colonialism website (Oxford and Colonialism Project Website, 2021). All colleges have been invited to contribute to this process. However, as the information on the website shows (Oxford and Colonialism Project Website, 2021), not all colleges have, as yet (February, 2021), engaged with the project.

The events surrounding the #RhodesMustFall campaign in South Africa has inspired students from around the world to engage in a dialogue between themselves as a body of people with different histories and from many cultural backgrounds. At the School of Oriental and African Studies (SOAS), an institution with close links to the history of British colonialism and with a strong representation from the former colonies, the students have contributed to the list of the school's priorities and a 'vision for itself for the next 100 years' (SOAS Students' Union, 2019). Under the title: *Decolonising SOAS: Confronting the White Institution*, the students' aims include the following:

- To address histories of erasure prevalent in the curriculum with a particular focus on SOAS's colonial origins and present alternative ways of knowing.
- If white philosophers are required, then to teach their work from a critical standpoint ... acknowledging the colonial context in which so called 'Enlightenment' philosophers wrote within.

Conclusion

The tone of these aims and their tentative nature relate to the students' evident awareness of the inadvisability of laying down a definitive and detailed curriculum for all disciplines and for all places (Garuba, 2015). They clearly see the necessity for dialogue, discussion and critical assessment of existing practice among students, teachers and university authorities. This is very much in line with the ideas of critical pedagogy and particularly that of Paulo Freire (1996), who has long promoted the need for oppressed groups and peoples of the Southern hemisphere to be part of this dialogue in which they are able to name the world and the problems they face. Such an attempt to develop the 'view from below' and to understand the history of the erasure of the ideas and cultures of Indigenous peoples is an essential element of such a dialogue.

Points for reflection and consideration in this chapter

This chapter has examined the enduring nostalgia for empire among many of the former colonial powers such as Britain and how this has been used to perpetuate a national myth of a glorious history that is still drawn on by many ordinary citizens and particularly nationalist politicians to mobilise support for their policies. So, rather than seeing the nation's colonial past as something requiring an open and honest debate, most British politicians see this issue as off-limits. As a result, the voices of the victims of colonialism and their descendants are not viewed as an essential part of the national historical narrative.

- What are your views on the English History National Curriculum? You can find information on Key Stages 1–4 and beyond at: https://www.history.org.uk/primary https://www.history.org.uk/secondary and https://www.history.org.uk/student

References

Al-e Ahmad, J. [1962] (1982) (trans. John Green and Ahmad Alizadeh) *Gharbzadeghi* (Westsruckness). Lexington, KY: Mazda.

Alatas, S.H. (1972) 'The captive mind in development studies'. *International Social Science Journal.* Vol. 34, No. 1, pp. 9–25.

Alatas, S.F. (2003) 'Academic dependency and the global division of labour in the social sciences'. *Current Sociology.* Vol. 51, No. 6, pp. 599–613.

Alatas, S.H. (2006) 'The autonomous, the universal and the future of sociology'. *Current Sociology.* Vol. 54, No. 7, pp. 7–23.

Anderlini, J. (2020) 'Britain's Colonial crimes come back to Haunt Trade negotiations'. *Financial Times.* 17 March. Available at: https://www.ft.com/content/224109be-6763-11ea-800d-da70cff6e4d3 (Accessed 17 March and 19 April).

Arday, J. (2020) *The Black curriculum: Black British history in the National Curriculum Report 2020.* Available at: file:///E:/Routledge%20Proposal%20%2025th%20April%202/Chapter%205%20decolonisation/The+Black+Curriculum+Report+2020.pdf (Accessed 20 April 2020).

Anderson, B. (2006) *Imagined Communities: Reflections on the Origins and Spread of Nationalism.* London: Verso.

Barnes, H. and Becker, H. (1938) *Social Thought: From Lore to Science* (Vols. 1–2). Washington, DC: Heath and Company.

BBC. (2019) 'General election 2019: Johnson will seek to reduce unskilled migration'. 14 November. Available at: https://www.bbc.co.uk/news/election-2019-50412772 (Accessed 17 April 2020).

Beard, M. (2016) 'Cecil Rhodes and Oriel College, Oxford', in *The Times Literary Supplement* December 2015. Available at: https://www.the-tls.co.uk/cecil-rhodes-and-oriel-college-oxford/ (Accessed 16 March 2019).

Behari-Leak, K. (2015) 'After protests, it can't be business as usual at South Africa's universities'. *The Conversation.* Available at: https://theconversation.com/after-protests-it-cant-be-business-as-usual-at-south-africas-universities-50548 (Accessed 22 April 2020).

Behari-Leak, K., Masehela, L., Marhaya, L., Tjabane, M. and Merckel, N. (2017) 'Decolonising the curriculum: It's in the detail, not just in the definition'. *The Conversation.* Available at: https://theconversation.com/decolonising-the-curriculum-its-in-the-detail-not-just-in-the-definition-73772 (Accessed 30 April 2020).

Berger, P. (1973) *The Social Reality of Religion.* Harmondsworth: Penguin University Books.

Birkbeck University of London. (2019) 'Equality and diversity law'. Available at: http://www.bbk.ac.uk/about-us/equality/law (Accessed 1 May 2020).

Boffey, D. (2018) 'Empire 2.0: The fantasy that's fuelling Tory divisions on Brexit'. *The Guardian.* 8 November. Available at: https://www.theguardian.com/politics/2018/nov/08/empire-fantasy-fuelling-tory-divisions-on-brexit (Accessed 13 April 2020).

Boronski, T. and Hassan, N. (2020) *Sociology of Education.* London: Sage.

Bourdieu, P. [1958] (1961) *The Algerians.* Boston: Beacon Press.

Bourdieu, P. [1963] (1979) *Algeria 1960.* Cambridge, UK: Cambridge University Press.

Bourdieu, P. (1990) *The Logic of Practice.* Stanford, CA: University of Stanford Press.

Cameron, D. (2011) 'PM's speech at Munich Security Conference'. *Speech.* Published 5 February 2011. Available at: https://www.gov.uk/government/speeches/pms-speech-at-munich-security-conference (Accessed 12 April 2020).

Coates, S. (2017) 'Ministers aim to build "empire 2.0" with African Commonwealth'. *The Times.* 6 March 2017. Available at: https://www.thetimes.co.uk/article/ministers-aim-to-build-empire-2-0-with-african-commonwealth-after-brexit-v9bs6f6z9 (Accessed 17 April 2020).

Collins, R. (1997) 'A sociological guilt trip: Comment on Randall'. *American Journal of Sociology.* Vol. 102, No. 6, pp. 1558–1564.

Connell, R. (1983) 'The black box of habit on the wings of history: Reflections on the theory of social reproduction', in R. Connell (ed.), *Which Way Is Up? Essays on Sex, Class and Culture.* Sydney: Allen and Unwin, pp. 140–161.

Connell, R. (1997) 'Why is classical theory classical?' *American Journal of Sociology*. Vol. 102, No. 6, pp. 1511–1557.
Connell, R. (2007) *Southern Theory*. Cambridge: Polity Press.
Dahlgreen, W. (2014) 'The British Empire is "something to be proud of"'. *YouGov*. Available at: https://yougov.co.uk/topics/politics/articles-reports/2014/07/26/britain-proud-its-empire (Accessed 12 April 2020).
Edwards, K. (2013) 'Gove's history curriculum needs to teach more equality'. *The Guardian*, 29 April. Available at: www.theguardian.com/teacher-network/teacherblog/2013/apr/29/gove-history-curriculum-more-equality (Accessed 15 January 2015).
Enan, M.A. (1979) *Ibn Khaldun: His Life and Work*. New Delhi: Kitab Bhavan.
Encyclopaedia Britannica. (2020) 'The most excellent order of the British Empire'. Available at: https://www.britannica.com/topic/The-Most-Excellent-Order-of-the-British-Empire (Accessed 15 April 2020).
Fanon, F. [1959] (1967) *Black Skin, White Masks*. New York: Grove Press.
Fanon, F. (1970) [1959] *Studies in a Dying Colonialism* [L'an V de la revolution algerienne]. Harmondsworth: Penguin.
Faulconbridge, G. and MacLellan, K. (2019) '"I'll make Britain great again", PM Johnson says, echoing Trump'. *Reuters*. 25 July. Available at: https://www.reuters.com/article/us-britain-eu/ill-make-britain-great-again-pm-johnson-says-echoing-trump-idUSKCN1UK0OG (Accessed 21 April 2020).
Faulkner, K. (2010) 'Children will learn poetry and monarchs of England by heart under Tory plans'. *The Mail Online*. 6 March. Available at: https://www.dailymail.co.uk/news/article-1255899/Children-learn-poetry-monarchs-England-heart-Tory-plans.html (Accessed 20 April 2020).
Ferguson, N. (2002) *How Britain Made the Modern World*. London: Penguin.
Flint, R. (1884) *Vico*. Edinburgh: W. Blackwood.
Freire, P. (1996) *Pedagogy of the Oppressed*. London: Penguin.
Garner, R. (2013) '"Jingoistic and illegal" – what teachers think of Michael Gove's national curriculum reforms'. *The Independent*. 12 June. Available at: https://www.independent.co.uk/news/education/education-news/jingoistic-and-illegal-what-teachers-think-of-michael-goves-national-curriculum-reforms-8656120.html (Accessed 21 April 2020).
Garton-Ash, T. (2016) 'Rhodes hasn't fallen, but the protesters are making me rethink Britain's past'. *The Guardian*, 4 March. Available online at: www.theguardian.com/commentisfree/2016/mar/04/rhodes-oxford-students-rethink-british-empire-past-pain (Accessed 7 March 2019).
Garuba, H. (2015) 'What is an African curriculum?' *Mail and Guardian*, 17 April. Available at: https://mg.co.za/article/2015-04-17-what-is-an-african-curriculum/ (Accessed 29 April 2020).
Gerth, H.H. and Mills, C.W. (eds) (1948) *From Max Weber*. London: Routledge and Kegan Paul.
Giddens, A. (1971) *Capitalism and Modern Social Theory: An Analysis of the Writings of Marx, Durkheim and Weber*. Cambridge: Cambridge University Press.
Goodman, D., Stirling, C. and McCormack, L. (2019) 'How a no-deal Brexit may become a problem for the world economy'. *Bloomberg*. 4 October. Available at: https://www.bloomberg.com/news/articles/2019-10-04/how-a-no-deal-brexit-may-become-a-problem-for-the-world-economy (Accessed 21 April 2020).
Gosling, H. (2016) 'Majority of Oxford students: Rhodes should stay' *Cherwell* 14 January. Available at: https://cherwell.org/2016/01/14/majority-of-oxford-students-rhodes-should-stay/ (Accessed on 15 March 2019).
Gov.UK. (2020) 'Nominate someone for an honour or award'. *Types of Honours and Awards*. Available at: https://www.gov.uk/honours/types-of-honours-and-awards (Accessed 14 April 2020).
Gumplowicz, L. (1980) *Outlines of Sociology*. New Jersey: Paine-Whitman Publishers.
Gunder Frank, A. (1969) 'The sociology of development and the underdevelopment of sociology'. *Catalyst*. Vol. 3, pp. 20–73.
Heath, D. (2017) 'British Empire is still being whitewashed by the school curriculum – historian on why this must change'. *The Conversation*. Available at: https://theconversation.com/british-empire-is-still-being-whitewashed-by-the-school-curriculum-historian-on-why-this-must-change-105250 (Accessed on 20 April 2020).
Heleta, S. (2016a) 'Decolonisation: academics must change what they teach, and how'. The Conversation. Available online at: https://theconversation.com/decolonisationacademics-must-change-what-they-teach-and-how-68080 (Accessed 5 April 2019).
Heleta, S. (2016b) 'Decolonisation of higher education: Dismantling epistemic violence and Eurocentrism in South Africa'. *Transformation in Higher Education*. Vol. 1, No. 1, p. a9. Available at: https://thejournal.org.za/index.php/thejournal/article/view/9/21 (Accessed 29 April 2020).
Hendricks, C. and Leibowitz, B. (2016) 'Decolonising universities isn't an easy process – but it has to happen'. *The Conversation*. Available at: https://theconversation.com/decolonising-universities-isnt-an-easy-process-but-it-has-to-happen-59604 (Accessed 21 April 2020).

The Historical Association. (2013) 'Poll on the new history curriculum draft proposal'. *Historical Association*. Available at: www.history.org.uk/resources/secondary_resource_6202_8.html (Accessed 15 January 2019).

Ho, J. (2013) 'Decolonizing Bourdieu: Colonial and postcolonial theory in Pierre Bourdieu's early'. *Sociological Theory*. Vol. 31, No. 1, pp. 49–74.

Hussain, M. (2015) 'Why is my curriculum white?' NUS. Available online at: https//www.nus.org.uk/en/news/why-is-my-curriculum-white/ (Accessed 9 April 2019).

Johnson, B. (1994) 'Goodbye, Brussels'. *Daily Telegraph*. 6 March.

Johnson, B. (2002) 'If Blair's so good at running the Congo let him stay there'. *The Telegraph*. 10 January. Available at: https://www.telegraph.co.uk/comment/personal-view/3571742/If-Blairs-so-good-at-running-the-Congo-let-him-stay-there.html (Accessed 20 April 2020).

Johnson, B. (2018) 'Denmark has got it wrong. Yes, the burka is oppressive and ridiculous – but that's still no reason to ban it'. *The Telegraph*. 5 August. Available at: https://www.telegraph.co.uk/news/2018/08/05/denmark-has-got-wrong-yes-burka-oppressive-ridiculous-still/ (Accessed 16 April 2020).

Keim, W. (2011) 'Counter hegemonic currents and internationalization of sociology. Theoretical reflections and one empirical example'. *International Sociology*. Vol. 26. No. 1, pp. 123–145.

Lach, E. (2020) 'Trump's dangerous scapegoating of immigrants at the State of the Union'. 5 February. Available at: https://www.newyorker.com/news/current/trumps-dangerous-scapegoating-of-immigrants-at-the-state-of-the-union (Accessed 15 April 2020).

Lane, J. (2000) *Pierre Bourdieu: A Critical Introduction*. London: Pluto Press.

Lawrence, B. (2005) *Introduction* to 2005 edn. Ibn Khaldun. *The Muqaddimah: An Introduction to History*. Translated by F. Rosenthal. Princeton, NJ: Princeton University Press.

Le Grange, L. (2016) 'Decolonisation involves more than simply turning back the clock'. *The Conversation*. Available online at: https://theconversation.com/decolonisation-involves-more-than-simply-turning-back-the-clock-62133 (Accessed 1 March 2019).

Merton, R. (1949) *Social Theory and Social Structure*. New York: Free Press.

Mishra, P. (2011) 'Watch this man'. *London Review of Books*, Vol. 33, No. 21. Available at: www.lrb.co.uk/v33/n21/pankaj-mishra/watch-this-man (Accessed 15 January 2020).

Mukerjee, M. (2010) *Churchill's Secret War: The British Empire and the Ravaging of India during World War II*. New York: Basic Books.

Ndvolu-Gatsheni, S. (2017) 'Decolonising research methodology must include undoing its dirty history'. *The Conversation*. Available at: https://theconversation.com/ decolonising-research-methodology-must-include-undoing-its-dirty-history-83912. (Accessed 25 April 2020).

Ngugi, wa T. (1972) *Homecoming (Studies in African Literature)*. London: Heinemann Educational Books.

Olusoga, D. (2016) 'Wake up, Britain. Should the empire really be a source of pride?' *The Guardian*. Available at: https://www.theguardian.com/commentisfree/2016/jan/23/britain-empire-pride-poll (Accessed 25 March 2020).

Oppenheim, M. (2018) 'Winston Churchill has as much blood on his hands as the worst genocidal dictators, claims Indian politician'. *The Independent*, 8 September. Available at: https://www.independent.co.uk/news/world/world-history/winston-churchill-genocide-dictator-shashi-tharoor-melbourne-writers-festival-a7936141.html (Accessed 22 April 2020).

Oriel College University of Oxford (2021) *Cecil John Rhodes (1853-1902)* Available at: https://www.oriel.ox.ac.uk/cecil-john-rhodes-1853-1902 (Accessed 20 February 2020).

Oxford and Colonialism Project. (2021) 'About the Oxford & Colonialism project'. Available at: https://oxfordandcolonialism.web.ox.ac.uk/about (Accessed 2 February 2021).

Parsons, T. (1937) *The Structure of Social Action: A Study in Social Theory with Special Reference to a Group of Recent European Writers*. New York: McGraw Hill.

Pett, S. (2015) 'It's time to take the curriculum back from dead white men'. *The Conversation*. Available at: https://theconversation.com/its-time-to-take-the-curriculum-back-from-dead-white-men-40268 (Accessed 30 April 2020).

Poole, S. (2018) 'What is a "vassal state"? Jacob Rees-Mogg's mid-Brexit vision explained'. *The Guardian*. 2 February. Available at: https://www.theguardian.com/books/2018/feb/02/word-of-the-week-steven-poole-vassal (Accessed 16 April 2020).

Prebisch, R. (1959) 'Commercial policy in the underdeveloped countries'. *The American Economic Review*. Vol. 49, No. 2, pp. 251–273.

Press Gazette. (2019) 'Boris Johnson's Telegraph column comparing Muslim women with 'letterboxes' led to Islamophobia spike'. 2 September. Available at: https://www.pressgazette.co.uk/boris-johnson-telegraph-column-muslim-women-letterboxes-bank-robbers-spike-islamophobic-incidents/ (Accessed on 15 April 2020).

Prince, R. (2010) 'David Cameron: Net immigration will be capped to tens of thousands'. *The Telegraph*. 10 June. Available at: https://www.telegraph.co.uk/news/politics/6961675/David-Cameron-net-immigration-will-be-capped-at-tens-of-thousands.html (Accessed 12 April 2020).

Rankin and Waterson (2019) 'How Boris Johnson's Brussels-bashing stories shaped British politics'. *The Guardian*. 14 July. Available at: https://www.theguardian.com/politics/2019/jul/14/boris-johnson-brussels-bashing-stories-shaped-politics (Accessed on 25 March 2020).

Rawlinson, K. (2016) 'Cecil Rhodes statue to remain at Oxford after "overwhelming support"'. *The Guardian*, 29 January. Available at: www.theguardian.com/education/2016/jan/28/cecil-rhodes-statue-will-not-be-removed--oxford-university (Accessed 7 March 2019).

Rostow, W.W. (1960) *The Process of Economic Growth*. London: Oxford University Press.

The Runnymede Trust. (2000) *The Future of Multiethnic Britain: The Parekh Report*. London: Profile Books.

Schultz, J. (2017) 'The ties that (still) bind: the enduring tendrils of the British Empire', in *The Conversation*. Available at: https://theconversation.com/the-tiesthat-still-bind-the-enduring-tendrils-of-the-british-empire-89308 (accessed on 18 March 2019).

Shapps, G. (2016) 'The Blog: Four things Britain must do now'. *The Huffington Post*. 30 June. Available at: https://www.huffingtonpost.co.uk/grant-shapps/brexit-uk-economy_b_10747900.html?guccounter=2 (Accessed 17 March 2019).

Shear, M. and McNeil, D. (2020) 'Criticized for pandemic response, Trump tries shifting blame to the W.H.O'. *The New York Times*. 14 April. Available at: https://www.nytimes.com/2020/04/14/us/politics/coronavirus-trump-who-funding.html (Accessed 15 April 2020).

Smith, M. (2020) 'How unique are British attitudes to empire?' *YouGov Report*. 11 March. Available at: https://yougov.co.uk/topics/international/articles-reports/2020/03/11/how-unique-are-british-attitudes-empire (Accessed 12 April 2020).

SOAS. (2019) '2016–2017 SOAS SU Educational priorities'. *SOAS Students' Union*. Available at: https://soasunion.org/education/educationalpriorities/ (Accessed 29 April 2020).

South African History Online. (2017) 'Cecil John Rhodes'. Available at: www.sahistory.org.za/people/cecil-john-rhodes (Accessed 4 March 2019).

South China Morning Post. (2017) 'Full text of President Xi Jinping's speech on "one country, two systems" and how China rules Hong Kong'. 1 July. Available at: https://www.scmp.com/news/hong-kong/politics/article/2100856/full-text-president-xi-jinpings-speech-one-country-two (Accessed 19 April 2020).

Soyer, M. and Gilbert, P. (2012) 'Debating the origins of sociology: Ibn Khaldun as a founding father of sociology'. *International Journal of Sociological Research*. Vol. 5, No. 1–2, pp. 13–30.

Studlar, D. (1976) 'Policy voting in Britain: The colored immigration issue in the 1964, 1966, and 1970 general elections'. *American Political Science Review*. Vol. 72, No. 1, pp. 46–64.

Swingewood, A. (1984) *A Short History of Sociology*. London: Macmillan.

Tell Mama. (2018) *Normalising Hatred: Tell Mama Annual Report 2018*. Available at: https://www.tellmamauk.org/wp-content/uploads/2019/09/Tell%20MAMA%20Annual%20Report%202018%20_%20Normalising%20Hate.pdf (Accessed 12 April 2020).

Thames Tv. (2014) 'Controversial | Enoch Powell interview | This week | 1976'. *Speech*. Available at: https://www.youtube.com/watch?v=OuH8kb1u1ig (Accessed 17 April 2010).

Tharoor, S. (2017a) *Inglorious Empire: What the British Did to India*. London: Harcourt.

Tharoor, S. (2017b) 'Interviewed by Ian Dale'. *LBC*. 6 March. Available at: https://www.lbc.co.uk/radio/presenters/iain-dale/empire-20-will-go-down-like-a-lead-balloon-india/ (Accessed 22 April 2020).

Tunzelmann, A. (2019) 'The Imperial Myths Driving Brexit'. *The Atlantic*. 12 August. Available at: https://www.theatlantic.com/international/archive/2019/08/imperial-myths-behind-brexit/595813/ (Accessed 20 April 2020).

Young, S. (2017) 'Shakespeare in Africa', in J. Levenson and R. Ormsby (eds), *The Shakespearean World*. London: Routledge, pp. 116–134.

6 Higher education as a site of liberatory practice

Introduction

Over the past four decades, universities around the world have been engaged in a process that challenges their very identities and purpose as places of 'higher education'. The question – 'what is a university for?' – has never been more relevant. As with all periods of dramatic change and reform, however, the emergence of a new synthesis brings with it varying sorts of benefits and potential opportunities as well as costs to those affected. Universities and other institutions of higher education globally are, just like other state-funded or partly state-funded organisations in the neoliberal era, being ineluctably drawn into the ways of thinking and organisation associated with the principles of neoliberal governmentality (Larner and Le Heron, 2005; Davidson-Harden, 2010; Maisuria and Cole, 2017). Michel Foucault (Foucault and Senellart, 2008) in his lectures at the *College de France* (1978–1979) identifies the primary purpose of government in the age of neoliberalism as that of financial accumulation and that universities are now expected to engage in this instrumental process of contributing to national economic growth. The role of the university has been recast from one of a place where knowledge and truth are pursued for their own sake (Kant, [1798] 1979; Newman, [1852] 2008), and from which extrinsic benefits may serendipitously arise, to one where they must justify their existence by demonstrating their 'success' in terms of government-imposed norms, such as their rates of graduate employment, 'measures' of academic excellence and their ability to monetise the knowledge they create (Peters, 2010).

Those who view such developments as an attack on the basic principles of a university talk of 'the university in crisis' (Peters, 2010), driven increasingly as they are now by market principles, business systems of organisation and performance as well as narrow and often contrived measures of excellence (Readings, 1996). These changes are becoming so pervasive that, according to Peters (2010), the more each institution adopts the new organisational and managerial systems, the more it loses its uniqueness as a seat of learning with a recognisable identity and becomes indistinguishable from any other corporate entity. The everyday lives of students and staff are increasingly dominated by the language of funding, employability, performance and efficiency and less by that of learning and pedagogy (Readings, 1995, 1996). Moreover, those who feel the need to challenge these processes and their consequences on students and teachers are usually silenced by declarations that there is no alternative (TINA) (Stanford, 2008), despite the fact that, as we have seen in previous chapters, there are many possible alternatives systems of human organisation that we are able to imagine and develop.

More cautious commentators and educators (McCowan, 2015) argue that, despite the objections we may have to these developments and their consequences, we need to be mindful of our moral position and the obligations we have to our students to support them within the current system and its constraints. This response is one of constructive criticism which is based on the premise that, as experts in the field, academics are able to present the evidence and arguments in a spirit of reasoned debate which is more likely to be taken seriously by those in power. Nevertheless, as Peters (2010) points out, those imposing such neoliberal policies are so committed to them that they have more or less given up any pretence that they are benefitting the nation and ignore evidence of the continuing and growing levels of inequality in terms of wealth and income (Wilkinson and Pickett, 2009, 2018), poor levels of social mobility (Savage et al., 2015) and punitive levels of debt experienced by young people from modest backgrounds due to rising tuition fees (IFS, 2017). Those with a more activist approach to the imposition of neoliberalism on the higher education sector are much more forthright in their responses, engaging in detailed critiques and political activism, whilst at the same time imagining alternatives to the current regime (Peters, 2010; Maisuria, 2014; Maisuria and Cole, 2017).

The modern university

In order to understand how we have arrived at this situation, it is necessary to examine how universities have been changing over the past few hundred years and the way their mission to teach and create knowledge has come to be seen by governments and business corporations as a key component of the knowledge economy. Despite the origins of the university in the ancient world (Naraghi, 1996), its endemic modern form emerged in Europe during the nineteenth century from the ideas of philosophers such as Immanuel Kant ([1798] 1979), John Henry Newman ([1852] 2008) and those of Wilhelm von Humboldt who established the University of Berlin in 1810 (Peters, 2010). Their founding principles, though influenced by their respective cultural outlooks, were based on the pursuit of knowledge and truth through an inclusion of philosophy into the curriculum, particularly that of the Ancient Greeks, the freedom of students to acquire a wide-ranging education and a belief in the idea of academic and institutional autonomy (Anderson, 2010). The Humboldtian model had a particularly strong influence throughout Europe with its emphasis not only on the teaching of students but also on the creation of knowledge. These founders of the modern university were particularly notable for their ideas on the organisation of the university into specialised disciplines in which the amateur gentleman scholar gives way to professional class of academics, at the top of which sit the professors, whose positions are achieved, rather than ascribed, by some form of peer assessment (Kant, [1798] 1979).

John Henry Newman: the idea of a university

In his discourses on *The Idea of a University Defined and Illustrated*, the Catholic philosopher and Cardinal John Henry Newman ([1852] 2008) explains at some length the purpose of a university. In particular, he defends and justifies the setting up of the new Catholic university in Dublin on the principles of liberal philosophy rather than theological ones. For Newman, this liberal education entails an open and reflective space where men (and only men), who are experts in their fields, engage in lively but mutually supportive discourse in their respective disciplines. In this atmosphere of intellectual openness and freedom, the student chooses from the variety of subjects in the arts and sciences and, guided by the masters who explain and interpret them, is able to acquire some understanding of the great wealth of human knowledge. When asked how one benefits from such an education and how they might profit from it, Newman responds with a simple answer that the purpose of this form of education is no more than the pursuit of knowledge for its own sake (Newman, 2008: 128):

> I am asked what is the end of University Education, and of the Liberal or Philosophical Knowledge which I conceive it to impart: I answer, that what I have already said has been sufficient to show that it has a very tangible, real, and sufficient end, though the end cannot be divided from that knowledge itself. Knowledge is capable of being its own end. Such is the constitution of the human mind, that any kind of knowledge, if it be really such, is its own reward.

For Newman then, the liberal university that he proposed was one that was devoted primarily to 'teaching universal knowledge' but not its 'advancement' or creation through research (Newman, [1852] 2008: ix). However, with the increasing influence of the Humboldtian ideal in which research and teaching are seen as mutually necessary in order for comprehensive learning to occur (Macheridis et al., 2020), the idea of modern university emerged. This joint mission of knowledge transmission and knowledge creation, driven by a liberal ethos, became its main identifying characteristic.

This was the ideal, but since their inception, universities have varied in terms of their purpose and organisation. McCowan (2015) suggests, however, that in their various forms they reveal some common characteristics. These can be reduced to two, though the way these are carried out and administered is historically and contextually dependent. The first is that of being places of teaching and learning, and, second, they are institutions where new knowledge is discovered and produced. Newman's position notwithstanding, McCowan (2015) suggests that in the process of teaching and imparting knowledge on the highest levels of human intellectual endeavour, there will inevitably be points at which new knowledge is created and, possibly also, new forms of practice. So, in terms of emphasising the purely intrinsic value and purpose of a university education, Newman's position does not in fact preclude the possibility that there may arise some outcomes of an extrinsic nature. This more nuanced interpretation of Newman's views is most clearly articulated by Collini (2012) in his book *What Are Universities for?* where he suggests that:

> A better way to characterise the intellectual life of universities may be to say that the drive towards understanding can never accept an arbitrary stopping-point, and critique may always in principle reveal that any currently accepted stopping-point is ultimately arbitrary.
>
> (Collini, 2012: 55)

Just as Dewey (1918) claims, the purpose of learning and the acquisition of knowledge is more learning which leads to 'growth' in the widest possible sense and there should be no arbitrary end or limit to learning for, by imposing a specific aim or purpose, we limit the process of growth. Moreover, as McCowan (2015) adds, by limiting learning to a specific point in time or to a specific instrumental purpose, we do not know how useful it might be in the future.

It would seem that there is no reason why higher education should not be implicated in developing new knowledge and practices that have extrinsic value beyond the pure thirst for its acquisition. However, as Collini (2012) suggests, this should be consistent with the normal academic endeavour of the university, rather than by some externally imposed criterion. Indeed, universities and institutes of higher learning have since ancient times been sites for the development of new knowledge and practice in fields such as medicine and science as much as of its transmission. During the Golden Age of Islam (762–1258), which started during the Abbasid caliphate in Baghdad (Naraghi, 1996), medicine was studied as an academic discipline, and hospitals, known as 'bimaristan' in Persian (Naraghi, 1996), were set up and attached to centres of learning, where the teaching and practice of medicine coincided. In the case of medicine, the common good can be seen from the original non-instrumental desire to know and understand the human body, including its pathological conditions, which informs external and instrumental practice.

Wittrock (1993) suggests that a unique feature of the modern university which marks it out as different from other institutions of post-school education is its role in advancing human knowledge through research. Moreover, it is accepted that research informs teaching and is an essential part of professional practice among university teachers (Macheridis et al., 2020). However, the modern university with its ethic of the pursuit and creation of knowledge guided by the principles of reason and academic autonomy is becoming increasingly difficult to sustain. The ability to pursue knowledge without externally imposed criteria is being undermined by a neoliberal regime of governmentality. States are now harnessing the intellectual potential of universities and yoking them to the principles of market capitalism as part of a double strategy of forcing them to justify their existence as publicly funded institutions, as well as ensuring they contribute to the new liberal *raison d'état* of promoting wealth creation and the nation's economic growth.

Universities and the reproduction of inequality

A further point about the modern university as an institution and the practice of learning and teaching is the way it has been associated with the reproduction of inequality and the maintenance of the position of elites within society (McCowan, 2015). This *positional* role that universities have had and continue to perpetuate (Savage et al., 2015) is not necessarily inherent in the idea of a university as expressed by its proponents so far, but it is the case that in countries such as England a university education was reserved for the political and cultural elites. Even in the age of mass higher education, we can see the existence of class difference and inequality within the system:

> Fundamentally, however, simply expanding the higher education system ... does not unsettle social hierarchies.... In fact differentiation of universities goes hand-in-hand with the institutionalisation of our elite class. The spread of meritocratic routes, allowing vast numbers of schoolchildren to gain access to higher education, does not, in itself, produce a more level playing field or spell an end to class division. Far from it. Within a highly competitive educational market-place, it is access to the elite institutions which conveys the glittering prizes.
> (Savage et al., 2015: 256–257)

The growing access to university, therefore, presents clear opportunities for the breaking down of barriers to the democratisation of higher education and its reconstruction as a site of liberation for poorer and marginalised groups. Instead, the encroachment of neoliberal principles has acted as a brake on the struggle for the right to an education around the world, particularly in developing countries. In poorer countries such as India, where education is seen as the only way out of poverty and of increasing an individual's life chances, there is a clear conflict between the constitutional right to an education and the exorbitant fees charged by private universities for medical degree courses (Nagasaila and Suresh, 1992).

The knowledge economy

The idea of a knowledge economy seems, on the face of it, a reasonable and seductively simple idea, particularly in the context of the growth of the knowledge society where human culture is increasingly mediated and experienced in nonphysical ways and where goods exchanged are increasingly of a symbolic form (Stehr, 1994). Similarly, in the fields of science and technology, highly skilled scientists are developing knowledge and understanding of biological and the physical worlds that can be used to create wealth in new forms that were previously unimaginable. The seemingly intuitive assumption that universities, as creators of high-quality knowledge and research by experts, can effectively be recruited as part of the process of knowledge production for the nation is understandable and has been presented by its proponents in an almost self-evident and unquestioning manner (Davidson-Harden, 2010). The development of this knowledge economy is specific to each country; however, we can identify particular landmarks as indicative of movements in such a direction. In Canada, Davidson-Harden (2010) claims that we can trace the origin of the debate back to the 1970s when governments at both the provincial and federal level identified the potential benefits of a closer link between 'centres of excellence' (i.e. universities) and the market (see Case study 6.1).

The spread of hegemonic Western knowledge through the knowledge economy

A further dimension of the generally uncritical assumptions associated with the knowledge economy, as well as its assumed self-evident benefits to the global and national economies, is the belief that there will be an increasing flow of knowledge around the world which has a benevolent and equalising effect. However, it is assumed that although in the developed world knowledge will be more equally distributed, there will be a much greater flow from the developed world to the developing world, that is, *from* the North *to* the South (Burton-Jones, 1999).

The notion of Northern/Western knowledge and practice as having a redemptive and progressive quality that will enable the South to grow and develop is inherent in the ethnocentric nature of the theory of a knowledge economy (Davidson-Harden, 2010). This, once again, demonstrates a blind spot of Northern postcolonial ideas and their academic origins in the colonial era. The intellectual foundations of Northern epistemology are based on the Enlightenment belief in human reason and the possibility of discovering universal truth. The knowing subject is able to understand the world in an objective manner through an act of reason, detached from place, time location and culture. Mbembe (2016) states that in the postcolonial era the emerging academic dependency of the South on Northern thinking has resulted in the creation of African universities in the Western image, with its mission to create and disseminate a 'uni-versal' knowledge, to the exclusion of alternative or Indigenous forms. These Western forms of knowledge have become so hegemonic that to

Case study 6.1: Canada's knowledge economy

What becomes quite evident from a review of Canada's situation is that the focus of universities on research and knowledge production has been dominated by the priorities of powerful and wealthy business interests to the detriment of other potential local, Indigenous, national or, indeed, global needs. Davidson-Harden (2010) shows how in Canada, during the period of the Liberal governments of Brian Mulroney (1984–1993) and Jean Cretienne (1993–2003), the National Advisory Board on Science and Technology (NABST) set up by the federal government urged universities to prioritise scientific and technological research to promote Canada's competitive position in the global market. The narrative of profit and wealth creation above that of any other priorities, including the risk of possible externalities, seems to be evident in decisions made at federal level. This policy was made easier to carry through by the elimination of more independent and democratic scientific bodies such as the Science Council of Canada (SCC). The SCC, though sympathetic to neoliberal idea of the knowledge economy, did retain some democratic functions in that it produced independent reports and committees were chaired by academics. Moreover, it reported to the Canadian Parliament where the nature and potential impact of such work was subjected to effective scrutiny. Under the Conservative government of Stephen Harper (2006–2015), the SCC was replaced by the Science Innovation and Technology Council (STIC) which lost all of these democratic functions and effectively became the 'vehicle for the hegemonic discourse' (Davidson-Harden, 2010: 579) of neoliberalism. Moreover, it is alleged that scientists working on government projects were prevented from speaking to the media or to attend conferences, which provoked scientists to hold a 'Death of Evidence March' in 2012 during which they protested against the restrictions on science communications and open scientific debate (Kinder, 2020). It is highly significant that the first chair of STIC was Dr Howard Alper, a research chemist, whose work in organic and inorganic chemistry has potential applications in the fields of 'pharmaceutical, petrochemical, and commodity chemical industries' (STIC, 2010, cited in Davidson-Harden, 2010: 579), which clearly indicates the kinds of scientific and technological fields that have been prioritised by recent Canadian governments.

Where the economic growth of one country is prioritised before that of any other, regardless of the effects of this policy such as the impact on other countries or, indeed the planet, then the consequences are likely to be potentially very serious for all of us, and universities around the world are implicated in such policies. Scientists and economists who adhere to neoclassical economic theory dominate university teaching, as well as research, and advise many political leaders on the need for continuous economic growth as the main measure of the nation's progress. In the US President Trump was so devoted to the extraction and use of fossil fuels to promote US economic growth that his administration targeted nearly eighty environmental protection regulations for abolition on the grounds that they are too burdensome on the fossil fuel industry (Popovich et al., 2018).

Since the election of the Liberal government of Justin Trudeau in Canada in 2015, there seems to have been some change of policy with scientists now able to speak more freely about their research, and there is a new Scientific Integrity Policy to protect the openness

> of government science introduced in 2018. Moreover, there has been a policy of promoting more open science generally and a priority on reconciliation in which the role of Indigenous traditional knowledge is receiving greater emphasis, particularly in the new impact assessment process in universities. Science policy in Canada has also seen 'an increasing focus on gender and issues of equity, diversity and inclusion' (Kinder, 2020). The long-term future and outcome of these policies are yet to be seen.

teach and do research using alternative ways of thinking and epistemologies is almost impossible (Ndvolu-Gatsheni, 2017) and becomes an act of 'epistemic disobedience' (Mignolo, 2009). By this Mignolo means challenging the colonial approach to understanding other cultures and rejecting the Western colonial epistemological position of ranking societies or cultures and defining who they are in relation to an ideal notion of what are modern or advanced forms of humanity. It also means 'de-linking' from Western epistemologies and advocating a complete transformational change of the knowledge structure, rather than merely accepting reform. It is therefore an act of defiance; a rejection of rules and procedures that the colonial masters have handed down to us from above. However, in all acts of disobedience there is the possibility of punishment or retribution.

Challenging Northern hegemonic knowledge

In Chapter 5, we saw how academic disciplines such as sociology were strongly associated with the colonial period and a response to contact with other 'strange' cultures that were in need of understanding and categorising according to evolutionary ideas of human development. Ethnographers from the colonial states cast an imperial gaze over the Indigenous people who had been 'discovered' and presented as if they had no conscious existence of their own prior to this discovery and needed to be told who they are and the position they occupy in the great classification system that is humanity or *humanitas* (Mignolo, 2009) (see Case study 6.2). In the words of Mignolo (2009: 1),

> From a detached and neutral point of observation (that Colombian philosopher Santiago Castro-Gómez describes as the hubris of the zero point), the knowing subject maps the world and its problems, classifies people and projects into what is good for them.

In the global knowledge economy then, universities in the global South have become satellites of the metropolitan North. They constitute a network of regional centres categorised as part of the field defined as 'area studies', rather than centres of serious knowledge production, because in this branch of the global knowledge economy there is a clear division of labour in which the South still provides the raw material for Northern intellectual elites who continue to dominate the process of creating universal knowledge.

The idea of a decolonised university: the re-centring of Africa

What is necessary, according to Mbembe (2016), is to move away from the outdated notion of the modern Western university and its concern with the Enlightenment notion of creating a single

Case study 6.2: Durkheim and the Arrernte

This indeed seems to have been the case regarding Durkheim's ([1912] 1976) classic study, *The Elementary Forms of Religious Life* (TEFRL). Australia is the example par excellence of a *terra nullius*, a place which the colonists considered a blank space in terms of law, politics, land ownership and also social scientific classification and definition. In the very concept we have the justification for disregarding the rights and prior title to the land of the Indigenous people. In Australia, Durkheim believed he had found the 'zero point' in the form of an original state of humanity and therefore the starting point for his theory of the evolution and classification of societies. As Connell (2007: 77–78) points out, 'Within the colonised world, Australia had the distinction of being **the most primitive of all, illustrating the extremity of its degradation or backwardness**' (emphasis in the original). However, Durkheim had not been to Australia. He made this assumption on the basis of a number of accounts of travellers as well as theorists of social evolution, most of whom had never been to Australia either. These accounts were usually suffused with highly racist judgements and often full of inaccurate claims (Connell, 2007). Nevertheless, following the evolutionary beliefs of the early social thinkers such as Comte and Spencer, Durkheim approached the study of the Indigenous people of the central desert region of Australia known as the Arrernte, with the assumption that they were in fact the most 'primitive' of peoples on the scale of human social evolution and as such they presented the opportunity to understand the most basic form from which all types of religions evolved. This was to be a crucial work upon which Durkheim's future reputation rested. Through this crude evolutionary approach, Durkheim claimed to have developed a universal theory of the origins of all human religions.

It is significant that in this famous ethnographic study, Durkheim did not engage in any dialogue with the Arrernte as part of his research, never having been to Australia, relying instead on the accounts by 'traders, police agents and priests' (Thomassen, 2016: 180), which were nonetheless assumed to be sufficiently sound data on which to build an entire theory. There was no attempt to check their accounts or their interpretations of what they claimed to have witnessed. This is hardly surprising, given that the thoughts of these supposedly 'primitive' people were deemed to be insignificant. They were considered mere cyphers in the whole process. Durkheim's thesis, as contained in this study, became the 'standard approach' to the sociology of religion and part of the core university curriculum in Western as well as Southern universities throughout the twentieth century (Connell, 2007; Thomassen, 2016). Those who challenged this orthodox narrative were not treated in the spirit of academic openness by the establishment. This was indeed the case when Arnold van Gennep (1913 in Connell, 2007; Thomassen, 2016) published a review of TEFRL in 1913. In a brief glimpse of the epistemological direction sociology could have progressed at that time, van Gennep (Thomassen, 2016) exposed the methodological deficiencies of the study, revealing Durkheim's weaknesses as an ethnographer and of his selective presentation of the data to fit his theory. van Gennep was particularly concerned that Durkheim did not conduct any direct observation through his own fieldwork and there was a complete lack of any element of human agency: 'Durkheim completely and categorically neglects the action of single, existing individuals in the formation of institutions and beliefs' (Thomassen, 2016: 182). No members of the Indigenous community were engaged in the study in terms of their personal views, feeling or definitions of themselves. Moreover, van Gennep was not reluctant to point out that Durkheim had completely underestimated the nature of Arrernte society and its level of sophistication, going so far as to suggest that the:

> more one knows of the Australians and the less one identifies the stage of their material civilization with that of their social organisation, one discovers that the *Australian societies are very complex, very far from the simple and the primitive, but very far advanced along their own paths of development*
> (van Gennep, 1913, cited in Lukes, 1985: 525). (Emphasis added)

Thomassen (2016) points out that van Gennep's critique of TEFRL was a significant moment in the history of sociology, yet we know very little about his work and its potential significance to the discipline because he was never formally accepted into French academia. It is suggested by Thomassen (2016) that Durkheim, then probably the most influential sociologist in France at the time, may have been responsible for blocking the academic appointments of 'one of France's most talented social scientist'. In fact, van Gennep 'never managed to land a teaching position, even at a provincial university' (Thomassen, 2016: 187). The reason is likely to be linked to what might be referred to as van Gennep's act of epistemological disobedience in the form of his critique of TEFRL and rejection of Durkheim's assumptions and generalisations about Indigenous peoples. As Durkheim himself states:

> He asks me that I support him. I fail to apprehend on which basis he may nurture such hopes, for he has no degrees, if I am not wrong. Nonetheless, after what he has written about me, I cannot help to say what I think about his candidature, which struck me as being over the top.
> (Durkheim cited in Thomassen, 2016: 186)

From this episode in the emergence of classical Northern sociology, it would appear that van Gennep, a highly skilled and gifted scholar, was critical of the way sociology was progressing. He objected to the way a crude evolutionary theory, based on unsubstantiated data and unfounded assumptions about so-called primitive societies, was being used to build a general theory of the foundations of society. In this respect, he believed that the leading figure of sociology in France at the time was pressing 'ethnography into service of a prefabricated theoretical scheme' (Thomassen, 2016: 181). In some unpublished notes relating to his academic encounters with Durkheim van Gennep writes:

> There arose then [after 1890] a fairly violent antagonism among the previously organized sciences of man by the renewal of Comtian sociology effected by Durkheim ... and in approximately twenty years made themselves masters. Whoever was not part of the group was 'marked'.
> (From Arnold van Gennep's unpublished notes, cited in Thomassen, 2016: 173)

> It is possible to claim that van Gennep was punished for his 'disobedience', and this was very severe in that it ended a very promising career in academic sociology. Some might argue that this was merely the outcome of a bitter but genuine academic debate; however, an academic debate, no matter how intense, should not have led to the end of an academic career that was so promising. This untimely removal of van Gennep from the development of French sociology merely served to pave the way for the kind of sociology that dominated modern university departments in the Southern as well as the Northern hemisphere for much of the past century.

universal truth and towards a 'pluriversity'. This is where there is an acceptance of a diversity of ways of seeing the world, and this should be reflected in the curriculum as well as in terms of research methodology. Mbembe is inspired by the ideas of the Kenyan educator Ngugi wa Thiong'o (1972) (see Chapter 5), who proposes a *re-centring* of Africa in the African university. By this he means that African universities need to reject Northern knowledge that tells Africans who they are and what they need to do to enter the 'modern world' of progress and development and replace it with a knowledge that enables Africans to define themselves and their place in the world.

This requires a liberation of the African mind from the undermining effects of Northern epistemologies to a position where Africans are able to see themselves as themselves (Ngugi, 1981). Such Northern knowledge shifts the blame for Africa's economic dependency away from the Northern metropole and its neocolonial domination of the South, to Africa itself. This can be seen in a speech given by the French president Nicolas Sarkozy to the assembled students and academics at the University of Dakar, Senegal in July 2007. Referring to the 'tragedy of Africa' (Purtschert, 2010: 1039), Sarkozy asserted that Africa has made little progress in cultural and economic terms because it has not yet moved from a state of 'natural consciousness' to one in which a reflective consciousness dominates thinking; that is, Africa had not 'entered into history' (Purtschert, 2010: 1039) where a record of achievement and contribution to humanity can be acknowledged. This is not an observation or an idea that Sarkozy had conjured up on his own. He was, in fact, more or less paraphrasing the ideas of the German philosopher Georg Wilhelm Friedrich Hegel in his *Philosophy of History* and *Philosophy of Spirit* (Mbembe, 2007). In *Philosophy of History*, Hegel describes how humanity moves from *nature* to *spirit* through various stages of historical development. However, rather than capturing the spirit of history, which involves reason and progress, Hegel claims that Africa is stuck at the lowest level of human progress; that is, at the start of history and the intersection between spirit and nature. Gilman (1980) adds that, having located Black people at the lowest level of humanity, Hegel believes, this limits their progression through history. Indeed, Purtschert (2010) suggests that in Hegel's theory of history, which traces the progress and development of civilisations and cultures located in time, direction and geographical space, from Asia to Europe and Africa, only the latter continent is seen to exist in space but not history. He sees Africa as trapped at the beginning of time, within a natural consciousness in which time is merely the repetition of seasons.

These ideas have certainly influenced the work of social theorists and ethnographers of the colonial period, but what is of concern is that such views are still given currency today. Hegel's racism is palpable in his treatment of Africa; however, McCarney (2003, cited in Purtschert, 2010) claims that to dismiss Hegel's work on these grounds would deny the contribution Hegel has made to philosophy and our understanding of historical development and gives licence to seek racism in Western philosophical thought throughout history. Perhaps, McCarney has actually missed the point: the fact that Hegel as well as other Northern thinkers have developed ideas and theories in which racist beliefs form an integral part needs to be acknowledged and critically assessed in this light. Racism is a theme that runs through many of the ideas of modernity. However, this does not mean that the ideas of Hegel, Kant or Hume should not be studied. As suggested in the previous chapter (Pett, 2015, SOAS Students' Union), they should still be taught, but from a more critical standpoint. As Chukwudi Eze (1997: 103) points out, 'In his important book, *This Is Race*, Earl W. Count observes that scholars often forget "Immanuel Kant produced the most profound raciological thought of the eighteenth century"', and goes on to advise in relation to the study of Kant: 'The so-called primitives surely ought to be wary of such Kantian "universalist-humanoid abstraction, which colonizes humanity by grounding the particularity of the European self as center even as it denies the humanity of others"' (Chukwudi Eze, 1997: 130–131).

The decolonised neoliberal university: an incompatible mix?

In the project of re-centring Africa in African universities and identifying them as not merely satellites of Northern knowledge systems, Ngugi (1981) emphasises the relevance of language in this process and how it influences thinking. The teaching of Indigenous African languages is therefore seen as essential particularly in terms of Africans thinking, as Africans. In addition, Ngugi proposes a corresponding expansion of outlook and perspective. He also seeks 'to pursue the African connection to the four corners of the Earth' (Ngugi, cited in Mbembe, 2016: 36). This is a significant aim in that extending the connections of Africa across the globe is not necessarily one of just wanting to learn more from the North but to show how the world has learned and gained from Africa and the African diaspora – both voluntarily and involuntarily –throughout the world over the centuries. The achievements of African Americans, African Caribbeans, Africans in Europe and Africans in Latin America in the fields of science, culture, music, politics, art and literature are all part of Africa's contribution to the world and demonstrate that Africa is not a mere footnote in the record of humanity's achievements. Moreover, it defies Hegel's idea of Africa as a place outside history.

If the decolonised African university requires a different focus and a shift from the universalising epistemologies of the North to a re-centring of Africa, then this also needs to be accompanied and supported by appropriate funding, administrative and organisational systems. However, a key obstacle to such reform in Africa, as well as other universities worldwide, is the way governments are prioritising economic growth above all else. This has been particularly evident in states where universities are being seen increasingly in instrumental, rather than pedagogical and emancipatory terms. Neoliberal principles are now dictating and shaping their priorities, and, it would seem, that the priorities of the neoliberal state are in fact incompatible with the notion of a decolonised and humanising university. In countries such as South Africa and Britain where there have been calls to decolonise the university and promote diversity in the curriculum and the composition of staff, the response by university administrators is a seeming willingness to respond to the demands of the 'consumer'; however, this usually takes the form of consultations, committees, staff and student surveys and the setting up of new departments and initiatives which often take up valuable scarce resources and usually end up causing confusion, if not resentment, about the whole process. Adebisi (2020) suggests that the neoliberal university's very logic is to function in such a way as to conceal its true nature, which is to maintain the existing systems of knowledge and inequality. In claiming to be responding to demands for social justice, increased recruitment of underrepresented groups and their appointment to senior and professorial roles, the neoliberal university's responses merely frustrate and hinder decolonisation, thereby acting to reinforce and maintain the existing order. This is because these policies are meaningless without the accompanying changes to the continuing domination of colonial-based knowledge systems which would enable universities to prioritise an *understanding* of why we do not have fair representations of minority ethnic groups in the academy or why there are so few authors from the geographic South on reading lists. Without this essential element, such reforms are likely to be misinterpreted and become a cause for resentment by those who may see them as tokenistic and merely the arbitrary fulfilment of quotas.

The implementation of performative and evaluative systems for assessing 'excellence' and 'value', therefore, actually contributes to the perpetuation of existing policies which also marginalise satellite institutions in the global South (Keim, 2011) and serve to provide a mechanism whereby the universities in the metropole can promote themselves as the preeminent global institutions of higher education. It is no coincidence that these systems of assessment, as well as the tables of world university ranking, were also devised and imposed by these very same institutions and are now being followed and even developed by countries in Asia (Mbembe, 2016; University World News, 2017). This can be seen clearly in the criteria used to measure excellence, and the weighting each criterion is given, in the process of ranking universities. For example, the *Times Higher Education* rankings introduced in 2004 was devised to more effectively position Britain in the international market in higher education, and this it certainly achieved (University World News, 2017). A key metric used by The Times Higher Education (THE) ranking system relates to performance in research: 'In many universities, meeting one or more comparative performance indicators – the [United Kingdom's] Research Excellence Framework, National Student Survey, Teaching Excellence Framework, or national or global rankings, or some combination – is the driving strategic objective' (Marginson, cited in University World News, 2017). The importance of the Research Excellence Framework (REF) in the UK cannot be overemphasised given that universities' revenues are highly dependent on their position in the REF rankings. The information provided by the University of Edinburgh (The University of Edinburgh, 2018) demonstrates this well, when it states that the REF is:

> used to provide information about the quality of a university's research for internal and external benchmarking and the allocation of research funding. Currently, the University of Edinburgh receives funding based on REF results from the Scottish Funding Council worth over £75 million each year. All publicly-funded universities take part.

The process is highly bureaucratic and time consuming for universities, but it has the potential for a huge payback to those institutions that deploy their staff in fields of research that are considered of 'value' to the state and the economy. Moreover, the system is presented as objective, transparent and fair, with panels of experts in four fields: medicine and the life sciences; physical science, engineering and mathematics; social science; and arts and humanities. These areas are divided into thirty-four subject-based units of assessment in which experts in specific subject areas judge the quality of outputs in the form of journal publications, chapters in books, performances and exhibitions, as well as 'their **impact** beyond academia, and the **environment** that supports research' (REF 21, 2020) (emphasis in original). However, as Hasan (2020) states, the kind of experts appointed in each subject area is highly significant, in that this is based on their position as recognised mainstream academics in their field. Hasan (2020) illustrates this with the example of the panels of experts who assess excellence in economics research. These are generally composed of orthodox neoclassical economists who judge work against this prevailing economic ideology. Moreover, as we saw in Chapter 4, the most high-ranking journals in which most academic economists aspire to have their work published are those that focus primarily on the explication and creation of new knowledge in neoclassical economics. As a result, academic freedom and integrity are compromised given that, first, any academic who wishes to progress to the highest levels of the academy in the field of economics is more or less obliged to develop an expertise in neoclassical economics, and, second, if a university wishes to maximise its potential funding from the government or wealthy philanthropic foundations (see Chapter 4) it is, once again, more or less obliged to employ academics with a narrow range of interests and expertise.

The implications of this for intellectual openness and freedom are clear. What it effectively does is give university administrators the power to direct the nature and funding of university research, and it also artificially hampers the development of alternative, challenging and original ways of thinking and understanding the world (Traianou, 2015). The consequences of government economic priorities and the growing imposition of wealth creation as the prime *raison d'état* constitute a direct threat to those who see the role of the university as a site for the promotion of intellectual openness and truth, no matter how unpalatable it may seem to those who defend the prevailing orthodoxy.

What might the university be?

Everywhere we look in the world we see institutions, including those of the state and democracy, that are becoming dominated by the values of the market and the priority of economic growth to the exclusion of all others. At the same time, the opportunity to question and challenge the consequences of this process are being increasingly denuded. Although it too is succumbing to the logic of neoliberalism, higher education still provides a place where young people and their teachers are able to ask some of the most important questions of humanity, including some of the most uncomfortable ones, and to offer insights into the kind of world we are heading towards, as well as to consider alternative ways of being. Without such spaces, the possibility to contemplate these questions and to offer alternatives would be lost. What can be seen from the preceding discussions is that history has not come to an end since the collapse of communism and the dominance of neoliberal capitalism; it has merely been rendered more nebulous and problematic, for what we are witnessing is the exacerbation of the problems that originated under capitalism. These include the potential destruction of the planet as we know it, growing and damaging levels of global inequality, and the flourishing of political leaders who are increasingly abusing the rights of their citizens and exploiting their positions for their own political ends. Moreover, neoliberalism has created an ideology of inevitability in which any attempts to seek alternatives have been foreclosed and branded as romantic and utopian dreaming.

What higher education can do is help restore our sense of possibility and the existence of alternatives to the current situation. It can educate hope (Levitas, 2013), but not in a way that is just fantasy. Universities are places where academics, researchers and students, together with ordinary citizens should collaborate to examine the evidence, create new insights into what is possible and test systems that may contribute to the creation a better world. If we leave these tasks to the existing class of politicians, corporate managers and billionaires, we are unlikely to move forward because their ethos is one of possessive individualism and the accumulation of wealth for its own sake. If educated hope is about growth and seeking a better future, then neoliberal capitalism means more of the same problems. Using one of Erich Fromm's ideas to describe the relationship (Freire, 1996 1: 41, citing Fromm), neoliberalism could be seen as 'necrophilic' because it does not lead to the growth and welfare of humanity and the planet, but instead it is one that thrives mainly on their suffering and destruction.

Conclusion

It should be considered as accepted practice that those who can see the moral and ethical problems, as well as the empirical evidence for the harmful or dehumanising consequences of a particular policy taken by our politicians and business leaders, are able to speak openly and without fear. However, as we have seen, academics and scientist have often been silent despite being aware of such injustices. In Canada, under the Conservative government of Stephen Harper (2006–2015) (Kinder, 2020), research scientists were banned from communicating with the press and the public about their work. In the US we now know of the policy of oil companies such as EXXON to silence the scientists who had evidence of the adverse effects of the growing use of fossil fuels on the climate (Goldenberg, 2015). And it is now evident that universities too are becoming less tolerant of academics speaking out against the negative effects of neoliberal policies on students' lives as well as their own as teachers and scholars (Traianou, 2015; Warner, 2015).

Those who do speak out or ask awkward questions clearly need more than just the requisite evidence and information to do this; they also need the moral strength and conviction to challenge those with the power and ability to silence them, or worse. We saw how Professor Philip Alston's (UNHRC, 2017, 2019) reports on extreme poverty in Britain and the US were greeted with derision and outrage by the two governments, particularly the claims in the reports that the former government was in breach of its human rights obligations, and the latter would be if it formally recognised such obligations.

Apart from the most extreme dictatorships in the world and a growing number of populist governments, it seems that it is in the regimes of neoliberalism that we find the policy of silence forced upon employees most stringently. Traianou (2015) notes that there has been a reduction in the amount of freedom academics in Britain have to speak critically about their own or other powerful organisations such as the government. She points to the increasing intolerance on the part of university authorities of criticisms by their employees, which are viewed as undermining the reputations of their institutions and affecting their ability to attract students and research funding, rather than as revealing potential problems or injustices. There seems to be a greater tendency by universities to use gagging, or nondisclosure, orders to prevent staff from openly criticising their employers. Given that these agreements, by their very nature, are usually undisclosed, it is difficult to know how extensively they are used and the issues being concealed; however, Marina Warner (2015) claims that there were over five-and-a-half thousand recorded cases of nondisclosure orders between 2007 and 2010 in the UK.

What makes this situation so concerning is that universities are supposed to be places for the free exploration, expression and production of ideas – no matter how controversial or unpopular they may be to those in authority. The imposition of performance criteria that direct and affect academic output, the shift from the pursuit and production of knowledge as a public good to the monetisation of all knowledge, and the reinvention of students as 'consumers' and 'customers' mean that universities have now become no different from any other business corporation, and this is very dangerous for any society that claims to be democratic (Giroux, 2011). Lord Robbins in his address to the British Academy in 1966 clearly saw the potential threat to academic freedom in the form of government managerialism and control (Williams, 2016), when he states that academic freedom is a form of freedom that goes much further than the right to free thought and speech of the ordinary citizen (Robbins, cited in Hasan, 2020):

> it is a demand that ... he shall have certain freedoms not necessarily involved in ordinary contractual relations and that the institutions in which he works shall likewise enjoy certain rights of independent initiative not necessarily granted to other institutions which are part of a state system.

This freedom in Robbins' view should enable students and academics to 'speculate and investigate as the spirit moves one, and to publish without restraint' (Robbins, 2020, cited in Hasan), in the same way that poets, novelists or artists should be able to create and write without restraint and restriction on any subject, though, of course, with due levels of consideration to the sensitivity and 'humility' regarding the subject matter (Kunzru et al., 2016).

Paulo Freire (1998) correctly points to the unfinishedness of ourselves as individuals and our understanding of the world. This applies also to the unfinishedness of a society. It is in the open and curious environment of the university, where dialogue between teacher and learner can occur, that we come to understand this unfinishedness and its ongoing nature. Under neoliberalism, there is instead an ideology of completeness in which teachers are increasingly trained and viewed as merely technicians with no need to understand the world of their students, and where students are expected to become mere vessels in which to deposit accepted and predefined knowledge. In Britain, this is most clearly illustrated by the nation's view of itself in history. It is through an acknowledgement of this unfinishedness as a society that growth will be possible.

Points for reflection and consideration in this chapter

The idea of a university is one that conjures up notions of 'civilization' and the freedom to learn about the world with all its mysteries, as well as a place to challenge conventional wisdom through open-minded disputation, dialogue and empirical research. Moreover, it should be a place where anyone from any background, colour or gender should have equal access, not merely the wealthy and powerful.

- How far would you agree with the above idea of a university?
- Would you change or add to it?
- Should universities be organised and controlled in such a way that their main task and purpose is to serve the state and the economy?

References

Adebisi, F. (2020) 'Decolonisation Is Not About Ticking a Box: It Must Disrupt'. *Critical Legal Thinking*, 12 March. Available at: https://criticallegalthinking.com/2020/03/12/decolonisation-is-not-about-ticking-a-box/ (Accessed on 15 March 2020).

Anderson, R.D. (2010) *European Universities from the enlightenment to 1914*. Oxford: Oxford University Press.

Burton-Jones, A. (1999) *Knowledge Capitalism: business, work, and learning in the new economy*. Oxford: Oxford University Press.

Chukwudi Eze, E. (1997) 'The color of reason: The idea of "race" in Kant's Anthropology', in E. Chukwudi Eze (ed.), *Postcolonial African Philosophy: A Reader*. Oxford: Blackwell, pp. 103–131.

Collini, S. (2012) *What Are Universities for?* London: Penguin.

Connell, R. (2007) *Southern Theory*. Cambridge: Polity Press.

Davidson-Harden, A. (2010) 'Interrogating the university as an engine of capitalism: Neoliberalism and academic 'raison d'état'. *Policy Futures in Education*. Vol. 8, No. 5, pp. 575–587.

Dewey, J. (2018) *Education and Democracy*. [1918] (2011) Simon and Brown.

Durkheim, E. [1912] (1976) *The Elementary Forms of Religious Life*. London: Allen & Unwin.

Foucault, M. and Senellart, M. (2008) *The Birth of Biopolitics: Lectures at the Collège de France, 1978–1979*. Basingstoke: Palgrave Macmillan.

Freire, P. (1996) *Pedagogy of Freedom: Ethics, Democracy and Civic Courage*. London: Rowman and Littlefield.

Gilman, S.L. (1980) 'The figure of the Black in the thought of Hegel and Nietzsche'. *The German Quarterly*. Vol. 54, No. 2, pp. 141–158.

Giroux, H. (2011) *On Critical Pedagogy*. London: Bloomsbury.

Goldenberg, S. (2015) 'Exxon knew of climate change in 1981, email says – but it funded deniers for 27 more years'. *The Guardian*. 8 July. Available at: https://www.theguardian.com/environment/2015/jul/08/exxon-climate-change-1981-climate-denier-funding (Accessed 18 May 2020).

Hasan, R. (2020) 'The Suffocation of Academic Freedom by the Research Excellence Framework'. *Quillette*. 1 February. Available at: https://quillette.com/2020/02/01/the-suffocation-of-academic-freedom-by-the-research-excellence-framework/ (Accessed 20 May 2020).

Institute for Fiscal Studies. (2017) *Higher Education funding in England: Past, Present and Options for the Future*. Available at: file:///E:/Routledge%20Proposal%20%2025th%20April%202/Chapter%206/IFS%20 2017%20Student%20debt.pdf (Accessed 7 May 2020).

Kant, I. [1798] (1979) *The Conflict of the Faculties*, trans. M. Gregor. New York: Abaris Books.

Keim, W. (2011) 'Counter hegemonic currents and internationalization of sociology. Theoretical reflections and one empirical example'. *International Sociology*. Vol. 26, No. 1, pp. 123–145.

Kinder, J. (2020) 'Science Policy in the 2010s: A Decade in Review'. *Institute on Governance News*. 16 January. Available at: https://iog.ca/about/news/science-policy-in-the-2010s/ (Accessed 12 May 2020).

Kunzru, H., Shamsi, K., Forna, A., Kennedy, A.L., Hensher, P., Duffy, S., Grant, L., Alderman, G., Gee, M., Shukla, N. and Cleave, C. (2016) 'Whose life is it anyway? Novelists have their say over cultural appropriation'. *The Guardian*. 1 October. Available at: https://www.theguardian.com/books/2016/oct/01/novelists-cultural-appropriation-literature-lionel-shriver (Accessed 20 May 2020).

Larner, W. and Le Heron, R. (2005) 'Neo-liberalizing spaces and subjectivities: Reinventing New Zealand universities'. *Organisation*. Vol. 12, No. 6, pp. 843–862.

Levitas, R. (2013) *Utopia as Method: The Imaginary Constitution of Society*. Basingstoke: Palgrave Macmillan.

Lukes, S (1985) *Emile Durkheim: His Life and Work – A Historical and Critical Study*. Stanford, CA: Stanford University Press.

Macheridis, N., Paulsson, A. and Pihl, H. (2020) 'The Humboldtian ideal meets employability? University teachers and the teaching–research relationship in marketized higher education'. *Industry and Higher Education*. Vol. 20, No. 10, pp. 1–9.

Maisuria, A. (2014) 'The neo-liberalisation policy agenda and its consequences for England: A focus on resistance now and possibilities for the future'. *Policy Futures in Education*. Vol. 12, No. 2, pp. 286–296.

Maisuria, A. and Cole, M. (2017) 'The neoliberalization of higher education in England: An alternative is possible'. *Policy Futures in Education*. Vol. 15, No. 5, pp. 602–619.

Mbembe, A. (2007) 'Nicolas Sarkozy's Africa'. Available at: https://www.africultures.com/index.asp?menu¼ affiche_article&no¼6816 (Accessed 13 May 2020).

Mbembe, A.J. (2016) 'Decolonizing the university: New directions'. *Arts and Humanities in Higher Education*. Vol. 15, No. 1, pp. 29–45.

McCowan, T. (2015) 'Should universities promote employability'. *Theory and Research in Education*. Vol. 13, No. 3, pp. 267–285.

Mignolo, W.D. (2009) 'Epistemic disobedience, independent thought and de-colonial freedom'. *Theory, Culture and Society*. Vol. 26, Nos. 7–8, pp. 1–23.

Nagasaila, D. and Suresh, V. (1992) 'Can the right to education be a fundamental right?' *Economic and Political Weekly*. Vol. 27, No. 45, pp. 2442–2446.

Naraghi, E. (1996) 'The Islamic antecedence of the Western Renaissance'. *Diogenese*. Vol. 44/1, No. 173, pp. 73–106.

Ndlovu-Gatsheni, S. (2017) 'Decolonising research methodology must include undoing its dirty history'. *The Conversation*. Available at: https://theconversation.com/decolonising-research-methodology-must-include-undoing-its-dirty-history-83912 (Accessed 12 May 2020).

Newman, J. H. [1852] (2008) *The Idea of a University Defined and Illustrated in Nine Discourses Delivered to the Catholics of Dublin*. Project Guttenberg. Available at: http://www.gutenberg.org/files/24526/24526-pdf.pdf (Accessed 5 May 2020).

Ngugi, wa Thiong'o (1972) *Homecoming (Studies in African Literature)*. London: Heinemann Educational Books.

Peters, M.A. (2010) *Policy Futures in Education*. Vol. 8, No. 2, pp. 151–165.

Pett, S. (2015) 'It's time to take the curriculum back from dead white men'. *The Conversation*. Available online at: https://theconversation.com/its-time-to-take-thecurriculum-back-from-dead-white-men-40268 (Accessed 25 March 2019).

Popovich, N., Albeck-Ripka, L. and Pierre-Louis, K. (2018) '78 environmental rules on the way out under Trump.' *The New York Times*. 28 December. Available at: https://www.nytimes.com/interactive/2017/10/05/climate/trump-environment-rules-reversed.html (Accessed 15 May 2020).

Purtschert, P. (2010) 'On the limit of spirit: Hegel's racism revisited'. *Philosophy and Social Criticism*, Vol. 36, No. 9, pp. 1039–1051.

Readings, B. (1995) 'From emancipation to obligation: Sketch for a heteronomous politics of education', in M.A. Peters (ed.), *Education and the Postmodern Condition*. Westport: Bergin & Garvey, pp. 193–208.

Readings, B. (1996) *The University in Ruins*. Cambridge, MA: Harvard University Press.

Robbins, L. (1966) 'Of academic freedom. Thank-offering to Britain fund lectures'. *Proceedings of British Academy*. Vol. 52, pp. 45–60.

Savage, M., Cunningham, N., Devine, F., Friedman, S., Laurison, D., McKenzie, L., Miles, A., Snee, S. and Wakeling, P. (2015) *Social Class in the 21st Century*. London: Penguin.

Stanford, J. (2008) *Economics for Everyone: A Short Guide to the Economics of Capitalism*, 2nd edn. London and Ottawa: Pluto Press.

Stehr, N. (1994) *Knowledge societies*. London: Sage.

The University of Edinburgh. (2018) 'What is the REF'. *University of Edinburgh, Institute for Academic Development*. Available at: https://www.ed.ac.uk/institute-academic-development/research-roles/research-only-staff/research-outputs/what-is-the-ref (Accessed 15 May 2020).

Thomassen, B. (2016) 'The hidden battle that shaped the history of sociology: Arnold van Gennep contra Emile Durkheim'. *Journal of Classical Sociology*. Vol. 16, No. 2, pp. 173–195.

Traianou, A. (2015) 'The erosion of academic freedom in UK higher education'. *Ethics in Science and Environmental Politics*. Vol. 15, p. 3. Available at: https://www.academia.edu/13166497/_2015_The_erosion_of_academic_freedom_in_UK_higher_education (Accessed 18 May 2020).

UNHRC. (2017) *Statement on visit to the USA, by Professor Philip Alston, United Nations Special Rapporteur on extreme poverty and human rights*. Available at: https://www.ohchr.org/EN/NewsEvents/Pages/DisplayNews.aspx?NewsID=22533 (Accessed 3 March 2020).

UNHRC. (2019) *Visit to the United Kingdom of Great Britain and Northern Ireland: Report of the Special Rapporteur on Extreme Poverty and Human Rights*. Available at: https://undocs.org/pdf?symbol=en/A/HRC/41/39/Add.1 (Accessed 18 July 2019).

University World News. (2017) 'Overall outcomes of university rankings are "junk"'. 13 October. Available at: https://www.universityworldnews.com/post.php?story=20171012083403751 (Accessed 17 May 2020).

Warner, M. (2015) *Learning My Lesson: A London Review of Books Winter Lecture*. Berlin: epubli GmbH.

Wilkinson, R. and Pickett, K. (2009) *The Spirit Level: Why More Equal Societies Almost Always Do Better*. London: Penguin.

Wilkinson, R. and Pickett, K. (2018) *The Inner Level: How More Equal Societies Reduce Stress, Restore Sanity and Improve Everyone's Well-being*. London: Allen Lane.

Williams, J. (2016) 'Why Academic Freedom Matters', in C. Hudson, and J. Williams. *Why Academic Freedom Matters*. London: Civitas, pp. 1–18.

Wittrock, B. (1993) 'The Modern University: The three transformations', in S. Rothblatt and B. Wittrock (Eds) *The European and American university since 1800: Historical and sociological essays*. Cambridge: Cambridge University Press, pp. 303–362.

7 Schools and the pursuit of social justice

Introduction

In the debates about the issues covered in this book so far, such as the crisis in welfare, the rising levels of global inequality, the impact of the knowledge economy on higher education, the responses by nations to the COVID-19 pandemic and the global climate crisis, all have a common thread running through them; the malign effect of neoliberal capitalism on the lives of ordinary people around the world, be they citizens of some of the most affluent nations or the poorest ones. Despite the promises made by the proponents of neoliberal capitalism that it will ultimately deliver more efficient services, that, if left to its own devices, the market will develop the technology and systems to create a cleaner planet, that by allowing the wealthy to accumulate limitless wealth there will be a trickle-down to the very poorest thereby improving their lives, that the deregulation and opening up of public services to non-state providers and the creation of internal markets in welfare and health will lead to more efficient and better welfare and health provision, that austerity was an essential response to the financial crisis of 2008, what we find in all of these is the emergence of false hopes of better times ahead amongst the poor and vulnerable. This is because under neoliberalism there emanates what Duncan-Andrade (2009) refers to as the 'enemies of hope' which together create an illusory view of the world that distorts reality and removes any belief in our ability to control our destiny. 'Hokey hope' relates to a constant hope against hope that things can only get better, despite the fact that there are no actual grounds to believe this. Hokey is a word derived from the American term 'hokum', which relates to the unreal, bunkum, sentimental or the deceptive practices of the huckster.

The sowing of false hope

Politicians and business leaders in the global neoliberal system constantly make declarations of concern and commitment to the welfare of all and pledge to make life better for the poor and the ordinary citizen. Billionaires such as Bill and Melinda Gates (Bill and Melinda Gates Foundation) and Mark Zuckerberg (Chan Zuckerberg Initiative), as we saw in Chapter 3, often claim to be committed to social justice and the elimination of a variety of social, educational, welfare or health problem or other 'injustice'. Through ostentatious and extravagant philanthropic declarations such as The Giving Pledge (2020), they are able to present themselves as concerned citizens who wish to 'give back' to society in a way that acknowledges their good fortune. However, as Hay and

Muller (2014) argue, what this merely amounts to is a feat of legerdemain in which supposed acts of selfless giving are magically turned into a self-serving system of 'philanthrocapitalism'. This constitutes a form of 'false caring' in which the super-rich present themselves as responsible individuals but who ultimately tend to act in their own financial interests.

Another dimension of such enemies of hope identified by Duncan-Andrade (2009) is 'mythical hope', which creates and perpetuates the myth that there is equality of opportunity and that anyone can succeed; all that is necessary is to work hard and overcome the obstacles that present themselves. These claims are supported by the identification of cases of heroic individuals who have succeeded, despite coming from disadvantaged backgrounds, but this merely belies the fact that such people are outliers who actually don't belong, rather than being the norm (Savage et al., 2015). Such exceptions do nothing other than to confirm the ongoing injustice of the system. The idea of meritocracy is a kind of vague policy equivalent of mythical hope, in that children from poor or modest origins are constantly being betrayed by the myth of being able to achieve success in educational and occupational terms, if only they work hard. In the field of welfare, we can see how the UK government has been promoting the notion of self-reliance and individual responsibility through paid employment, by implementing the cuts to welfare benefits and the new system of Universal Credit as the way out of poverty. However, the evidence in the UK reveals that over the past twenty-five years, the in-work poverty rate has actually gone up from 13 to 18 per cent (Bourquin et al., 2019).

The third dimension of the enemies of hope Duncan-Andrade (2009) refers to is 'hope deferred', in which the state effectively carries out a strange act of implicating itself in the lack of progress in reducing social inequalities by blaming 'the system', including such factors as 'the economy' or 'the lack of social services' (Duncan-Andrade, 2009: 184). This is a somewhat audacious form of hope deferral in that the 'the system' was actually created and/or is perpetuated by the state itself and its economic partners. It is, of course, the existing system that most of us have no power over which needs to be changed. However, any prospect of the alleviation of hardship is always indefinitely postponed and 'hope deferred' on spurious grounds, such as the poor state of national finances, a crash in the markets or simply through acts of 'God'.

The myth of care

These forms of hope frustration can be seen as a way of understanding a variety of issues concerning which politicians claim to care about their citizens and yet preside over regimes that cause and perpetuate growing inequality. This is particularly evident in countries such as the UK where privilege is so entrenched and inequalities in wealth and income becoming so extreme, that politicians who promote neoliberalism are obliged to constantly resort to blaming mythical forces and creating spurious initiatives in order to give the impression that they are doing something positive to address these issues. This can be clearly illustrated when Michael Gove asserts that state schools in England need to raise their standards and reduce the achievement gap between themselves and the independent sector, and between children from more affluent and those from poorer backgrounds, claiming that this was the reason for his education reforms during the Conservative-led coalition government of 2010–2015 (Gove, 2013). In presenting the government's reforms as 'progressive' and designed to reduce the attainment gap as well as to meet the needs of the economy, and to create a proud and patriotic nation at ease with itself in the world, Gove invokes the bogeyman of 'the Blob' as the enemy of progress and reason. The Blob is 'an amorphous, bloated education establishment opposing him at every turn; a mass of bureaucrats, unions and academics who eschew rigour for a left-wing, child-centred, progressive agenda' (Bell, 2013): these people might alternatively be seen as educationalists who show a degree of concern about the consequences of such reforms on the education system as well as their potential illegality (see Chapter 5). In presenting the Blob as a vague group of left-leaning and anti-patriotic academics, journalists and trades unions, Gove manages to create a scare object against which to focus blame for the continuing failure of governments to reduce the attainment gap, whilst at the same time supporting a divisive education system that continues to promote privilege, exclusivity and a highly nationalistic ideology.

The narrative, then, is one in which political leaders avow their dedication to the needs of *all* citizens and point to malign forces and divisive and unpatriotic sections of the population who are preventing him from fulfilling his mission to bring about a 'better' society.

Conspiracies by the left

Even more insidious is the claim by US President Trump to have found evidence of a 'deep state' in the US that is made up of forces within important national state institutions such as the Central Intelligence Agency (CIA) and the Federal Bureau of Investigation (FBI) to undermine the power of the president as well as the freedoms and liberties of Americans. David Rhode (Rhode, 2020), who has investigated this conspiracy theory which feeds into Trump's claims that these institutions and certain branches of the media, are creators of 'fake news', believes that there is no evidence to support such allegations. Rhode suggests that they actually serve to enhance presidential powers by casting suspicion on and undermine the role of institutions set up to provide effective oversight over the actions and powers of the president or that serve the public, such as local government services and public education. So, despite the lack of any evidence, the idea has been planted in the minds of many Americans, that there is an ever-growing state that seeks to implement greater bureaucratic control over them, such as the setting up of a 'socialist' national health service which would be taxpayer-funded. These suspicions are such that even local firefighters, public school teachers and local government officials are implicated in this alleged conspiracy of the deep state (NPR, 2020).

Trump's attacks on a supposed enemy within, and his distrust of 'experts', particularly in their capacity as advisers to the government, are highly reckless and potentially dangerous. It has led the President to undermine these people in public, thereby exposing them as well as ordinary citizens to personal danger (Rogers et al., 2020). In the case of Dr Anthony Fauci, director of the National Institute of Allergy and Infectious Diseases (NIAID) and the government's chief medical adviser during the COVID-19 pandemic who challenged Trump's strategy of wanting to relax some of the social distancing regulations, he was accused by Trump of exaggerating the seriousness of the COVID-19 threat. In a series of online messages Trump, amongst other things, called Fauci a 'Fraud-ci', prompting some of president's supporters to issue death threats to the doctor (NPR, 2020). The implication of such an approach to government and the desire to scapegoat others, including accusing other nations such as China of threatening America's security and of being responsible for American deaths, once again, is a means by which populist and right-wing governments are able to deflect blame for policy failures away from themselves and on to others. Such manipulation of the public through the creation of moral panics is becoming an increasing feature of such regimes and, no doubt, helps them at election time, but can expose innocent and vulnerable groups to potential danger (Moffitt, 2015; Cheesman et al., 2018).

The assault on state education

In the US, public education has been the subject of concerted attack by those who see it as an obstacle to raising standards and innovative ways of funding education, proposing privately managed charter schools as the solution. Kolderie (1996) suggests that by acting as laboratories for research and development, as well as being sources of constructive competition for public schools in terms of working practices and cost savings through economies of scale, charter schools should ultimately be seen as replacements for districts as providers of education in the US (Finn et al., 2017).

However, researchers have been investigating the way the policy of expanding charter schools is not only reducing the role of the state in public education but is also effectively destroying the ability of state-run public schools to function. Moreover, the education system is being handed over to private organisations such as charities and businesses that are controlled by wealthy individuals who are able to make huge profits from running them (Black et al., 2019; Gardner Kelly, 2019). Once again, we hear the names of philanthrocapitalists such as Bill Gates who present themselves as civicminded citizens, lobbying for the further expansion of charter schools as the austerity measures imposed on public services after the 2008 financial crisis continue to affect the ability of states to fund their education systems (Leachman et al., 2017). These demands for a greater role of charter schools in educational provision for kindergarten up to year 12 students (K-12) are also fuelled by federal grants, that is, direct aid from the central government which is dominated by anti-union, conservative politicians dedicated to removing education from the district sphere (Blume, 2018). In Los Angeles, which has the highest proportion of charter schools and charter students in the country (Blume, 2018), wealthy individuals such as Bill Gates and the Walton Family Foundation have been heavily involved in their funding which, according to John Rogers, Professor of Education at the University of California Los Angeles (cited in Blume, 2018), is beginning to destabilise and undermine the whole system. Although charter schools are public schools, they are privately run and most are non-unionised, making it easier for their employers to impose working conditions that may otherwise be challenged in a non-charter public school. They have grown rapidly throughout the whole country since 2006, when there were about 1m students, to 3.2m students in 2017/2018 (National Alliance for Public Charter Schools, 2018). This has had a detrimental impact on public schools in many districts because the greater the number of charter school students in any district, the less funding is available for local public schools. In a system based on per capita funding, every school place lost in a district when a student moves to a charter school also means their pro-rated share of funding moves with them, yet the district is still responsible for the full ongoing costs of services within their schools (Lafer, 2018).

Moreover, there is a good deal of evidence to show that because the setting up and running of charter schools is so poorly regulated with little oversight by any authority, there are charter school operators who are increasingly 'self-serving private entities built on funds derived from lucrative management fees and rent extraction which further compromise the future provision of "public" education' (Barker and Miron, 2015). Indeed, even the Inspector General of the US Department of Education reports that the way charter school systems operate poses a 'financial risk, which is the risk of waste, fraud, and abuse' (Office of the Inspector General, 2016: 2). As Black et al. (2019)

claim, many charter contracts are signed that enable these schools to operate in ways that would never be allowed in the 'real' world of business, not least because many of them would be illegal. From the evidence available, what is most alarming is the almost total lack of concern on the part of the federal government about such practices (Black et al., 2019) and the lengths to which neoliberal policymakers and their supporters are prepared to go to destroy the state education system in the US.

Impact on the poor

A further examination of the evidence regarding the impact of budget cuts on communities reveals that it is those districts with the highest levels of deprivation that are most affected (Knight, 2017), and Gardner Kelly (2019) believes that the expansion of charter schools in these areas is further exacerbating the situation. The long-term consequences of these policies are likely to add to their existing detrimental effects on educational attainment and occupational prospect of the young people in poorer districts (Baker, 2018).

In Britain, the government has also been forcefully pushing for the wholesale removal of state-run primary and secondary schools from the public sphere and placing them under the control of independent bodies that run schools on behalf of the state but independently of it (Vasagar and Stratten, 2010; Reilly, 2019). This has been part of a wider and longer-term pattern of right-wing politicians around the world deregulating and privatising state public services and subjecting them to the disciplines and principles of governmentality (Davidson-Harden, 2010; Ball, 2013). British governments have been engaged in a policy of privatisation since 1979, when Mrs Thatcher embarked on the wholesale privatisation of state businesses, assets and services. However, this did not stop with the sale of assets that could be seen as having obvious potential commercial value – coal, gas or steel; it also involved the gradual privatisation of public goods such as social care and education.

Since then there has been a relentless process of privatising education driven by two main ideological principles. From what has been referred to as the supply-side position (Ball, 2013; Walford, 2014), neoliberals argue for reform on the grounds that state education is inherently inefficient, claiming that it ultimately lets down working-class children due to its domination by 'trendy' left-wing teachers guided by notions of child-centredness, a reluctance to impose discipline in the classroom and a refusal to demand high standards from their pupils (Phillips, 1997; Gove, 2013). The government in this perspective sees itself as an enabler for a quasi-market in schools to provide the competition needed for the efficient functioning of the system.

Moreover, as we saw from the ideas of Kolderie (1996), relating to the justification for the introduction of charter schools in the US, privately run state-funded schools are viewed as sources of creative competition for state-run schools which leads to greater efficiencies and flexibilities. However, according to Walford (2014), what this usually means is the implementation of systems where teachers are not protected by nationally agreed contracts and pay levels.

Second, there is the demand-side position which is predicated on the libertarian principle of the freedom of likeminded citizens to set up their own schools, free from government control, based on particular pedagogical, religious or philosophical principles. This, on the face of it, sounds inherently more sensitive to local democratic and community needs; however, as Walford (2014) points out, access to many of these new schools is based on various types of selection, thereby often excluding local children.

The result of these two motives for creating a quasi-market in education is an array of schools, some of which were the result of demand (demand-side) by religious and charitable groups, as well as parental and local requests which were met under the 1993 Education Act. This allows them to set up schools themselves that would be funded by a grant directly from the government (grant-maintained status) but run independently and partly funded by sponsors. In addition, there are free schools, promoted (supply-side) by the government under the 2010 Education Act, as part of its policy of opening up the school system to business models and systems of efficiency. They can be set up by a range of proposers, such as parent and teacher groups and charities, but are modelled on and inspired by the Swedish system of free schools and American charter schools that are primarily run by education businesses and, as we have seen from the case of US, are able to make a profit from the 'business' of education. It is this combination of different schools in competition with each other and the existing independent sector, driven by market principles, ideas of traditional standards as well as libertarian notions of freedom, that Gove believes will solve the 'problem' of England's underperforming schools.

The issue of selection and social justice

A key issue raised by these reforms, however, is the impact of selection on social justice. As Walford (2013) points out, selection has been a key aspect of all the new schools created by the reforms in England since 1979, be it religious, academic or general aptitude. Moreover, there has long been selection based on ability to pay. Selection sits comfortably with the philosophy of competition which already exists in some local authorities with grammar schools as well as the independent sector; however, selective systems generally act in favour of wealthier middle-class families and at the expense of poorer ones. Much of the evidence suggests that selection does not occur on a level-playing field (Walford, 2014; Boronski, 2016; Pickett, 2016; Burgess et al., 2017). Be it for selection to grammar schools, faith schools, specialist academies or newly created free schools, the criteria for selection tend to be biased in favour of the middle-class parents rich in cultural capital that is passed on to their children: 'With the entirely new free Schools, parents, teachers and others have been able to construct schools that have a particular appeal to certain types of families' (Walford, 2014: 326).

The impact on vulnerable children

Moreover, social justice is further compromised by the permissive legislation giving free schools and academies greater autonomy over the implementation of their own exclusion policies (West and Wolf, 2018). This has had significant consequences for pupils with special educational needs (SEN) (Tomlinson, 2005; DfE, 2018; Rogers, 2019). It was feared that with the expansion of the academies and free schools programme under the coalition (2010–2015) and Conservative governments (2015-), children with SEN would become particularly vulnerable, given schools' increasing consciousness of the need to maintain their position in school league tables, as well as due to the additional cost of teaching and supporting such children (Weal and McIntyre, 2018). Rogers' (2019) research confirms that these fears have been borne out by the evidence. Figures from the Department for Education (DfE, 2018) show that exclusions are increasing, with a rise from 6,685 in 2015/2016 to 7,720 in 2016/2017. Weal and McIntyre (2018) report that according to official estimates, in 2018 there were around 4,500 pupils with statutory rights to special needs support still waiting for appropriate educational provision at the start of that year. However, this probably greatly underestimates the real number, given that only about 253,000 of the 1.2m children with some form of SEN possess SEN statements or education and healthcare plans (EHC), which are the passports to special needs support. This is because, despite the introduction of a new Special Educational Needs Code of Practice in 2014, that is supposed to be more sensitive to the views of children with special needs and their parents, it would seem that the decisions to grant EHC plans are based increasingly on financial considerations (Tickle, 2017). Due to a decade of austerity local authorities are increasingly unable to meet their obligations to some of our most vulnerable people (NAHT, 2018; Butler, 2019, 2020).

Justice is also denied to those who feel they have been unfairly excluded from academies. Under the current system of appeals, the local government ombudsman has no jurisdiction to investigate complaints of maladministration over exclusion decisions made by panels run by academies (West and Wolf, 2018).

In the four decades of continuous reforms and 'experimentation' with privatisation and the marketisation of state education by both Conservative (1979–1997, 2010-) and New Labour (1997–2010) governments in England, we are still in a situation where government ministers are making the same claims; working-class children are being let down by state schools in England, as if they and their parents are responsible for education policies, when in fact they had no part to play in them at all. In effect, teachers and state schools continue to be scapegoated for the poorer performance of vulnerable children and those from working-class backgrounds compared to those from the middle class, as well as for the associated lack of progress in terms of upward social mobility of working-class children (May, 2016). The myth of neoliberal efficiency and the constant deferral of hope regarding the creation of a more just and meritocratic society are clearly wearing thin. However, they are periodically revived and given new life. This can be seen in recent government campaigns and high-profile policies that were announced but soon abandoned or have, once again, come to nothing (see Case study 7.1).

The continuing myth of social mobility in neoliberal times

In Britain, the effects of austerity on the nation, particularly the poor, have been devastating for public service, welfare and the health and care service (Royal College of Physicians, 2016; National Association of Head Teachers, 2018; Butler, 2019, 2020). The economic policy of the Conservative-led coalition (2010–2015) implemented by the Chancellor George Osborne was presented as an approach that had no alternative. However, when Theresa May became Conservative prime minister in 2016, following David Cameron's failed Remain campaign in the Brexit referendum, rumours grew of some possible relief after six years of deep cuts in public spending. Despite the announcement of a continuation of the policy of austerity, the government had pledged to protect education from further cuts until 2020 (Perraudin and Wintour, 2015). Nevertheless, it soon became clear that schools in Wales and England were heading for a huge financial crisis. In a poll conducted by the National Association of Head Teachers (NAHT, 2018) of 589 school leaders in Wales and England, more than a fifth stated that their budget for 2017/2018 was in deficit, and three quarters said that they would have to set a deficit budget in the following year. Due to years of declining funding, most claimed they had no reserves left to draw on (NAHT, 2018). Paul

Whiteman, General Secretary of the NAHT, warns that 'the entire state-funded school system is rapidly heading towards insolvency. And as this research shows, the cuts are beginning to have an impact on children and education' (NAHT, 2018). Moreover, schools are increasingly having to rely on food banks to support children's families and to provide services that would otherwise be provided by local authorities. As Emma Knights, Chief Executive of the National Governance Association, the organisation that represents school governors, states:

> There is an increasing demand on schools to take responsibility for more areas of children's lives than simply their education.... School staff have an increased burden of providing welfare services because of chronic underfunding in other areas and particularly cuts to local authority services.
>
> (Knights, cited in Coughlan, 2019)

The importance of factors beyond the school

In their analysis of social class and social mobility in Britain, Savage et al. (2015) examine different forms of capital assets, their uneven distribution and their impact on class formations. Whereas politicians and academics on the Right see educational performance in very narrow terms whereby individuals, if taught 'effectively' and they work hard, can achieve what they deserve (Saunders, 2010, 2012), others who take a multidimensional approach through an examination of the social class origins of children, their ethnic/'racial' origins, their gender, their cultural background, the economic position of their families and the extent of economic inequality in society reveal a more complex picture and a better understanding of the nature and patterns of educational inequality (Wiederkehr et al., 2015). Not only is it intuitively self-evident that children's experience of education and educational performance is bound up with factors both in and outside the classroom, it is also demonstrably clear from the evidence (Wiederkehr et al., 2015; Masci et al., 2018; Wilkinson and Pickett, 2018). It is, it seems, only the least intellectually curious politicians and their supporters who, perhaps for ideological reasons, refuse to take this evidence seriously.

In their research on class and social mobility in the UK Savage et al. (2015) conducted a survey on 160,000 respondents in the UK. In analysing the data, they apply what they refer to as the capitals, assets and resources (CAR) approach. This is influenced by the ideas of Pierre Bourdieu (1984, 1986) who sees class position as based on the differing levels of access to, or possession of, various types of assets: economic, cultural and social. Unlike Marxists who see class as determined by a person's relationship to the means of production, and the exploitative nature of the relationship between the workers and the owners of capital, or Weberians, who see class as based on status differences between occupational groups and the way they use their market position to maximise their access to economic benefits, Bourdieu sees class in terms of how the three forms of assets are used by particular classes in strategic ways to secure their interests against other class groups (Bourdieu, 1986). In the study by Savage et al. (2015), this involved assessing their respondents and classifying them in terms of three main categories: first, in terms of such things as income levels, house values and savings, which are conventionally associated with economic capital. Second, in terms of factors such as educational background, leisure and cultural pursuits

Case study 7.1: Creating the 'great meritocracy'

It is against this background of increasing austerity and growing levels of inequality, that in 2016 Theresa May made a speech to the British Academy (May, 2016) in which she outlined her vision for Britain as the 'great meritocracy'. Responding, it seems, to evidence from the government's own Social Mobility Commission (2016a, 2016b, 2017) of a lack of progress in terms of social mobility in Wales, Scotland and England, May proposed a strategy for creating 'the great meritocracy' where 'working class people have more control over their lives and the chance to share fairly in the prosperity of the nation' (May, 2016: 2) and 'to give ordinary, working class people the better deal they deserve' (May, 2016: 3).

May's plan

Under the original Child Poverty Act 2010, the Blair government committed its 2001 aim of ending child poverty by 2020 into law. In order to achieve this, the act imposed a legal duty on future governments to focus on four areas: the reduction of children living in relative poverty (those living in families below 60 per cent of the median income) to less than 10 per cent, the reduction of absolute poverty (those living in families below 60 per cent of an adjusted base amount, with the base year as 2010/2011) to less than 5 per cent, for fewer children to be living in persistent poverty over long periods with targets to be set at a future date and, finally, less than 5 per cent of children to experience material deprivation in low-income families (low income measured as below 70 per cent of median income; CPAG, 2020).

In addition, the act established the Child Poverty Commission (CPC) staffed by experts in social policy to monitor and report to the government on progress being made in relation to its targets. There was an explicit recognition by the Labour government as well as the CPC of the inseparable link between levels of inequality in society and the educational performance not only of those at the bottom of the socioeconomic system but also of society as a whole (Wilkinson and Pickett, 2009, 2018): the more unequal the society, the less likely are poorer children to achieve their full potential. Moreover, extremes of inequality in affluent societies drag down whole societies, not just the poor.

However, under the coalition government (2010–2015) led by the Conservatives, the Child Poverty Commission was renamed the Social Mobility and Child Poverty Commission, and then, under the Conservative government of 2015–2017, it became the Social Mobility Commission (SMC). What we can clearly see is the gradual removal of the original focus of the commission on child poverty, which was part of its original title, to one that focuses only on social mobility. Indeed, this seems to be part of the Conservative government's strategy of removing 'child poverty' entirely from the political and educational agenda, whilst at the same time following policies that are resulting in its increase. With the introduction of the Welfare Reform Act of 2016, the Child Poverty Act of 2010 was abolished along with its four targets. The Conservative government had effectively relieved itself of a government pledge to abolish child poverty by 2020. It has been left to other organisations such as the Child Poverty Action Group (CPAG, 2019), the Resolution Foundation (Corlett, 2019) and the

Joseph Rowntree Foundation (Wright and Anderson, 2018) to monitor the effects of government austerity measures on poorer children and the growth of child poverty in the UK. It is significant that during the period of the Labour government 1997–2010, these organisations report a reduction in child poverty 'on a scale and at a pace unmatched by other industrial nations' (PSE, 2019). However, 'they warn that the government's policies since 2010 risk wiping out all the gains made' (PSE, 2019).

It is at this policy and legislative juncture that Theresa May made her 'great meritocracy' speech in 2016 and was able to do so without once mentioning the word 'poverty'. In it she makes two key assumptions which, it can be suggested, will merely lead to a continuation of the existing inequalities in education. However, what it does is provide a further episode in the manufacture of hokey hope, whereby the government makes some dramatic headline-grabbing declarations of its desire to promote social justice (May, 2016), together with some ostentatious policy proposals that are likely to end in the further postponement of hope.

More examples of perverse logic

The first assumption is that schools alone can bring about greater social justice and a fairer society for all, regardless of the levels of social and economic inequality. Hence Michael Gove's assertion that 'a difficult start in life can be overcome, with hard work and good teaching' (Gove, 2012). Second, the belief that this can be achieved within the existing elitist and divided English education system, in which a wealthy and privileged minority has access to the most exclusive private schools, as well as to the best-funded selective state schools, i.e. grammar schools. Mr Gove is suggesting that, even under the present regime of austerity, ordinary state schools can be as successful as the most exclusive private and selective schools. The perversity of Gove's logic is palpable here and suggests a degree of 'hokum' which defies all credibility, particularly as most of the evidence, both national and international, suggests otherwise (Jerrim and Macmillan, 2015; Savage et al., 2015; Wilkinson and Pickett, 2018).

Mrs May's speech starts by resorting to the familiar theme of blaming 'the system' and malign influences for Britain's problems. She does this first by implicating foreign forces in the form of the European Union as preventing Britain from following its desire to be a free and 'confident, global trading nation' (May, 2016: 2) and then by talking of anonymous 'politicians' who have failed to respond to the concerns 'of ordinary, working class people' (May, 2016: 2). There are also 'vested interests' that need to be challenged, and Mrs May says she wants a society where everyone 'plays by the same rules' (May, 2016: 2). Foreign forces, mysterious groups of domestic politicians and vested interests are alluded to as the obstacles to change and the national desire to make Britain 'great' again. This is summed up in the following: 'They want to take back control of the things that matter in their lives. They want a government that listens, understands and is on their side. They want change. And this government is going to deliver it' (May, 2016: 2). It should be pointed out that it is not entirely clear who 'they' are. Presumably it is 'the ordinary, working class people' (May,

2016: 2), and if it is, did they ever really have control? It could be argued that here, once again, we see another example of hokey hope being created, in which the government presents itself, once more, as a champion of the people, making ostentatious claims to tackle mythical enemies with vague promises that are lacking in substance or credibility.

Rather than proposing a truly meaningful change that would actually enable the voices of 'ordinary, working class people' to be heard, Mrs May actually declares her intention to deliver them further into the hands of the 'privileged few', 'those with the loudest voices', 'special interests', those with 'the greatest wealth' and 'access to influence', that is, those who run our most powerful and influential educational institutions, businesses and interest groups: the very people who, earlier in her speech, she vowed not to be influenced by. In her bid to raise standards in state schools, Theresa May proposes to enlist the support of Britain's top private schools, elite universities and most successful businesses and academy chains. In addition, she proposes to expand the selective education sector by allowing grammar schools to grow and spread their knowledge and experience of good practice to underperforming state schools.

Playing the game

Not so much listening to ordinary people then, as deciding for them and actually increasing the influence of powerful vested interests. The plan involves these privileged groups 'sharing' their business, leadership, pedagogical and organisational skills as well as their facilities and resources with state schools in order to raise their standards and performance. In doing so, independent schools would play a key role in this meritocratic mission, thereby serving to justify their existence, including their preferential tax status (Verkaik, 2019). The metaphor of playing a game is apt, but self-implicating, in that games usually imply there will be winners and losers. Also, there is no mention of whose 'rules' everyone should be playing by, but the evidence suggests that in order to become a 'winner' in the 'game of education' in England, it is essential to be very familiar with the rules (Savage et al., 2015). It also suggests that the system works in favour of a minority who come to the game with distinct advantages (Savage et al., 2015; Masci et al., 2018; Wilkinson and Pickett, 2018).

that symbolically mark a group out from others and which indicate levels of *cultural capital*. Finally, they were assessed in terms of their social networks that link members of a class fraction and how these can be used at appropriate times to pursue or reinforce their individual and collective interests. This is referred to as *social capital*.

By using such capitals, resources and assets approach, Savage et al. (2015) have been able to examine the strategies employed by those most successful at negotiating the complexities of the English education system through the effective deployment of economic assets, the display of cultural symbols and the use of social networks. In the process they have created a new social classification system in which seven classes are identified and ranked according to levels of economic capital and rated in terms of their possession of cultural and social capital.

What Savage et al. (2015) found is that those classes richest in all three types of capital tended to be in the highest levels of the class system, whereas those at the bottom of the class system tend to have the lowest amounts of these assets. This 'homology', as Bourdieu (1984) calls it, is much less evident between these two extremes. At the top is the *ordinary elite*, who make up 6 per cent of the sample. They are much better off economically than any of the other class groups, though distinct from the super-rich (see Chapter 4), with incomes double that of the next-placed group. This ordinary elite is made up of top professionals such as lawyers, city financiers and traders as well as those in the medical profession. They score highly in relation to 'high-brow' culture as measured by activities such as attending the opera, classical concerts and visiting museums. They also have wide social networks that include high-status individuals among the major institutions of education, the law and politics. This ordinary elite is increasingly pulling away from all the other classes in terms of income. Below this elite sits a group of five classes: the *established middle class*, made up of highly skilled professionals in IT, engineering and science; the *technical middle class*; the *new affluent workers*; the *traditional working class*; and the *emerging service class*. These five classes that sit in the middle display less homology and are therefore much more difficult to assess and classify. However, at the bottom of this hierarchy is a clearly identifiable class named by Savage et al. (2015) as the *precariat*, who make up approximately 15 per cent of the population. They score lowest on the three types of capital, having few influential social connections, low levels of participation in high-status cultural activities and, predictably, limited economic assets in the form of income, savings and property. The name was devised by Guy Standing to denote 'a class-in-the-making' (Standing, 2011: Preface) that shows high levels of similarity with other workers around the world enduring low pay, lack of job security and poor conditions of work, all of which mean that they tend to be forced to rent accommodation in an increasingly deregulated and volatile rental sector. The term precariat is a portmanteau, combining the words 'precarity' and 'proletariat' to highlight their increasingly precarious working and domestic lives due to declining or non-existent levels of welfare support and protection for workers by the neoliberal state. The term is also used as an alternative to the names often used to describe the poorer members of society that tend to stigmatise them and perpetuate stereotypes that justify their harsh treatment by the state: lower class, the undeserving poor, welfare-dependent scroungers or chavs (Jones, 2011). The poor and low-paid working class is demeaned in ways that are rarely used to stigmatise the wealthy or super-rich for their excesses (see Chapters 1 and 3). Furthermore, the evidence shows that there are high levels of self-recruitment at this end of the class system (Bukodi et al., 2015; Savage et al., 2015; Bukodi, 2019). Savage et al. (2015) found that 65 per cent of people born into the precariat remain there, and only 11 per cent of the elite is made up of those who originated from the precariat.

The inheritance of privilege

What separates the elite from the established middle class is not so much their levels of skill or expertise as their membership of the 'gentlemanly' professions such as the bar (barristers) that tend to recruit from the most exclusive educational institutions; the top public schools and the universities of Oxford and Cambridge. The evidence collected by Savage et al. (2015) reveals that the elite, just like the precariat, is highly self-recruiting with 51 per cent coming from backgrounds in which their parents were also employed in the higher professions, as CEOs or senior managers. The privileged backgrounds of most elite members means it is a class made up of families that have, over the generations, developed a distinct identity and in which members have been able to accumulate ever higher levels of capital to pass on to their descendants. These combined factors make the elite extremely difficult to access from below. It is this class that effectively sets the rules of the game and is also most adept and applying them.

Within the elite, then, a combination of high levels of economic resources, particular modes of behaviour and disposition as well as an exclusionary and a reciprocating network of connections enable its members to effectively manoeuvre around the complexities of the education market as well as most other important systems and institutions. They are, in effect, better able to access advantage by confidently gaining entry and moving within the systems and institutions that are essential as a means of becoming part of the elite. Just as economic capital is passed on by parents, so too is cultural capital through which 'highly cultured' parents prepare their children for the encounters they will have in prestigious educational institutions and elite professions. Such preparation, however, is inchoate without the economic means to pay for an exclusive education, which is usually an advantage when applying to an elite university. The Sutton Trust (Montacute, 2018) reports that independent school pupils are seven times more likely to attend Oxford or Cambridge university than those from non-selective state schools. It is at these points and locations in the education system that not only knowing the rules of the game is important, but so also is having the confidence and demeanour to demonstrate that one belongs. The Sutton Trust (2018) significantly points to the poor understanding of the rules, not just amongst pupils from state schools applying to the top universities but also by their teachers when it reports that 'many young people are not getting the right advice' (Montacute, 2018: 2), as if this is the fault of the teachers in state schools for not knowing or understanding the rules. Most teachers in state schools are not from elite backgrounds and are therefore not in possession of the levels of cultural or social capital required for such a task either.

The problem of elitism

A further significant and related point made in the Sutton Trust report (Montacute, 2018) is the level of applications by very able students from state schools, particularly those from poorest areas, compared with those from independent schools to elite universities such as Oxford. Using A*A*A (A* being the highest possible grade for A Level) as the standard by which to identify very able students, the figures show that 37 per cent of very able students attending independent schools, 25 per cent from state schools generally and 14 per cent from the most deprived areas of the country applied to Oxford in 2017/2018. It appears that it is not primarily ability and merit that influence applications. The Sutton Trust makes a number of recommendations to the top universities in order to encourage poorer students to apply. However, such students clearly do not feel motivated to apply, and this situation is hardly surprising given the potential feeling amongst pupils from modest backgrounds that they do not 'belong' (Reay et al., 2005). Once again, it is those without the kinds of dispositions and cultural capital who are expected to know the rules and adapt accordingly, rather than the system upon which England's elitist system of education rests, that is seen as in need of change.

Race and ethnicity

In terms of 'race' and ethnicity, there are even more deeply entrenched problems. Savage et al. (2015) found that minority ethnic groups are relatively well represented in the established middle class and the emerging service class at 13 and 21 per cent, respectively. This is probably a reflection of high staying-on rates after the age of 16 among some ethnic minorities (See et al., 2011). However, when it comes to the elite they are relatively poorly represented (4 per cent). This is also reflected in the proportion of minority ethnic students, particularly Black students attending elite universities. Although Black students make up 8 per cent of the UK student population, only 1.2 per cent of Oxford undergraduates in 2016 were Black (*The Guardian*, 2016). The figure for Cambridge was 1.5 per cent. At 4 per cent, Black students are better represented in the Russell Group universities, but this is still only half of their overall representation in higher education (*The Guardian*, 2016). Evidence from Savage et al. (2015) suggests that attendance at an elite university such as Oxford or Cambridge or a Russell Group university provides a distinct advantage to anyone aspiring to elite class membership, but research by Robson et al. (2017) suggests that students from minority ethnic backgrounds often don't apply to Oxford or Cambridge because they are not generally encouraged to by their teachers and are led to believe that they will not 'fit in' (Robson et al., 2017).

This experience of not belonging is revealed in a book of poetry, prose and essays entitled *A Fly Girl's Guide to University: Being a Woman of Colour at Cambridge and Other Institutions of Power and Elitism*, by Lola Olufemi, Odelia Younge, Waithera Sebatindira and Suhaiymah Manzoor-Khan (2019), four women of colour who attended Cambridge University. What they found was that as women of colour at Cambridge, they felt both highly visible in a world of white privilege, and yet highly invisible, as manifested by the lack of a record or official recognition of the stories and narratives of such women in the curriculum. The book is a way of redressing the issue, thereby providing support for others in the same situation and showing them that they are not alone. Their experiences could have been very isolating, as no doubt it is for many in their situation; however, these women were determined not only to ensure that they were able to fully engage in university life but also to support other women of colour through FLY, Cambridge University's network and forum for women and non-binary people of colour.

By validating the feelings of other young women in similar situations of isolation and not belonging, Olufemi, Younge, Sebatindira and Manzoor-Khan have tried to show that it is not they who are the problem, but the structure of white elitism and privilege which needs to be completely dismantled and replaced 'with spaces that nurture women of colour' (Adulawoye, 2019). This would involve making people of colour more visible through new structures and curricula that give space for the voices of oppressed groups (see Chapter 4). The establishment of FLY by Odelia Younge and its development with her fellow students have provided a positive response to the experiences of women of colour in elite universities, wherever they may be, through political activism, cultural experiences and bringing important issues, such as the narrowness of the curriculum, to wider public attention in order to bring about major changes in such institutions.

The independent sector

The elitism of the English education system is further perpetuated by the existence of a thriving independent education sector. Approximately 7 per cent of pupils attend independent schools (Kynaston and Kynaston, 2015; Verkaik, 2019), and, clearly, not all private schools are as exclusive or as well-known as Eton, the school attended by the Prime Minister Boris Johnson; however, members of the Headmasters' and Headmistresses' Conference (HMC) represents nearly three hundred of 'the world's leading independent schools' (HMC, 2020). The educational performance of these schools, particularly the most prestigious ones, is very high, and the children who attend them experience a very strong boost to their life chances in terms of employment prospects, future earnings as well as the social capital that enhances their access to positions of power and influence. Indeed, this is something that those spending anything from £18,000 a year for a day-pupil to over forty thousand pounds a year for a boarder (UK Boarding Schools, 2018) might expect from such a service. And, indeed, this seems to be the case, as Savage et al. (2015: 245) state: 'almost two-thirds of those taking the "royal road" – coming from a senior managerial or traditional professional home, and going to an independent school and then to Oxford – reach the elite', illustrating that the independent school sector still plays a significant role in perpetuating class privilege and advantage over the rest of the population. This is particularly evident in the field of politics, where two-thirds of Boris Johnson's first cabinet in 2019 attended a public school (Walker, 2019). Peter Lampl, chairman of the Sutton Trust, which monitors social mobility in the UK, states that 'Social mobility – the potential for those to achieve success regardless of their background – remains low' (cited in Walker, 2019).

Once again, we see a much-publicised government initiative to help children in poorer communities come to nothing. Theresa May's promise to make Britain the great meritocracy with a declaration that 'This government's priorities are those of ordinary, working class people' has pretty much disappeared without trace amid the confusion caused by the government's main priority: 'taking back control' from Europe. Under Boris Johnson, the situation became very much business as usual, with Angela Rayner, the shadow education secretary, declaring that it is 'no surprise that the Tories have failed to honour their pledge to rethink the tax loopholes that benefit private schools, and Johnson instead plans yet another giveaway for the super-rich' (cited in Walker, 2019).

The notion that independent schools would jeopardise their dominant position and premium status in the English as well as the international market in education by sharing their facilities, their expertise as well as their exclusivity with the poorest in the country seems fanciful. Moreover, it is just as unrealistic to believe that a government which represents the privileged classes and professes to support a deregulated quasi-market in education would seek to regulate a highly successful independent education sector.

Conclusion

This discussion of the educational system in England reveals that ability and effort alone are generally not sufficient to help children from poorer and modest family backgrounds reach their full potential. To focus merely on schools, then, is inadequate if the intention is to see greater social justice. Moreover, it shifts the blame away from governments and onto teachers in schools, who are increasingly struggling against the challenges of continuous cuts in school funding, as well as the impact of increasing levels of poverty on the children they teach. A growing amount of evidence from British and international research suggests 'that education is important but not enough to change inequalities around the world' (Volante and Jerrim, 2018). Education in any society is not a purely technical or mechanical process. Children's development, both physical and psychological, are intimately bound up with their material, social and environmental experiences. Savage et al. (2015) remind us that 'equality of opportunity can only be made real when it is associated with equality in general' (Savage et al., 2015: 215).

Points for reflection and consideration in this chapter

This chapter has examined education policies pursued by neoliberal states such as England and the US. In particular, it has shown how these states have portrayed themselves as supporters of greater equality of opportunity and social justice, whilst actually carrying out policies that have the opposite effect in entrenching and deepening social inequality.

- What do you think of Michael Gove's claim that 'a difficult start in life can be overcome, with hard work and good teaching'?
- Is it logically coherent for politicians who claim to support equality of opportunity and a level-playing field in education to also believe in the right of a wealthy elite to pay for an exclusive education that gives their children much better life chances than the rest of the school population?

References

Adulawoye, D. (2019) 'A FLY Girl's Guide to University: "Giving women of colour something to read that better reflects their world"'. *Varsity* 4 June. Available at: https://www.varsity.co.uk/news/16834 (Accessed 4 June 2020).

Baker, B. (2018) *Educational Inequality and School Finance: Why Money Matters for America's Students*. Cambridge, MA: Harvard Educational Press.

Baker, B. and Miron, G. (2015) 'The Business of Charter Schooling: Understanding the policies that charter operators use for financial Benefit'. *National Education Policy Center*. Available at: https://nepc.colorado.edu/sites/default/files/rb_baker-miron_charter_revenue_0.pdf (Accessed 27 May 2020).

Ball, S. (2013) *The Education Debate*. Bristol: Policy Press.

Bell, D. (2013) 'Michael Gove must stop fighting "The Blob" and listen to the education experts'. *The Conversation*. Available at: https://theconversation.com/michael-gove-must-stop-fighting-the-blob-and-listen-to-the-education-experts-22659 (Accessed 22 May 2020).

Black, D. Baker, B. and Green, P. (2019) 'Charter schools exploit lucrative loophole that would be easy to close' *The Conversation*. Available at: https://theconversation.com/charter-schools-exploit-lucrative-loophole-that-would-be-easy-to-close-111792 9 (Accessed 2 April 2020).

Blume. (2018) 'L.A. teachers union rallies supporters with call for cap on charter schools'. *Los Angeles Times*, 21 December. Available at: https://www.latimes.com/local/education/la-me-edu-teachers-union-charter-cap-20181221-story.html (Accessed 26 May 2020).

Boronski, T. (2016) 'Grammar schools: A very English solution to a very English problem'. *The Conversation*. Available at: https://theconversation.com/grammar-schools-a-very-english-solution-to-a-very-english-problem-65389 (Accessed 16 April 2019).

Bourdieu, P. (1984) *Distinction: A Social Critique of the Judgement of Taste*. London: Routledge & Kegan Paul.

Bourquin, P., Cribb, J., Waters, T. and Xu, X. (2019) *Why has in-work poverty risen in Britain?* Institute for Fiscal Studies. IFS Working Paper W19/12. Available at: https://www.ifs.org.uk/uploads/WP201912.pdf (Accessed 26 May 2020).

Bukodi, E., Goldthorpe, J.H., Waller, L. and Kuha, J. (2015) 'The mobility problem in Britain: New findings from the analysis of birth cohort data'. *The British Journal of Sociology*. Vol. 66, No.1, pp. 93–117.

Bukodi, E. (2019) 'Britain's social mobility problem has been misunderstood – education is not the great leveller'. *The Conversation*. Available at: http://theconversation.com/ britains-social-mobility-problem-has-been-misunderstood-education-is-not-the-greatleveller-109125 (Accessed 2 March 2019)

Burgess, S., Crawford, C. and Macmillan, L. (2017) 'Grammar schools: Why academic selection only benefits the very affluent'. *The Conversation*. Available at: https://theconversation.com/grammar-schools-why-academic-selection-only-benefits-the-very-affluent-74189 (Accessed 24 May 2020).

Butler, P. (2019) 'One in five councils face drastic spending cuts within months'. *The Guardian* 2 July. Available at: https://www.theguardian.com/society/2019/jul/02/one-in-five-councils-face-drastic-spending-cuts-within-months (Accessed 26 May 2020).

Butler, P. (2020) 'Councils in crisis with more tax rises and service cuts due'. *The Guardian* 5 February. Available at: https://www.theguardian.com/society/2020/feb/05/councils-in-crisis-with-more-tax-rises-and-service-cuts-due (Accessed 26 May 2020).

Cheesman, N., Casal Bertoa, F., Storm, L. and Dodsworth, S. (2018) 'How populism can be turned into an opportunity, not a threat'. *The Conversation*. Available at: https://theconversation.com/how-populism-can-be-turned-into-an-opportunity-not-a-threat-96934 (Accessed 27 May 2020).

Corlett, A. (2019) *The Living Standards Outlook 2019*. Available at: www.resolutionfoundation.org/publications/the-living-standards-outlook-2019/ (Accessed 30 May 2019).

Coughlan, S. (2019) 'Food banks increasing in schools for pupils' families'. *BBC News*. 3 September. Available at: https://www.bbc.co.uk/news/education-49515117 (Accessed 27 May 2020).

CPAG. (2019) 'Child poverty promise and child poverty act'. Available at: www.cpag.org.uk/content/child-poverty-promise-andchild-poverty-act (Accessed 11 June 2019.

CPAG. (2020) *Recent history of UK child poverty*. Child Poverty Action Group. Available at: https://cpag.org.uk/recent-history-uk-child-poverty (Accessed 27 May 2020).

Davidson-Harden, A. (2010) Interrogating the University as an Engine of Capitalism: neoliberalism and academic 'raison d'état'. *Policy Futures in Education*. Vol. 8, No. 5, pp. 575–587.

Department for Education. (2018) *Permanent and Fixed Period Exclusions in England: 2016 to 2017*. 19 July 2018. Available at: https://assets.publishing.service.gov.uk/government/uploads/system/uploads/attachment_data/file/726741/text_exc1617.pdf (Accessed 26 May 2020).

Duncan-Andrade. (2009) 'Note to educators: Hope required when growing roses in concrete'. *Harvard Educational Review*. Vol. 19, No. 2, pp. 181–194.

Finn, C., Manno, B. and Wright, B. (2017) 'The purpose of charter schools'. *US News*. 8 May. Available at: https://www.usnews.com/opinion/knowledge-bank/articles/2017-05-08/how-charter-schools-improve-traditional-district-education (Accessed 23May 2020).

Gardner Kelly, M. (2019) 'Charter school cap efforts gain momentum'. *The Conversation*. Available at: https://theconversation.com/charter-school-cap-efforts-gain-momentum-112918 (Accessed 5 May 2020).

Gove, M. (2012) 'Education secretary Michael Gove's speech to Brighton College'. Available at: www.gov.uk/government/speeches/education-secretary-michaelgoves-speech-to-brighton-college (Accessed 14 January 2020).

Gove, M. (2013) 'I refuse to surrender to the Marxist teachers hell-bent on destroying our schools: Education Secretary berates "the new enemies of promise" for opposing his plans'. *The Mail* 23 March. Available at: https://www.dailymail.co.uk/debate/article-2298146/I-refuse-surrender-Marxist-teachers-hell-bent-destroying-schools-Education-Secretary-berates-new-enemies-promise-opposing-plans.html (Accessed 20 May 2020).

Hay, I. and Muller, S. (2014) 'Questioning generosity in the golden age of philanthropy: Towards critical geographies of super-philanthropy'. *Progress in Human Geography*. Vol. 38, No. 5, pp. 635–653.

HMC. (2020) *Welcome to HMC*. Available at: https://www.hmc.org.uk/ (Accessed 5 June 2020).

Jerrim, J. and Macmillan, L. (2015) 'Income inequality, intergenerational mobility, and the Great Gatsby curve: Is education the key?' *Social Forces*. Vol. 4, No. 2, pp. 505–133.

Jones, O. (2011) *Chavs: The Demonization of the Working Class*. London: Verso.

Knight, E. (2017) 'Are high-poverty school districts disproportionately impacted by state funding cuts?: School finance equity following the great recession'. *Journal of Education Finance*. Vol. 43, No. 2, pp. 169–194.

Kolderie, E. (1996) 'The Charter idea: Updates and prospects'. *Centre for Education Reform*. Available at: https://edreform.com/edreform-university/resource/the-charter-idea-update-and-prospects-1996/ (Accessed 23 May 2020).

Kynaston, D. and Kynaston, G. (2015) 'Education's Berlin Wall: Does a better social mix make these schools acceptable? The Left has been silent on these issues for 40 years'. *New Statesman*, 3 February 2014. Available at: www.newstatesman. com/2014/01/education-private-schools-berlin-wall (Accessed 21 November 2019).

Lafer, G. (2018) *Breaking Point: The Cost of Charter Schools for Public School Districts*. In The Public Interest. Available at: https://educationvotes.nea.org/wp-content/uploads/2018/05/ITPI_Breaking_Point_May-2018FINAL.pdf (Accessed 27 May 2020).

Leachman, M., Masterson, K. and Figueroa, E. (2017) 'A punishing decade for School funding'. *Centre on Budget and Policy Priorities*, 29 November. Available at: https://www.cbpp.org/research/state-budget-and-tax/a-punishing-decade-for-school-funding (Accessed 26 May 2020).

Masci, C., Johnes, G. and Agasisti, T. (2018) 'Student and school performance across countries: A machine learning approach'. *European Journal of Operational Research*, Vol. 69, No. 3, pp. 1072–1085.

May, T. (2016) 'Britain, the great meritocracy: Prime Minister's speech'. *Department of Education*. 9 September. Available at: www.gov.uk/government/speeches/britain-the-great-meritocracy-prime-ministers-speech (Accessed 7 December 2018).

May, T. (2017) Engagements. *Hansard*. 19 April 2017, Vol. 624, Column 667. Available at: https://hansard.parliament.uk/commons/2017-04-19/debates/E28A633C-8DC8-4FAF-9258-2835F24836CB/Engagements (Accessed 27 May 2020).

Moffitt, B. (2015) 'Populism and democracy: friend or foe? Rising stars deepen dilemma'. *The Conversation*. Available at: https://theconversation.com/populism-and-democracy-friend-or-foe-rising-stars-deepen-dilemma-39695 (Accessed 27 May 2020).

Montacute, R. (2018) *Access to Advantage: The Influence of Schools and Place on Admissions to Top Universities*. London: The Sutton Trust.

NAHT. (2018) 'New poll reveals full impact of school funding crisis'. *NAHT News*. Available at: https://www.naht.org.uk/news-and-opinion/press-room/new-poll-reveals-full-impact-of-school-funding-crisis/ (Accessed 28 May 2020).

National Alliance for Public Charter Schools. (2018) *Estimated Public Charter School Enrollment 2017/18*. Available at: https://www.publiccharters.org/sites/default/files/documents/2018-03/FINAL%20Estimated%20Public%20Charter%20School%20Enrollment%2C%202017-18.pdf (Accessed 26 May 2020).

National Public Radio. (2020) '"In deep" challenges president Trump's notion of a deep-state conspiracy'. *Terry Gross*. Gary Rhode interviewed by Terry Gross. 15 April. Available at: https://www.npr.org/2020/04/15/834874400/in-deep-challenges-president-trump-s-notion-of-a-deep-state-conspiracy (Accessed 22 May 2020).

Office of The Inspector General (2016) *Nationwide Assessment of Charter and Education Management Organizations: Final Audit*. Washington: United States Department of Education.

Olufemi, L., Younge, O., Manzoor-Khan, S. and Sebatindira, W. (2019) *A Fly Girl's Guide to University: Being a Woman of Colour at Cambridge and Other Institutions of Power and Elitism*. Glasgow: Verve Poetry Press.

Perraudin, F. and Wintour, P. (2015) 'Tories will protect "per pupil spending", says Cameron'. *The Guardian*. 2 February. Available at: https//www.theguardian.com/ education/2015/feb/02/tories-will-protect-per-pupil-spending-says-cameron (Accessed 17 March 2020).

Phillips, M. (1997) *All Must Have Prizes*. London: Little Brown.

Pickett, K. (2016) 'To move forwards on inequality we must not go back to grammar schools'. *The Conversation*. Available at: https://theconversation.com/to-move-forwards-on-inequality-we-must-not-go-back-to-grammar-schools-65199 (Accessed 18 May 2019).

Poverty and Social Exclusion (PSE) (2019) *Ending child poverty by 2020: Progress Report*. Available online at: www.poverty.ac.uk/report-child-poverty-government-policy/ending-child-poverty-2020-%E2%80%93-progress-report (Accessed 9 June 2019).

Reay, D., David, M. and Ball, S. (2005) *Degrees of Choice: Class, Race and Gender in Higher Education*. Stoke-on-Trent: Trentham Books.

Reilly, K. (2019) 'How the debate over charter schools is fueling the Los Angeles teacher strike'. *Time*. 14 January. Available at: https://time.com/5499164/la-teacher-strike-charter-schools/ (Accessed 20 May 2020).

Rhode, D. (2020) *In Deep: The FBI, the CIA, and the Truth about America's 'Deep State'*. New York: W.W. Norton and Company.

Robson, J., O'Sullivan, K. and Winters, N. (2017) 'Black students on going to Oxbridge: "It's not even asked or pushed for, it's just assumed no one is applying"'. *The Conversation*. Available at: https://theconversation.com/black-students-on-going-to-oxbridge-its-not-even-asked-or-pushed-for-its-just-assumed-no-one-is-applying-87279 (Accessed 4 June 2020).

Rogers, C. (2019) 'Too many children with autism are let down by schools and end up in prison'. *The Conversation*. Available at: https://theconversation.com/too-many-children-with-autism-are-let-down-by-schools-and-end-up-in-prison-107376 (Accessed 26 May 2020).

Rogers, K., Hauser, C., Yuhas, A. and Haberman, M. (2020) 'Trump's suggestion that disinfectants could be used to treat coronavirus prompts aggressive pushback'. *New York Times*. 24 April. Available at: https://www.nytimes.com/2020/04/24/us/politics/trump-inject-disinfectant-bleach-coronavirus.html (Accessed 24 May 2020).

Royal College of Physicians. (2016) *Underfunded, underdoctored and overstretched: The NHS in 2016*. Available at: file:///C:/Users/tomas/AppData/Local/Packages/Microsoft.MicrosoftEdge_8wekyb3d8bbwe/TempState/Downloads/Underfunded, %20underdoctored, %20overstretched_0_0%20(1).pdf (Accessed 27 May 2020).

Saunders, P. (2010) *Social Mobility Myths*. London: Civitas.

Saunders, P. (2012) *Social Mobility Delusions: Why So Much of What Politicians Say about Social Mobility in Britain is Wrong, Misleading or Unreliable*. London: Civitas.

Savage, M., Cunningham, N., Devine, F., Friedman, S., Laurison, D., McKenzie, L., Miles, A., Snee, S. and Wakeling, P. (2015) *Social Class in the Twenty 21st Century*. London: Penguin.

See, B.H., Torgerson, C., Gorard, S., Ainsworth, H., Low, G. and Wright, K. (March 2011) 'Factors that promote high post-16 participation of some minority ethnic groups in England: A systematic review of the UK-based literature'. *Research in Post-Compulsory Education*, Vol. 16, No. 1, pp. 85–100.

Social Mobility Commission. (2016a) 'Social mobility and the professions'. Available at: https://assets.publishing.service.gov.uk/government/uploads/system/uploads/attachment_data/file/545822/The_Professions_factsheet.pdf (Accessed 23 December 2018).

Social Mobility Commission. (2016b) 'Social mobility and higher education'. Available at: https://assets.publishing.service.gov.uk/government/uploads/system/uploads/attachment_data/file/545821/Higher_Education_factsheet.pdf (Accessed 23 December 2018).

Social Mobility Commission. (2017) *State of the Nation 2017: Social mobility in Great Britain*. Available at: https://assets.publishing.service.gov.uk/government/ uploads/system/uploads/attachment_data/file/662744/State_of_the_Nation_2017_-_ Social_Mobility_in_Great_Britain.pdf (Accessed 25 March 2019).

Standing, G. (2011) *The Precariat: The New Dangerous Class*. London: Bloomsbury.

The Giving Pledge (2020) *A Commitment to Philanthropy*. Available at: https://givingpledge.org/ (Accessed 2 April 2020).

Tickle, L. (2017) '"People give up": The crisis in school support for children with special needs'. *The Guardian*. 5 September. Available at: https://www.theguardian.com/education/2017/sep/05/crisis-in-support-for-sen-children-ehc-plans (Accessed 26 May 2020).

Tomlinson, S. (2005). *Education in a Post Welfare Society*. London: Routledge.

Vasagar, J. and Stratten, A. (2010) 'Michael Gove: Academies bill needs to be rushed through to improve schools'. *The Guardian*. 19 July. Available at: https://www.theguardian.com/education/2010/jul/19/michael-gove-schools-academies-plan (Accessed 23 May 2020).

Verkaik, R. (2019) 'Public Schools claim to help the taxpayer. But they serve only the rich'. *The Guardian*. 29 April. Available at: https://www.theguardian.com/commentisfree/2019/apr/29/private-schools-help-taxpayer-rich-study-billions (Accessed 1 June 2010).

Volante, L. and Jerrim, J. (2018) 'Education does not equal social mobility'. *The Conversation*. Available at: https://theconversation.com/education-doesnot-always-equal-social-mobility-106386 (Accessed 7 February 2019).

Walford, G. (2014) 'From city technology colleges to free schools: Sponsoring new schools in England'. *Research Papers in Education*, 2014. Vol. 29, No. 3, pp. 315–329.

Walker, A. (2019) 'Two-thirds of Boris Johnson's cabinet went to private schools'. *The Guardian*. 25 July. Available at: https://www.theguardian.com/education/2019/jul/25/two-thirds-of-boris-johnsons-cabinet-went-to-private-schools (Accessed 5 June 2020).

Weal, S. and McIntyre, N. (2018) 'Thousands of children with special needs excluded from schools'. *The Guardian*. 23 October. Available at: https://www.theguardian.com/education/2018/oct/23/send-special-educational-needs-children-excluded-from-schools (Accessed 24 May 2020).

West, A. and Wolf, D. (2018) 'Academies, the school system in England and a vision for the future'. *Clare Market Papers No. 23*. Available at: http://www.lse.ac.uk/social-policy/Assets/Documents/PDF/Research-reports/Academies-Vision-Report.pdf (Accessed 23 May 2020).

Wilkinson, R. and Pickett, K. (2009) *The Spirit Level: Why More Equal Societies Almost Always Do Better*. London: Penguin.

Wilkinson, R. and Pickett, K. (2018) *The Inner Level: How More Equal Societies Reduce Stress, Restore Sanity and Improve Everyone's Well-being*. London: Allen Lane.

Wright, D. and Anderson, H. (2018) 'Unacceptable rises in child poverty as more working parents left unable to make ends meet'. *Joseph Rowntree Foundation Home/Press*. Available at: www.jrf.org.uk/press/rises-child-poverty-moreparents-left-unable-make-ends-meet (Accessed 3 June 2019).

8 Critical pedagogy and promoting social justice

Introduction

In this final chapter, there will be an examination of the ways in which the injustices and perverse logics of the current global neoliberal system, or 'hypercapitalism' (Piketty, 2020), can be challenged and addressed. The role that education can play in this project to humanise the world will be discussed, not just in terms of understanding ways in which resources of the planet can be more equitably and sustainably distributed so that all, including vulnerable, oppressed, and excluded groups, are able to live more fulfilling lives, but also as a mechanism to engage everyone in a process that recognises and acknowledges past and continuing injustices. This will be conducted in a spirit of utopian hope in which the education of desire can be nurtured and mobilised.

Utopian visions and the education of hope

It could be argued that we are entering a unique period of social, political, economic and environmental turmoil that coincides in such a way as to be highly favourable to the emergence of what Brossard (2019) refers to as a *chain* of utopian *niches*. He defines a utopian niche as an episode during which there is an upsurge in utopian activity, be it in terms of thinking, art, text or political action; a feeling or milieu arises in which change is seen not only as desirable but possible. Chains relate to the network of connections between these niches, all of which together provide an understanding of the factors leading to a growth in 'utopia production' (Brossard, 2019). Brossard gives several examples of such social conditions and events that have created utopian niches in the past, one of which is the events in Spain that took place between 1932 and 1933, during which there were attempts at large-scale agrarian reform. With the ending of the Spanish Civil War in 1939, this desire for reform endured. Despite continuing rule by the dictator General Franco until 1975, there was in parts of Spain an upsurge of experiments in agricultural and manufacturing cooperatives led and managed by workers, some of which continue to prosper today (Brossard, 2019).

A growing chain

In recent years, the growing frequency and pace of these niches and the resulting chains have, like time-lapse photography, presented a moving picture of past and continuing injustices of many contemporary so-called democratic systems: the destruction of the natural world and the warming

Case study 8.1: The Mondragon Corporation

The Mondragon Corporation founded in 1956 in the Basque region of Spain is a federation of cooperatives that is the result of ordinary workers and farmers coming together to tackle the poverty, hunger and destruction resulting from civil war. A Catholic priest, Fr Arizmendiarrieta, who moved to Mondragon in 1943, set up a technical college based on humanist principles to train local people the skills of engineering, agronomy and horticulture. These humanist principles were to be the institutional guide to the eventual setting up of enterprises based on cooperation, democracy and the sharing of profits (Mondragon S Coop, 2020). In 1956, Fr Arizmendiarrieta chose a group of five of his graduates to set up Mondragon's first enterprise, producing domestic heaters. This led to the creation of other successful cooperatives in agriculture and in the field of electronics. Mondragon Corporation is now the tenth largest company in Spain (Mondragon S Coop, 2020). As we can see, particular niches or episodes can lead to positive and humanising outcomes that benefit the community and not merely individuals who are often motivated by and seek total control and unlimited wealth for themselves. They are usually responses to particular types of social or political upheavals or injustices that lead to demands and popular mobilisations for new ways of doing things and being. What is also significant to note is the role that education, particularly its humanist foundations, has played in the development of a corporation that exists mainly for the benefit of its workers and the community. Moreover, it indicates the importance of such a humanising education for those being trained in any occupation or profession as a means of providing the appropriate moral and ethical guidelines for its practice, and it is a lesson to be acknowledged and acted upon by all educators and trainers (Arizmendiarrieta, 2016).

of the planet (National Geographic, 2020), resulting from the unregulated and uncontrolled activities of powerful and reckless international energy corporations; the plunging of millions of ordinary workers and homeowners into financial ruin during the financial and banking crisis of 2007 and 2008 due to the activities of a deregulated and greedy financial services sector; the structural racism inherent in the systems of (in)justice whereby Black people in the US are regularly killed by the police or in racially motivated attacks by white racists; and the inequalities in health that have been starkly revealed in daily news reports in the UK and the US during the Covid-19 pandemic, showing that people from minority ethnic backgrounds are more likely to contract the virus and to die from it (BMJ, 2020; Honigsbaum, 2002).

Each of these niches has led to a growth of utopia production and output that point to alternative ways of conducting politics, justice, education and environmental policy in a chain that links them together. This can be seen in the actions of youth climate activists such as Greta Thunberg (Jordans, 2020), the connections she has made between the climate crisis and the unrestrained demand for economic growth, and, more recently, in the Black Lives Matter (BLM) movement, following the death of yet another Black man at the hand of the US police in May 2020. George Floyd was suffocated to death in Minneapolis in full public view whilst in the custody of police officers. His killing sparked protests around the world against the institutional racism of the American justice system and has led to demands for new approaches to policing. George Floyd's cries of 'I can't breathe' as he lay face down on the ground with a policeman's knee on his neck, is symbolic of the way African Americans have experienced Covid-19, a disease that also chokes the life out of its victims and disproportionately affects Black people in Britain as well as the US. The Nigerian writer Ben Okri sums it up succinctly when he states: 'The pandemic itself is about the very issue of breathing. I think that it helped to strike a chord in people' (cited in Honigsbaum, 2002). Covid-19 and racism are both diseases that create injustices which demand the destruction of old systems and the construction of new ones.

Demands for 'debating overhauling, dismantling' and 'cutting funding for police departments' (Press Association, 2020) were a key feature in the establishment of the Capitol Hill Autonomous Zone (CHAZ) or Capitol Hill Organised Protest (CHOP), in Seattle on 8 June 2020, which lasted until 1st of July. Setting up a 'No Cop Co-op', the occupiers created spaces for free and open debate as well as demands for the defunding of the police department and the redirection of the money to increase investment in health, education and community services. Hardly the 'domestic terrorists' (cited in Golden, 2020) that President Trump had branded them. Beyond the sign declaring 'You are now entering Free Capitol Hill' (Golden, 2020), there were teach-ins and discussion areas on justice and the environment, art exhibitions, documentaries and points serving free water, food, hand sanitisers and face masks for the community, as well as a station providing free medical care. Moreover, there was a shrine to the memory of George Floyd which, together with their demands, provided the salient reasons for the gathering of ordinary people calling for justice and reform. These are not so much unreasonable expectations, as things one might expect from the world's wealthiest democracy that once called itself the leader of the 'free world'. As one of the protesters, Dae Shik Kim Jr., stated: 'I think what we're seeing in CHAZ is just a snippet of a reality that the people can have' (cited in Golden, 2020).

The global demand for justice

Across the globe, in countries with dark colonial pasts, such as Britain, Belgium and Australia, there have also been protests in solidarity with the BLM movement against institutional racism in America and the death of George Floyd, but there have also been attacks on the origins and symbols of white colonial power within those countries. In Belgium (Keating, 2020), thousands of protesters marched in Brussels on the eve of George Floyd's funeral, demanding the removal of the statue of King Leopold II (1885–1908) who, as the imperial ruler of the Congo, personally presided over a regime of exploitation and, during whose 44-year reign, it is estimated that ten million Africans were killed (Keating, 2020). As many as fourteen statues of the monarch are dotted around Belgium, but despite attempts by anti-racist groups to alert the nation to the way Belgium's capitalist development and prosperity was in large part the result of such ruthless colonialism, white politicians in Belgium, as in Britain, Germany and elsewhere, have been in denial of their countries' colonial legacies (Keating, 2020; Melber and Kossler, 2020). As recently as 2010, a former Belgian foreign minister, Charles Michel, called Leopold II a 'Belgian hero', describing the accusations against the monarch as 'exaggerations' (Keating, 2020).

The events in Belgium followed those in Britain, where protests in support of the BLM movement led to the toppling of a statue of Edward Colston (1636–1721), a sea merchant from Bristol who worked for the Royal Africa Company and made his fortune in the slave trade. He has been directly linked to the transportation of 84,000 Black slaves, 19,000 of whom perished on the middle passage from Africa to the Caribbean (Watts, 2020). During the Victorian period, Colston became lauded as a local hero and philanthropist, and a statue to commemorate his work was funded by public subscription and erected in 1895. However, all this was done with little if any reference to his deeds as a slave trader (Dresser, 2016). Indeed, there was very little record in the Bristol City archives of this activity, where he is presented as a trader in wine, ivory and sugar (though these commodities were also linked to slavery). There seems to have been an attempt to erase from history the role Black people played in creating the wealth of the city.

During a protest on 6 June 2020, the statue of Colston was toppled from its plinth, dragged through the streets and then dumped into the waters of the harbour, but not before a protester was pictured with their knee pressed against the neck of the prostrate effigy of Colston. This was a powerful symbolic re-enactment of the death of George Floyd that caught many by surprise and caused outrage. And this is the key point; most people in Britain are unaware of the sheer number of monuments and statues that exist around the country that 'celebrate' and 'commemorate' individuals and organisations that are, or should be, an affront to anyone who knows what they stand for. The question is, why is this the case? Why is there such ignorance on these matters? Why does the National Curriculum not teach children about such people who are still commemorated in our very communities? In Bristol and other cities such as Edinburgh, Cardiff and Manchester, there have long been campaigns by anti-racist groups for local councils, if not for the removal of such monuments, then at least to provide contextual and educational information for ordinary citizens, as well as the teaching of a history curriculum that includes the voices of the victims of colonialism (see Chapter 5). Yet despite such campaigns in Bristol and these other cities, little has been done. Instead of berating these local authorities for not acting on the legitimate concerns of many citizens and the continuing offence caused by such monuments, thereby precipitating such situations, the government attacked the protesters as vandals and of having committed a 'criminal act' (Boris Johnson, cited in BBC News, 8 June 2020). This response reveals the government's greater concern for the basic principle of upholding the law rather than of bringing about justice. It is significant that at the time the police opted for the latter by choosing not to prosecute any of the statue-topplers. Moreover, there was even a denial by ministers that any of the issues that the BLM protesters were raising had any relevance to Britain today (Mason and Siddique, 2020), a comment that clearly reveals a government and political party in denial. According to Dawn Butler, a former Labour minister and first Black woman to speak at the Dispatch Box in the House of Commons, how can such a position be held against the background of continuing discrimination and poverty amongst minority ethnic groups in Britain and the consequences of such institutional racism that has led to the Windrush scandal, the Grenfell Tower fire of 2017 and the way minority ethnic groups are disproportionately affected by the COVID-19 pandemic (Mason and Siddique, 2020)?

A pedagogy for change through action

All these events around the world, even the violent ones, though not the ideal way of learning or seeking justice (Blunt, 2019), are highly educational. They are indeed forcing the nations that have, until now, been reluctant to confront their colonial pasts and to engage in the debate about their often-concealed histories (Keating, 2020).

However, these opportunities have occurred and need to be grasped before those with an interest in preserving the existing situation manage to present, yet again, false pledges of bringing

Case study 8.2: Decolonising the curriculum: the ethics of using 'stolen' or 'looted' artefacts

The extract below is the introduction to one of the activities carried out by students of education studies at a university in the UK as part of their philosophy of education module.

Trip to the British Museum: the search for philosophers and the ethics of using 'looted' or 'stolen' treasures

The trip to the British Museum will give you the opportunity to see artefacts and displays from all over the world in one of the world's greatest museums. One thing to remember is that many of the artefacts displayed at the British Museum are the subject of much controversy in terms of how they were acquired as well as their cultural significance to the people from whom they were 'acquired'. There is a strong resistance from the trustees and administrators of museums to demands (Alberge, 2019) that these artefacts and treasures be returned to their places of origin. Probably the most famous of these treasures are the Parthenon Marbles that once formed part of the temple of the Parthenon on the Acropolis in Athens (447–432 BCE). However, just as significant in terms of Africa's cultural heritage are the Benin Bronzes (Horton, 2018) looted from the Kingdom of Benin in West Africa by the British in 1897.

We will, therefore, be looking at and using many artefacts that are the subjects of contention and dispute as to their ownership. You might like to think about the ethics of the situation. Is it 'right' for us to benefit from the use of potentially stolen cultural treasures? However, despite these disputes we are privileged as a nation to have access to some of the most superb examples of human creativity, art and intellectual endeavour ever produced: some of the first examples of human writing (Sumer, Mesopotamia 3rd Millennium BCE modern-day Iraq), some of the contents of the first ever library (Nineveh, Mesopotamia 7th C BCE), statues of famous philosophers of the Ancient world.

Nevertheless, Britain's past is often elided in the presentation, and therefore the viewing of these artefacts, particularly as the information provided in the display cases usually contains minimal and very basic descriptions. There is little sense of the moral, ethical or possible criminal nature relating to their provenance. They are often displayed purely as pieces of civilisations to be admired but not necessarily interrogated. When examining the information on the artefacts, you might like to see if there are any references to Britain's historical and colonial connections to them and how they have ended up here in central London. This lack of awareness of the problematic nature of empire seems to be an example of what Brian Kwoba refers to as Britain's imperial 'blind spot' (Kwoba cited in Rawlinson, 2016).

Points to reflect on

- Have you ever visited a museum in Britain with artefacts and treasures from other parts of the world?
- Did you ever consider how they were acquired?
- What are the moral and ethical issues this raises?
- Do any of these issues have implications for the way history is taught in English schools?

about justice. This requires concerted and coordinated campaigns to completely rethink the history curriculum, as well as a national programme for the reassessment of the display of civic statues and monuments celebrating public figures, and the information presented about them to the public. Moreover, this is a highly apposite niche in which to press for the return of artefacts looted or otherwise acquired from the civilisations conquered during empire (Horton, 2018), as well as the appropriate contextual presentation of artefacts linked to the colonial period in national and civic museums, and those attached to institutions of higher education (insightshare, 2020).

Tackling the injustice of inequality

In the concluding comments of the previous chapter it was pointed out that in order to achieve greater fairness and equality of opportunity, and to enable poorer and vulnerable children to achieve their academic potential, it is necessary to tackle the debilitating effects of the structural inequalities that affect them from birth. It is futile and unfair on schools and teachers to expect education alone to rectify these inequalities, particularly if children are attending school hungry and troubled by the effects of poverty on their lives. In Scotland, where responsibility for education rests with the Scottish government in Holyrood, rather than Westminster, there is a much more holistic approach which acknowledges the national and international evidence and recognises the need to tackle poverty and the extremes of inequality as a first step towards creating an education system that provides greater equality of opportunity and justice for all. As the Scottish government states: this 'will also require the government to work collaboratively with employers, councils, schools and universities. They all have a key role to play' (Scottish Government, 2018).

However, Conservative governments in England refuse, for ideological reasons, to accept this evidence and continue to perpetuate false hopes when promising to create an education system that meets the interests of 'ordinary working-class people' (May, 2016: 2), without first tackling the extremes of inequality and the elitist education system. The sense of hokey hope about the plight of ordinary working people's educational progress is betrayed by a general lack of interest in the effects of poverty by the government, and its pursuit of policies that actually exacerbate poverty and inequality, thereby perpetuating a divisive elitism in education. In his book *Capital and Ideology*, Thomas Piketty (2020) suggests that inequality, particularly the extreme forms it is taking around the world, is illegitimate and morally wrong, particularly in the current era of neoliberal hypercapitalism in which there are levels of inequality only last seen in the early part of the last century. Moreover, Piketty suggests that such levels of inequality are unsustainable against a background of rapid climate change and the need for a coordinated global effort to prevent planetary temperatures reaching a fatal tipping point. As Satterthwaite (2009) claims, it is not the growth in the population of the poor that is threatening the future of the planet, but the growing wealth of the few who, the richer they become, the more they pollute due to the increasingly disproportionate amount of the world's scares resources they consume. However, as Piketty (2020) suggests none of this is inevitable. Growing inequality is not something that will continue indefinitely; it is contingent on the success of competing ideologies to influence society's conceptions of justice and fairness and how different groups in society mobilise themselves to promote their positions at crucial points in time. It could be argued that at present we are at what Piketty calls another potential 'switch point' at which alternative pathways to more just types of societies can be followed (Piketty, 2020). This position is based on the extensive research Piketty has conducted on systems of inequality, or *inequality regimes*, globally over the past millennium. What he found is that there has been a tendency over time for the 'reduction of inequality' (Piketty, 2020: 7) and from this has emerged some of our most prised institutions and practices that have enhanced humanity as a whole. These include the principle and institutionalisation of universal suffrage, the key elements of a welfare society where progressive taxation, universal health insurance and free public education have served to improve the quality of life for all in those societies where they have been established. Piketty identifies wider access to education, in particular, as playing a vital role in economic prosperity and social well-being of all citizens and not merely the elite.

The great transformation

The period 1914–1945 is what Piketty (2020: 417) refers to as the '*Great Transformation* of attitudes' towards conventional capitalist property relations, the market and wealth. It was a time when most of the major nation-states of Europe – Germany, France and the UK – whose propertied classes were accumulating unimaginable levels of property and capital through their acquisition of foreign assets facilitated by colonialism, 'boasted of portfolio assets unequalled to this day' (Piketty, 2020: 416). However, within little more than three decades the colonial empires of powerful European nation-states were being dismantled in the wake of the Second World War. The term *The Great Transformation* is taken from the book of the same name by Karl Polanyi (1944), the Hungarian economist who claimed that in early-twentieth-century Europe there was a growing doubt in the ability of free market liberal capitalism to regulate itself sufficiently to prevent a breakdown in relations between the great powers of Europe and thereby avoid major conflict. This scepticism was clearly justified as witnessed in the terrible events of the two world wars. Nor was liberal market capitalism seen as capable of delivering the kinds of benefits and 'maximum happiness' for all members of society that had been promised (Werner, 2005: 3) (see Chapter 4). Indeed, the First World War, the Bolshevik Revolution of 1917 and the Great Depression of the 1930s were clear warning signs of the instability of the system. What Polanyi (1944) identifies so convincingly is the realisation by many European states of the need to 'socially embed' market capitalism. He believed in the possibility of achieving democratic socialism, as distinct from oppressive Soviet-style socialism, by introducing state systems for the control of the excesses and instability of the market economy. Moreover, Polanyi (1944) pointed to the clear failure of the free market to regulate itself with regard to the infinite demand for land and natural resources and their finite quantities, or scarcity, making it even more imperative to socially embed capitalism. This is what led many European nation-states to experiment with new forms of social democracy in the inter-war period, particularly in Germany and Sweden, that involved such measures as highly progressive taxes on wealth and income as well as new ways of power sharing and co-management of enterprises (Piketty, 2020), all of which led to higher wages and standards of living for working people, including their access to education. It would seem that Piketty's approach to the problem of inequality is very much influenced by Polanyi's thesis in *The Great Transformation* regarding the persistent political and ideological struggle on the one hand to socially embed the market and, on the other hand, the forces of economic liberalism seeking to spread and expand the role of the market in new areas such as education, health and welfare, as we are experiencing today. Piketty fully endorses Polanyi's claim that nothing is inevitable. We have choices and there are alternatives to the current regimes of inequality.

A time of opportunity and hope

Nevertheless, in the last century, competition between the major European powers, spurred on by nationalism, led to the Second World War, resulting in a huge loss of life and their almost total destruction. From this post-war devastation new social democratic and welfare societies arose led by governments committed to greater equality and social justice. By 1945, the world was dominated by the ideological and political conflict between Soviet-style communism in Russia and Eastern Europe and Western-style social democracy. In the former, private property virtually ceased to exist, creating highly egalitarian but very oppressive regimes. In the latter, inequality was radically reduced through a combination of nationalisation of key industries and national assets, highly progressive taxation on income and property and free public education. From the late 1940s onwards, starting with India, which gained its independence from Britain in 1947, the process of decolonisation began, though it was one that was in many cases forced on the colonial powers (Siddique, 2020). In this 'golden age of social democracy' as Piketty (2020: 487) calls it: 'Income equality settled at a level noticeably lower than in previous decades in the United States and the United Kingdom, France and Germany, Sweden and Japan, and nearly every European and non-European country for which adequate data are available' (Piketty, 2020:487).

A new Jerusalem

It is hard to comprehend the significance of the Labour Party's victory in Britain after the war ended in 1945. It was to be a 'New Jerusalem' – in other words, a new promised land created by a democratically elected government with a programme dedicated to the care of its people from 'cradle to grave'. For those who had not experienced access to a properly organised and funded healthcare system, free education from primary to university level, and sickness benefits, all paid for through national insurance and a progressive taxation system, it seemed like a utopian dream come true. The Beveridge Report of 1942 captured the spirit of the times stating, this 'revolutionary moment in the world's history is a time for revolutions, not for patching' (The Beveridge Report, 1942: 6).

What was the alternative? Winston Churchill's Conservative Party had little to offer the returning soldiers after the war, but more of the same inequality and deprivation that existed antebellum. Not only had the country been devastated by the bombing, there was also the huge class divide in terms of education as well as the squalor caused by poor housing and the massive health divide that was a product of these poor living conditions and the lack of a proper health service. Clearly, a welfare state would not be free but, instead, based on the idea that everyone received what they needed and that the fortunate members of society, those who had received a free higher education and therefore greater occupational rewards, including higher pay, would probably put more into the system than they received. This is a sound and fair principle that all would benefit from. However, the system soon came under threat, particularly by those privileged enough not to have to be concerned about the consequences of poverty on their lives and who derisively described this welfare society as 'the nanny state' (Macleod, 1965). However, this denigration of arguably one of the greatest achievements of human civilisation was part of an ideological assault on those who sought social and economic justice by those who enjoyed access to a privileged education and wished to restore their rights to unlimited property and wealth accumulation and who, ironically, were the ones most likely to have had nannies. By conflating a rather overcautious approach to life with a caring and humane social philosophy that aims to provide for the welfare and care of all citizens, politicians such as Margaret Thatcher and her predominantly privileged colleagues in the Conservative Party have been able to trivialise and condemn the welfare state as wasteful and unnecessary and also to conveniently and inappropriately link it to the oppressive Soviet system. It is part of the ideological attempt to re-embed market capitalism which predominantly Conservative-led governments seem to have been achieving since the 1980s, having been victorious in eight of the eleven general elections between 1979 and 2019.

An unfinished process

The problem remains, then, that economic liberalism has not died, as Polanyi had claimed, because the aims of social democracy remain unfinished. Despite the trend towards greater equality, Piketty (2020) points to a continuous battle against regressive ideologies that challenge the benefits and justice of greater equality by constantly invoking the need of society and the economy for a super-wealthy and enterprising elite, claiming that without them there would be no innovation or economic growth. It is significant that, according to Piketty, at a time of hypercapitalism in which there has been a huge rise in inequality since 1980, we have actually experienced a decline in rates of economic growth. Nevertheless, politicians such as Boris Johnson (2013) continue to 'naturalise' inequality, claiming that to curb the 'rights' of the rich to accumulate limitless wealth would be damaging to us all. This battle of ideologies is constantly being fought using ideas that create doubt and uncertainty amongst those who experience disadvantage of the need for change. And, of course, it is the people who control the main sources of mass communication who are able to more effectively promote their ideas and demonise their critics. We can identify many examples from the past and present, in which those with power and privilege mount a defence of the indefensible. This can be seen in Europe and the US in the eighteenth and nineteenth centuries when slave owners argued that ending slavery would infringe their property rights and lead to social and political instability and who were, moreover, eventually compensated financially for the ending of this 'right' to own other human beings (Piketty, 2020). Such was the ideology that 'sacralized' private property and the rights of slave owners. It is also revealed in what Piketty calls the appeal to *nativism*, so prevalent in the right-wing press, which plays on the threat of foreigners as well as a nostalgia for the past 'glories' of empire, with its domination of other peoples and their lands, thereby providing further evidence that the process of decolonisation has not been completed (see Chapter 5).

The historical evidence, as revealed by Thomas Piketty (2020) is, therefore, a cause for optimism, given the historical tendency towards greater equality in wealth and income distribution and that, moreover, the more widely wealth and education are distributed in a society, the more everyone benefits. Nevertheless, as Piketty points out (2020: 41), 'ideologies count', and this is shown by historical data as well as events which also reveal that during periods when regimes of inequality have been seriously challenged, unless the disadvantaged groups can be convinced of the need and possibility of reform, such as through the ballot box and a united mass social movements, it is very difficult to achieve progress in terms of the sustained reduction and permanent elimination of the extreme levels of inequality. Moreover, there has, until recently, been a persistent reluctance by the political establishment as well as charitable trusts that fund universities (Shankleman, 2020), and wealthy corporations, whose assets were built on proceeds of slavery (Faulconbridge and Holton,

2020), to confront the legacy of colonialism, racial discrimination and structural racism in countries such as Britain and the US. In most theories of 'development' looked at so far, the focus has been on poorer countries and how to make them more like the developed ones in the geographical North. What is actually needed is for these affluent Northern nations to change and develop in more humane and socially responsible ways, and to face their obligations, not only to their own citizens but also to the peoples of other countries in the South whose lives are still being adversely impacted by the long-term consequences of colonialism.

We have, arguably, reached a point at which the key elements of the neoliberal inequality regime and the legacy of colonialism are once again being seriously challenged. Groups of citizens around the world, both Black and white, have been galvanised into action by the unequal impact of the COVID-19 pandemic, racist police and justice systems, the consequences of unregulated economic and industrial activity on the planet, and the growing levels of inequality within and between nations (Wilkinson and Pickett, 2009, 2018; Piketty, 2020).

Education, education...

The evidence suggests that increasing access to and investment in education is one of the keys to bringing about greater social and economic progress as well as justice: 'History shows that economic development and human progress depend on education and not on the sacralisation of inequality, property and stability' (Piketty, 2020: 546). A particularly glaring issue in hypercapitalism however relates to the 'meritocratic myth' (Piketty: 712) which has been examined already. Piketty's most recent research reveals the unequal nature of educational investment. What we find in most countries is that children hailing from the working class and the middle class do not receive the same levels of spending on their education as the children of upper classes and the elite. This is particularly evident in those countries with high levels of inequality such as the US, the UK and France and the highly divided countries of the South and Middle East (Piketty, 2020).

An important step forward in increasing social justice and enhancing democracy in all societies would be the right of every child to the same educational funding. However, this needs to be done in conjunction with a reduction in the wider inequalities in society given that, as we have seen, education on its own cannot make up for the effects of such differences, but it helps if the school system does not add to the problems children experience in their home and family lives (Wilkinson and Pickett, 2018).

Constitutional safeguards

This can only be achieved if certain fundamental rights are guaranteed by the constitution and cannot be abrogated on the whim of a political party that commands a majority in the legislature and seeks to take advantage of the electorally and politically most vulnerable groups in society. There are some issues so morally compelling and urgent that they transcend political ideology and electoral mandates and should be subject to constitutional safeguards. In Britain, as we have seen, the last Labour government (1997–2010) enshrined in law a pledge to eliminate child poverty by 2020 under the Child Poverty Act 2010. This would have enabled all children to grow up and live in a society that protects them from the consequences of poverty and austerity. However, the current nature of the British constitution prevents any parliament from binding a future parliament:

'no Parliament can pass laws that future Parliaments cannot change. Parliamentary sovereignty is the most important part of the UK constitution' (Parliament UK, 2020). This may seem like an effective constitutional and democratic safeguard against arbitrary government decisions or legislation that is clearly outdated. However, it has enabled Conservative-led governments to abolish the Child Poverty Act of 2010, thereby removing its responsibilities to the nation's poorest and most vulnerable children. In the current political climate and the impact of Covid-19, there is an urgent need to protect such groups, including the extremely vulnerable (Hoskins and Finch, 2020), and also for all children to be treated equally or, in the case of the extremely vulnerable, in terms of their specific needs in relation to social and educational funding.

In Britain, this is particularly problematic given the impact of austerity, evidence of government manipulation of data relating to education funding (Coughlan, 2018; UKSA, 2019), the autonomy of academies in terms of admission and exclusion policies (see Chapter 7) and also the government's actions promoting an elitist education system by giving independent schools the right to operate in the quasi-market in education alongside state schools. There is a clear contradiction here in terms of the British government's stated aim of being committed to a meritocratic system in which all children have equal opportunities (May, 2016) and a belief in the right of wealthier parents to educate their children separately from the rest of the school population at exclusive private institutions (Kynaston and Kynaston, 2015). This issue is extensively documented by Piketty (2020), who found that even in France where the education system is notionally public, schools in poorer districts receive less funding and are more poorly resourced than schools in affluent ones. Moreover, there are also private primary and middle schools as well as *lycées* that not only benefit from public funding but also from preferential tax status. It is also the case that they have the right to admit children according to their own selection criteria. Such access to an exclusive private education provides the more affluent parents and the elite with a clear advantage over the rest of the population (Piketty, 2020).

Ancient does not mean benevolent

In Britain, there still seems to be a good deal of support for a system based on a tradition that includes some of the most ancient educational institutions in the country, such as Eton, Harrow and Winchester School (ComRes, 2019). Robert Verkaik (2018) points to this strange allure public schools hold over the British public. Just as we have seen with regard to the monarchy and the empire, there seems to be a perverse logic at work here. These ancient institutions attract a high level of support, despite the unwarranted privilege and elitism they represent, and the fact that the vast majority of the population have no prospect of being able to send their children to such schools. This is particularly significant given that the most ancient and prestigious 'public schools' were originally set up for the benefit of the children of the less well-off (Verkaik, 2018). In the 2019 UK general election, Labour's proposal to integrate independent schools into the state sector was therefore a vote loser (Weal, 2019). Nevertheless, there is certainly the need for a national debate on the issue, given that a disproportionate number of pupils from the independent sector end up in the most prestigious universities and the highest paid jobs (Savage et al., 2015).

The labour economist, Francis Green (2019), has suggested just such a national debate is necessary in Britain. Given that most of us have very little knowledge or experience of how the independent education sector works, we are unlikely to have well-informed opinions about such schools and, despite the fact that not all schools in the sector are as exclusive as Eton or Harrow, it is nonetheless a rarefied world that involves only 7 per cent of the school population and their parents with whom very few of us are likely to have any meaningful contact. As with all highly contested and controversial issues, a certain level of knowledge and understanding is essential. Once again, it can be argued that education is a key factor; a critical understanding of the issues is one of the most effective ways of establishing justice regarding an ancient system that allows a small percentage of exclusive fee-paying schools to help perpetuate extreme class inequalities in Britain and other countries around the world.

A just and inclusive curriculum

However, it is not just the right of every child to equal funding for their education and access to a fair and non-exclusionary system of education that are imperative. What is also important is the kind of education and curriculum they experience. If, as already suggested, the education of our children is a sacred process, then it should be carried out in the spirit of sanctity that it deserves. The notion of education as a sacred thing is neither extravagant nor overstated. It is one of the foundations upon which our relationship with our children is based and in which they are expected to place their trust in adults to help prepare them for their future lives and to become responsible, reflective and ethical beings, not just future workers. This was certainly advocated by Bertrand Russell, one of Britain's most respected philosophers (Park, 2013).

Moreover, if any system of education is to have credibility it must honestly and fairly represent a nation's past, and it must also do so in a manner that is not tendentious or one-sided to the exclusion of weaker and less powerful groups in society. All children from all backgrounds and cultures that are part of a nation's growth and development should be included in that story. Any attempt by the state to conceal inconvenient truths, silence voices or otherwise manipulate the narrative is clearly betraying its young people.

Yet this is what is happening in England, where Michael Gove has introduced a curriculum to 'celebrate the distinguished role of these islands in the history of the world' presenting it as 'a beacon of liberty for others to emulate' (Gove, cited in Higgins, 2011). In doing so, he took the focus away from Britain's multicultural past and present, as well as a more critical and reflective approach to Britain's historical role in the world. Such a curriculum, instead, promotes a one-dimensional and mythical white image of the nation and its achievements implying that this island's story is primarily one of white British people bringing civilisation and liberty to the world. Although Gove made some concessions to those who described his curriculum as entering the realms of 'propaganda' (Higgins, 2011) by allowing the optional study of Black history, it is still the case that most children are unaware of the role of Black and Asian people on these islands over many centuries (Olusoga, 2017). According to the evidence, only '11% of GCSE students are studying modules that refer to black people's contribution to Britain' (Leach et al., 2020).

Recent events such as the #rhodesmustfall campaign, and the brutal murder of George Floyd in the US in May 2020, which led to widespread support for the BLM movement around the world, have pushed this issue once more on to the political and educational agenda. In England, hundreds of thousands have signed petitions calling for a reform of the National Curriculum to include the stories of Black people in Britain and the Empire, as well as their contribution to British culture (Lock, 2020, Change.org, 2021) and children around the UK are requesting a change to the curriculum by making colonialism and Black history integral parts of their studies (Banner, 2020; Sutter, 2020).

Youth activism and pedagogy through activism

Such requests, as we saw in Chapter 3, are part of a growing activism among young people whose traditional status as passive actors in a political system which has excluded them from important decisions that affect them and their future is being challenged on a variety of issues such as the climate crisis, racism and gun control (Hudson, 2018; Shear, 2018). This activism reveals a growing awareness and frustration amongst children and young people over the way that so-called responsible adults are proving incapable of dealing with some of the most pressing issues that face humanity.

The evidence seems to show that in former colonial powers such as Britain, young people are becoming increasingly aware of their need and, indeed, their right to know more about the diverse peoples and cultures that helped to create their society and what it is today. Their seeming awareness of the problem with imposed 'national histories' is leading some to challenge the cultural literacy approach of E. D. Hirsch adopted by Michael Gove (see Chapter 3). They can see how we have become stuck in the cultural literacy trap. The nation's history has been appropriated by the self-appointed keepers of the way we should see the past, and it is one that seems to suit their ideological purposes by adhering to a heroic and self-justificatory narrative on the issue of Empire. There are indeed things to celebrate, particularly how Britain stood up against the Nazi threat in 1939, as well as its involvement in the development of democratic institutions, but there are also wrongs that need to be understood and acknowledged, not just for the historical record but also for potential acts of restitution (Hirsch, 2020).

History is not a once-and-for-all account of the past. It is a living and developing story which not only challenges and questions existing hegemonic views but must also be open to new knowledge and evidence that have hitherto been either unavailable or ignored (Olusoga, 2017). This is precisely the issue with the existing English History National Curriculum; it is preventing children from developing the very skills that any good historian should be acquiring. Indeed, there seems to be a clear contradiction in the government's position on this as well as those who criticise attempts to examine the historical evidence relating to eminent and respected British figures and institutions and their links to colonialism. In the case of Cambridge University's inquiry to find out whether the university and its libraries or museums benefited in any way from the Atlantic slave trade (Cambridge University, 2019), the *Daily Mail* journalist and historian Dominic Sandbrook, seems more concerned about the potential impact of this inquiry on the reputation of his alma mater than the need for us to examine the evidence and to gain a better understanding of the university's *history*, when he opines: 'For good and ill – generally good – our history happened, and *there's no point* apologising for or *trying to rewrite it*' (Sandbrook, 2019) (emphasis added). It is as if such an inquiry does not constitute history, that we do not need to know any more about the university and that history does not need to be reassessed or even *rewritten* in the light of new evidence and information. If this is the case, how are we to develop an authentic and honest appraisal of British society and examine ways 'to address its impact' (Cambridge University, 2019)? Should historians and scholars shy away from studying the history of powerful or influential individuals and institutions that may produce inconvenient truths?

The honourable thing to do

Most nations are keen to see themselves in a positive light (Goodman, 2017). Britain, as we saw in Chapter 5, having been one of the most powerful nations on earth in the form of the British

Empire, still has a self-image of being exceptional in terms of exerting a benign influence on the world through its values of being honourable and having a sense of fairness and justice (Treadell, 2019). Indeed, the guardians of British identity and the constitution officially present their politicians as representatives of *all* the people with Members of Parliament designated as 'Honourable' or 'Right Honourable' member. Many venerable British institutions, be they business, cultural or financial, which also contain such prefixes as 'honourable' or 'worshipful' in their official titles, have either direct or indirect connections with the colonial period and slavery (Reclaim EC1, 2020). If such designations are to be more than just titles and to have any real meaning, then these institutions and our political leaders also need to *act* honourably. Only in this way is Britain's reputation and standing in the world likely to be warranted, particularly amongst its former colonies. This would include such policies as introducing an inclusive curriculum that is truly representative of all those who had a part to play in the nation's past; a programme for the repatriation of stolen and looted cultural treasures and artefacts; the development of programmes and public debates in collaboration with former colonies to identify the most appropriate ways to provide restitution for the damage caused by colonialism; further inquiries by universities and cultural institutions, such as that being carried out by Cambridge University, to know and understand more clearly whether they have benefitted from slavery and, if so, to find positive ways of working together with the peoples of those societies to achieve justice and redress. If this is done in good will and in a spirit of reconciliation, rather than retribution, all parties are likely to benefit.

In France, such issues are already being publicly discussed, and action is being taken to collaborate with its former colonies to 'see the conditions put in place so as to allow for the temporary or definitive restitution of African cultural heritage to Africa' (Macron, cited in Nayeri, 2018). A report on the issue was commissioned by Emmanuel Macron, the French president, and published in 2018 (Sarr and Savoy, 2018). Its recommendations, based on discussions with representative of four African countries – Mali, Senegal, Benin and Cameroon –who were invited to meet with French government officials, museum directors and art specialists, suggests a formal framework for the return of artefacts and treasures to these countries. The outcome of negotiations over these artefacts are likely to be drawn out and controversial, not just in France, but within the African countries involved (Price, 2020). However, the change in the French state's position on the future of such looted treasure is a cause for hope among these African states. Thomas Piketty (2020) also raises the issue of restitution by France to her former colonies in the form of financial compensation for the effects of colonialism and slavery, stating the 'argument that all this is ancient history cannot withstand scrutiny' (Piketty, 2020: 226), given that the former French colony of Haiti was forced by the French state to pay crippling compensation *to* French slave owners as the price for the emancipation of its slaves in 1825, a debt that was only finally paid off in 1950. Moreover, the victims of Nazi persecution during the Second World War are still to this day being paid by Germany and allied regimes such as Vichy France, US compensation paid to Japanese Americans detained and interned during the War was only agreed in 1988, and compensation is being paid by the former Communist regimes to citizens of Eastern Europe for the expropriations they experienced after 1945. It seems, Piketty (2020) suggests, that there is a degree of 'ethno-racial' discrimination at work in relation to decisions regarding which victims of international crimes and other form oppression are worthy of compensation. The issue is not likely to go away and will no doubt escalate given the growing pressure from a number of French groups that are demanding justice in regard to this matter. In any case, Piketty suggests that the French state should be involved in the setting up of national and regional museums, exhibitions and educational programmes given that, even now, there is 'no museum of slavery worthy of the name in France' (Piketty, 2020: 227). As previously noted, such acts, though inexpensive when compared to the cost of a full programme of compensation, would yield great pedagogical as well as reputational benefits.

Conclusion

Every age brings with it 'wicked problems' (Rittel and Webber, 1973) that relate to issues of policy and equity in relation to such things as housing provision and homelessness, dealing with growing levels of inequality, the provision of welfare and care for the elderly and vulnerable, environmental policy, or how to teach a nation's history to its children. These are highly contested areas that are often settled in each country by democratically elected governments. However, some of the problems we face today are so overwhelming and intractable that they pose a threat to all of us on the planet and require urgent international cooperation and action if humanity is to avoid global catastrophe. These include the threat of global pandemics such as Covid-19, global warming, the renewed proliferation of nuclear weapons and a global water shortage. Levin et al. (2012) refer to these as *super wicked problems* and, despite their significance and the magnitude of their threat, those who are responsible for solving them seem either reluctant or incapable of doing so. This is primarily because the people and organisations that were responsible for causing the problem in the first place are usually the ones that are also responsible for finding the solutions, and their particular interests usually conflict with the sorts of policies that are needed to act in the interests of all and not just a powerful minority.

It is suggested by some geographers and geologists that we are now in an era they refer to as the 'Anthropocene'. This can be defined as a geological period which is so dominated by human behaviour, such as the production of carbon dioxide and plastic waste, that evidence of this will be found in rock deposits and sediments millions of years in the future (Maslin and Lewis, 2020). More pressingly, the consequences of this human behaviour, constitute a threat to humanity here and now. Potentially, the most devastating consequences are global warming to a point that may result in another 'mass extinction' which could include the human race. Research by Lewis and Maslin (2015) suggests that although humans have from their evolutionary origins had an impact on the planet, it was not until the advent of capitalism, which took off so spectacularly during the fifteenth and sixteenth centuries in Europe, that this impact has been so globally significant. It led to a period characterised by rapacious invasions of the Americas, Africa and Asia by Europeans that involved the destruction of ancient civilisations and their collective knowledge and wisdom, in a desire for treasure, land and natural resources. Added to this, the introduction of disease and the imposition of a system of slavery based on an ideology of racism that remains alive today in the beliefs and institutions of the former colonial nations. The result was a system that became devoted to the single-minded exploitation of conquered peoples and the planet for profit which disproportionately benefits the rich and powerful of the colonial nations, even after decolonisation. With the temporary but ultimately failed attempt by communist dictators during the twentieth century to impose a global egalitarian system, neoliberalism has now gained almost complete freedom to exploit millions of landless and powerless human beings, as well as the planet further, with its ideology of the self-regulating market that was supposed to create a better world for all.

What is clear is that neoliberal hypercapitalism is unfit to deal with these problems, making it essential to challenge this ruthless system. Its continued expansion can only mean greater hardship for ordinary people and inflict even greater damage to the planet. Through movements motivated by social and economic justice and dedicated to change the world, particularly those led by young people from all nations and backgrounds, be it in terms of developing new ways of thinking in relation to the economy (Rethinking Economics, The Post-Crash Economics Society, coreecon), the environment (Zero Hour, Youth Strike 4 Climate), social and educational justice (Advocacy Academy), anti-racism (Black Lives Matter) or human rights (Amnesty International National Youth and Student Program), young people seem to be uniquely placed to think beyond existing ways of doing things and of planning for their future. They need to be much more involved in this process with both their teachers and politicians, rather than being subjected to a banking system of education which is failing us all. Under the UN Convention of the Rights of the Child, Articles 12 and 15, children and young people have the right to be heard and their views to be taken into consideration on issues that affect them and their future. Moreover, they also have the right to peaceful association and assembly (Lansdown, 2011) as part of this process, and our political leaders must respect these rights. Children and young people need to be at the centre of the political, social, economic, educational and environmental agenda, and, through dialogue, they should be able to both help *define* the problems in the world they will inherit and to *contribute* to their solution.

Points for consideration and reflection in this chapter

In this chapter, it has been suggested that we are entering a global period of social, political, economic and environmental disorder, precipitated by the effects of neoliberalism which has pushed to the limits the ability of humanity and the planet to endure the levels of exploitation they are experiencing. This ideology, that promotes unbounded possessive individualism and which benefits primarily the very wealthy who consume hugely disproportionate levels of the world's resources, is totally unsuited to the current needs of humanity. This is a period, then, that can be viewed as providing opportunities to develop new ways of being and doing such things as education, producing food and energy, as well as creating a more just and fairer world in terms of the distribution of these scarce resources. In identifying these new ways, there should be a preferential option for the young, who will be the inheritors of the world of the future, and also of vulnerable groups such as those with disabilities, the elderly and the poor.

- What is your view of the claim that we are entering a new global and geological era which requires new ways of thinking and acting in relation to politics, economics, welfare and the environment?
- Do you think a nation's story as taught to its children in school should be primarily a celebration of the nation rather than a historical record that not only takes account of diverse sources and views but should also be reassessed and perhaps even rewritten in the light of new evidence and knowledge?

References

Alberge, D. (2019) 'British Museum is world's largest receiver of stolen goods, says QC'. *The Guardian*. 4 November. Available at: https://www.theguardian.com/world/2019/nov/04/british-museum-is-worlds-largest-receiver-of-stolen-goods-says-qc (Accessed 20 July 2020).

Arizmendiarrieta, J.M. (2016) *A letter from Mondragon*. Available at: https://static1.squarespace.com/static/58292a54cd0f681af51bccd1/t/586f0c3f5016e17f5f528c57/1483672644724/Armi%CC%81n_Isa%CC%81sti-A_Ltr_from_Mondragon.pdf (Accessed 28 July 2020).

Banner, G. (2020) 'More than 1,300 in county sign petition to put colonialism on curriculum' *Shropshire Star*. 22 June. Available at: https://www.shropshirestar.com/news/local-hubs/shrewsbury/2020/06/20/more-than-1300-in-county-sign-petition-to-put-colonialism-on-curriculum/ (Accessed 21 June 2020).

Beveridge, W. (1942) *Beveridge Report on Social Insurance and Allied Services*. London: His Majesty's Stationery Office.

Blunt, G.D. (2019) *Global Poverty, Inequality and Injustice*. Cambridge: Cambridge University Press.

Brossard, B. (2019) 'Elements for a Theory of Utopia Production'. *Utopian Studies*, Vol. 30, No. 3, pp. 422–443.

Cambridge University. (2019) 'Cambridge University launches inquiry into historical links to slavery'. *News*, 30 April. Available at: https://www.cam.ac.uk/news/cambridge-university-launches-inquiry-into-historical-links-to-slavery (Accessed 29 July 2020).

Change.org. (2021) 'Make Black British History Compulsory in Schools'. Petition. Available at: https://www.change.org/p/secretary-of-state-for-education-make-black-british-history-compulsory-in-schools-8e94c175-6e3d-47d7-adce-c789bd4c909d (Accessed 18 April 2021).

ComRes. (2019) 'Independent Schools Council – GB Omnibus: A survey of GB adults about attitudes to independent schools'. *Savanta:ComRes*. Available at: https://comresglobal.com/polls/independent-schools-council-gb-omnibus/ (Accessed 7 July 2020).

Coughlan, S. (2018) 'School funding "exaggerated" by ministers, says watchdog'. *BBC News* 8 October. Available at: https://www.bbc.co.uk/news/education-45784644 (Accessed 27 May 2020).

Dresser, M. (2016) *Slavery Obscured: The Social History of the Slave Trade in an English Provincial Port*. London: Bloomsbury.

Faulconbridge, G. and Holton, K. (2020) 'Update: Lloyd's of London apologizes for its "shameful" role in Atlantic Slave Trade'. *Insurance Journal*. 18 June. Available at: https://www.insurancejournal.com/news/international/2020/06/18/572696.htm (Accessed 8 July 2020).

Green, F. (2019) 'Why Britain's private schools are such a social problem'. *The Conversation*. Available at: http://theconversation.com/why-britains-privateschools-are-such-a-social-problem-111369 (Accessed 17 April 2019).

Golden, H. (2020) 'Seattle protesters take over city blocks to create police-free "autonomous zone"'. *The Guardian*. 12 June. Available at: https://www.theguardian.com/us-news/2020/jun/11/chaz-seattle-autonomous-zone-police-protest (Accessed 9 July 2020).

Goodman, M. (2017) 'The Myth of American Exceptionalism'. *Counterpunch*. 27 July. Available at: https://www.counterpunch.org/2017/07/27/the-myth-of-american-exceptionalism/ (Accessed 1 April 2020).

Higgins, C. (2011) 'Historians say Michael Gove risks turning history lessons into propaganda classes'. *The Guardian*. 17 August. Available at: https://www.theguardian.com/politics/2011/aug/17/academics-reject-gove-history-lessons (Accessed 5 July 2020).

Hirsch, A. (2020) 'The case for British slavery reparations can no longer be brushed aside'. *The Guardian*. 9 July. Available at: https://www.theguardian.com/commentisfree/2020/jul/09/british-slavery-reparations-economy-compensation (Accessed 27 July 2020).

Honigsbaum, M. (2002) 'Epidemics have often led to discrimination against minorities – this time is no different'. *The Conversation*. Available at: https://theconversation.com/epidemics-have-often-led-to-discrimination-against-minorities-this-time-is-no-different-140189 (Accessed 10 June 2020).

Horton, M. (2018) 'Returning looted artefacts will finally restore heritage to the brilliant cultures that made them'. *The Conversation*. Available at: https://theconversation.com/returning-looted-artefacts-will-finally-restore-heritage-to-the-brilliant-cultures-that-made-them-107479 (Accessed 8 July 2020).

Hoskins, J. and Finch, J. (2020) 'How disabled people have been completely disregarded during the coronavirus pandemic'. *The Conversation*. 21 July. Available at: https://theconversation.com/how-disabled-people-have-been-completely-disregarded-during-the-coronavirus-pandemic-142766 (Accessed 1 August 2020).

Hudson, M. (2018) 'Is the "Zero Hour" youth climate march a turning point, or more of the same?' *The Conversation*. Available at: https://theconversation.com/isthe-zero-hour-youth-climate-march-a-turning-point-or-more-of-the-same-100173 (Accessed 23 March 2020).

Iacobucci, G. (2020) 'Covid-19: Review of ethnic disparities is labelled "whitewash" for lack of recommendations'. *BMJ* 3 June 2020. Available at: https://www.bmj.com/content/369/bmj.m2208 (Accessed 9 June 2020).

insightshare (2020) 'Realigning the narratives'. *insightshare*. Available at: https://insightshare.org/maasai/ (Accessed 8 July 2020).

Johnson, B. (2013) 'Boris Johnson: 3rd Margaret Thatcher Lecture (FULL)'. Available at: www.youtube.com/watch?v=Dzlgrnr1ZB0 (Accessed 15 December 2019).

Jordans, F. (2020) 'Thunberg has hope for climate, despite leaders' inaction'. *Associated Press*. 19 June. Available at: https://abcnews.go.com/International/wireStory/thunberg-hope-climate-leaders-inaction-71358741 Accesses on 19 June 2020).

Keating, D. (2020) 'How Belgium is being forced to confront the bloody legacy of King Leopold II'. *New Statesman*. 9 June. Available at: https://www.newstatesman.com/world/europe/2020/06/belgium-king-leopold-congo-statue-atrocities-belgian-colonialism (Accessed 10 June 2020).

Kynaston, D. and Kynaston, G. (2015) 'Education's Berlin Wall: Does a better social mix make these schools acceptable? The Left has been silent on these issues for 40 years'. *New Statesman*, 3 February 2014. Available at: www.newstatesman.com/2014/01/education-private-schools-berlin-wall (Accessed 21 November 2019).

Lansdown, G. (2011) *Every Child's Right to Be Heard: A Resource Guide on the Un Committee on the Rights of the Child General Comment No.12*. London: UNICEF/Save the Children.

Leach, A., Voce, A. and Kirk, A. (2020) 'Black British history: the row over the school curriculum in England' *The Guardian* 13 July. Available at: Black British history: the row over the school curriculum in England | Education | *The Guardian* (Accessed 3 April 2020).

Levin, K., Cashore, B., Bernstein, S. and Auld, G. (2012) 'Overcoming the Tragedy of Super Wicked Problems: Constraining Our Future Selves to Ameliorate Global Climate Change'. *Policy Sciences*. Vol. 45, No. 2, pp. 123–152.

Lewis, S.L. and Maslin, M.A. (2015) 'Defining the Anthropocene'. *Nature*. Vol. 519, pp. 171–180.

Lock, H. (2020) 'Hundreds of Thousands of Brits Sign Petitions to Get Black British History Taught in School'. *Global Citizen*. Available at: https://www.globalcitizen.org/en/content/black-curriculum-education-race-equality-uk/ (Accessed on 12 April 2020).

Maslin, M.A. and Lewis, S.L. (2020) 'Why the Anthropocene began with European colonisation, mass slavery and the "great dying" of the 16th century'. *The Conversation*. Available at: https://theconversation.com/why-the-anthropocene-began-with-european-colonisation-mass-slavery-and-the-great-dying-of-the-16th-century-140661 (Accessed 2 August 2020).

Mason, R. and Siddique, H. (2020) 'Ministers face backlash after claiming Britain is not racist'. *BBC News*. 7 June. Available at: https://www.theguardian.com/us-news/2020/jun/07/ministers-face-backlash-over-suggestions-that-britain-is-not-racist (Accessed 10 June 2020).

Macleod, I. (1965) '70-mph'. *The Spectator*. 3 December. Available at: http://archive.spectator.co.uk/article/3rd-december-1965/11/70-mph

Melber, H. and Kossler, R. (2020) 'Colonial amnesia and Germany's efforts to achieve "internal liberation"'. *The Conversation*. Available at: https://theconversation.com/colonial-amnesia-and-germanys-efforts-to-achieve-internal-liberation-138840 (Accessed 10 June 2020).

Mondragon S Coop. (2020) *About US*. Available at: https://www.mondragon-corporation.com/en/about-us/ (Accessed 9 June 2020).

National Geographic. (2020) 'Flood, drought, and climate change photos'. *National Geographic*. Available at: https://www.nationalgeographic.com/environment/photos/climate-change/ (Accessed 19 June 2020).

Nayeri, F. (2018) 'Museums in France should return African treasures, report says'. *The New York Times*. 21 November. Available at: https://www.nytimes.com/2018/11/21/arts/design/france-museums-africa-savoy-sarr-report.html (Accessed 9 August 2020).

Olusoga, D. (2017) 'Black people have had a presence in our history for centuries. Get over it'. *The Guardian*. 13 August. Available at: https://www.theguardian.com/commentisfree/2017/aug/12/black-people-presence-in-british-history-for-centuries (Accessed 21 July 2020).

Park. J. (ed.) (2013) *Bertrand Russell: On Education*. London: Routledge.

Parliament UK. (2020) 'Parliament's authority'. Available at: https://www.parliament.uk/about/how/role/sovereignty/ (Accessed 11 July 2020).

Piketty, T. (2020) *Ideology and Capital*. Translated by A. Goldhammer. Cambridge, MA: Belknap Harvard.

Polanyi, K. [1944] (2001) *The Great Transformation*. Boston, MA: Beacon Books.

Press Association. (2020) 'George Floyd's body arrives at church for private funeral'. *PA Media*. 9 June. Available at: https://www.msn.com/en-gb/news/world/george-floyd-s-body-arrives-at-church-for-private-funeral/ar-BB15fGKk?ocid=spartan-dhp-feeds (Accessed 9 June 2020).

Price, S. (2020) 'Has the Sarr-Savoy report had any effect since it was first published?' *Apollo*. 6 January. Available at: https://www.apollo-magazine.com/sarr-savoy-report-sally-price-dan-hicks/ (Accessed 8 August 2020).

Rawlinson, K. (2016) 'Cecil Rhodes statue to remain at Oxford after "overwhelming support"'. *The Guardian*. 29 January. Available at: www.theguardian.com/education/2016/jan/28/cecil-rhodes-statue-will-not-be-removed--oxford-university (Accessed 7 March 2019).

Reclaim EC1. (2020) 'The City of London and the Slave Trade Part 1'. *reclaimec1*. 20 June. Available at: https://reclaimec1.wordpress.com/2020/06/17/the-city-of-london-the-slave-trade-part-1/ (Accessed 4 August 2020).

Rittel, H.W.J. and Webber, M.M. (1973) 'Dilemmas in a general theory of planning'. *Policy Sciences*. Vol. 4. No. 2, pp. 155–169.

Sandbrook, D. (2019) 'Of course slavery was abhorrent. But Cambridge dons who now feel guilty about our Empire are narcissistic cowards'. *Mail Online*. 1 May. https://www.dailymail.co.uk/debate/article-6978591/DOMINIC-SANDBROOK-course-slavery-abhorrent-Cambridge-dons-guilty-Empire-cowards.html (Accessed 29 July 2020).

Sarr, F. and Savoy, B. (2018) *The Restitution of African Cultural Heritage. Toward a New Relational Ethics*. Available at: http://restitutionreport2018.com/sarr_savoy_en.pdf (Accessed 8 August 2020).

Satterthwaite, D. (2009) 'The Implications of Population Growth and Urbanisation for Climate Change'. *Environment and Urbanisation*. Vol. 21, No. 2, pp. 545–567.

Savage, M., Cunningham, N., Devine, F., Friedman, S., Laurison, D., McKenzie, L., Miles, A., Snee, H. and Wakeling, P. (2015) *Social Class in the 21st Century*. London: Pelican.

Scottish Government. (2018) 'Tackling poverty'. Available at: www.gov.scot/ news/child-poverty-and-social-mobility/ (Accessed 25 June 2019).

Shankleman, J. (2020) 'Oxford faces pressure to change as Universities confront racism'. *Bloomberg*, 7 July. Available at: https://www.bloomberg.com/news/articles/2020-07-07/oxford-faces-new-pressure-over-statue-as-colleges-confront-racism (Accessed 8 July 2020).

Shear, M.D. (2018) 'Students lead huge rallies for gun control across the U.S'. *The New York Times*. Available at: https://www.nytimes.com/2018/03/24/us/politics/students-lead-huge-rallies-for-gun-control-across-the-us.html (Accessed 21 July 2020).

Siddique, H. (2020) 'Home Office urged to correct false slavery information in citizenship test'. *The Guardian*. 22 July. Available at: https://www.theguardian.com/politics/2020/jul/22/home-office-urged-to-correct-false-slavery-information-in-citizenship-test (Accessed 24 July 2020).

Sutter, G. (2020) 'Hundreds call for Britain's colonial history to become part of school curriculum'. *Daily Echo*. 22 June. Available at: https://www.bournemouthecho.co.uk/news/18533226.hundreds-call-britains-colonial-history-become-part-school-curriculum/ (Accessed 21 July 2020).

Treadell, V. (2019) *Universal Values: Justice & Fairness: 9th Annual Michael Kirby Justice Oration* Speech Delivered on: August 2019. Available at: https://www.gov.uk/government/speeches/universal-values-justice-fairness (Accessed 3 August 2020).

UKSA. (2019) 'What is the cost of UK government education?' Available at: www.ukpublicspending.co.uk/uk_national_education_analysis (Accessed 14 March 2019).

Verkaik, R. (2018) *Posh Boys: How the English Public Schools Ruin Britain*. London: Oneworld.

Watts, J. (2020) 'Edward Colston statue toppled: how Bristol came to see the slave trader as a hero and philanthropist'. *The Conversation*. Available at: https://theconversation.com/edward-colston-statue-toppled-how-bristol-came-to-see-the-slave-trader-as-a-hero-and-philanthropist-140271 (Accessed 26 June 2020).

Weal, S. (2019) 'Labour's plan for private schools based on "desire to damage"'. *The Guardian*. 30 September. Available at: https://www.theguardian.com/politics/2019/sep/30/labours-plan-for-private-schools-based-on-desire-to-damage (Accessed 7 July 2020).

Werner, R.A. (2005). *New Paradigm in Macroeconomics*. London: Palgrave.

Wilkinson, R. and Pickett, K. (2009) *The Spirit Level: Why More Equal Societies Almost Always Do Better*. London: Penguin.

Wilkinson, R. and Pickett, K. (2018) *The Inner Level: How More Equal Societies Reduce Stress, Restore Sanity and Improve Everyone's Well-being*. London: Allen Lane.

INDEX

Abensour, Miguel 23, 26–28, 30
Abramovich, Roman 33
'abstract utopia' 31
academic autonomy 99
academic buoyancy 48
academic dependency 82–86, 100
academic disciplines 87, 99, 102
academic excellence 96
academic freedom 108, 110
academic integrity 108
academic neocolonialism 82–83, 86–87
academic open-mindedness 86
academic resilience 47–48
academies 118, 119, 142
act of defiance 102
act of symbolic violence 81, 89
acts of disobedience 50, 102
Adebisi, F. 107
Adorno, T.: *Dialectic of Enlightenment* 26
A Fly Girl's Guide to University: Being a Woman of Colour at Cambridge and Other Institutions of Power and Elitism (Olufemi; Younge; Manzoor-Khan and Sebatindira) 126
age of imperial domination 83
age of neoliberalism 96
Alatas, Syed Hussain 82–83, 86
Al-e Ahmad, J.: *Gharbzadeghi* 35, 83
Allison, M.A. 30
Alper, Howard 101
Alston, Philip 42, 109
Anambiguous utopia (Le Guin) 29

American charter schools 118
American Dream 21
ancient educational institutions 142–143
ancient institutions 4, 10, 142
ancient public schools 10
Anderson, B. 79
'Anglobalisation' 77
'Anthropocene' 146
anti-Muslim incidents 79
'anti-political politics' 24
anti-racist groups 134, 135
anti-union 116
anti-utopian belief 22
'anti-wealth egalitarianism' movement 5
arbitrary government policies 51
arguments for change 5
Arizmendiarrieta, J.M. 133
Arrernte 103–104
Ashcroft, B. 34
assessment-driven education policy 46
Atlantic slave trade 144
austerity 3, 7, 46, 79, 113, 116, 119, 121, 122, 141, 142; continuing threat of neoliberalism 66–67; critical economics 68–70; ethics of excessive wealth 57–58; evidence against philanthrocapitalism 64–66; government 8, 52; 'hypercapitalism' 67–68; impact on education 64; managing the poor 59–60; minimal state 60–61; neoliberal 41–42; philanthrocapitalism 62–64; unlimited wealth without responsibility 59; welfare state 61–62
authentic human relationship 11

'balanced and broadly based' approach, history curriculum 80
balance sheet approach to history 77
banking model of education 14
banking system of education 43, 44, 147
Barton, Geoff 42
Barton, Len 47
Beard, Mary 90
Beaumont, Matthew 30
Behari-Leak, K. 87, 90
Being Some Chapters from a Utopian Romance (Morris) 28
Bengal famines 77
Berger, Peter 34
Bernanke, Ben 70
Beveridge Report of 1942 139
'bimaristan' in Persian 99
Birrell, G. 45
Black Lives Matter (BLM) movement 133, 134, 143
Blair, Tony 121
BLM movement *see* Black Lives Matter (BLM) movement
the Blob 115
Bloch, Ernst 23, 25, 31
Bloom, P. 64
blueprint utopianism 25
'bodies remember' 42
Bolshevik Revolution of 1917 138
Bookchin, Murray 29
Bourdieu, Pierre 120, 124; *The Logic of Practice* 85
Bregman, R. 58
Brexit 81; campaign 87; referendum 76, 119
Britain 24, 76, 77, 110, 119, 144; Africa and 87–90; Black people in 134, 143; encroachment of neoliberalism in 6; exceptionalism of 81; freedom of academics in 109; legislation 90; policy process in 5; poverty in 3; social class and social mobility in 120; Thatcherism in 67; wealth and income inequality in 57
British and Western imperialism 78
British colonialism 91
British colonial rule 77, 78
British Empire 76, 77, 87
British government's policies 42
British national identity and sovereignty 2
British sovereignty 2, 79
Britons 76
Brossard, B. 132
Brown v Board of Education 65
Buffet, Warren 62
Butler, Dawn 135

Cameron, David 5, 8, 79, 119
Canadian PISA data 45
Capital and Ideology (Piketty) 137
Capital in the 21st Century (Piketty) 67
Capitalism and Modern Social Theory (Giddens) 83
capitalist development 134
capitalist global economy 58
capitals, assets and resources (CAR) approach 120
Capitol Hill Autonomous Zone (CHAZ) 134
Capitol Hill Organised Protest (CHOP) 134
'captive mind' 83
CAR approach *see* capitals, assets and resources (CAR) approach
Cervone, J. A. 65
charitable organisations and philanthropy 61
charity 59, 62, 66
Charity Organisation Society of Britain 59
charter schools 116–118
CHAZ *see* Capitol Hill Autonomous Zone (CHAZ)
child-led approach to schooling 12
Child Poverty Action Group (CPAG) 121
Child Poverty Act of 2010 121, 141, 142
Child Poverty Commission (CPC) 121
children 10; Black and Indigenous 45; education (*see* education); educational achievement 48; mental health of 5; physical development 42, 127; poverty 2, 121, 122; quasi-market imposed on 11; rights 51; vulnerable 51, 118–119, 137, 142; working-class 117, 119
CHOP *see* Capitol Hill Organised Protest (CHOP)
Cho, Seehwa 1
Christian fundamentalism 65
'chronic underachievement' 47
Churchill, Winston 77, 78, 139
'civilised' democracies 51

Clarke, Kenneth 8
Clarkson, Jeremy 32
class privilege, role of education 9–10
classroom: critical pedagogy in 13–14; discipline in 117
Climate Accountability Institute 32
Clinton, Hilary 6
Coalition Provisional Authority 41
CoE *see* community of enquiry (CoE)
cognitive skills and knowledge development 44
Coles, Tait 49
Collins, Randall 87
Collini, S. 98; *What Are Universities for?* 98
colonial-based knowledge systems 107
colonial domination 35, 83
colonialism 25, 32–36, 76, 82–83, 85, 86, 88, 91, 135, 138, 141, 143–145
'colonial legacy' 91
colonial powers 81, 83, 87, 91, 139
colonies 32, 34, 35, 76, 77, 81–83, 86, 91, 145
Colston, Edward 134, 135
Common Market 77
'common sense' arguments 3
Commonweal 27
commonwealth 76, 77, 79–81
communal activism 50
communism 24, 108
Communist Manifesto (Marx and Engels) 27
Communist Party of Great Britain (CPGB) 24
community education, re-investment in 13
community of enquiry (CoE) 52
competitive individualism 45
competitive quasi-market principles 68
Comte, Auguste 103
Connell, R. 85–87, 103
conscientizacao 15
Conservative government 57, 61, 77, 80, 87, 101, 109, 118, 121, 137
Conservative leadership 77, 79
Conservative-led coalition government 114, 119
Conservative Party 76, 78, 139, 140
constitutional safeguards 141–142
consumer-citizens 40
content-oriented skills and knowledge 44

conventional capitalist property relations 138
conventional wisdom 110
Count, Earl W.: *This Is Race* 106
CPAG *see* Child Poverty Action Group (CPAG)
CPC *see* Child Poverty Commission (CPC)
CPGB *see* Communist Party of Great Britain (CPGB)
CPS *see* Crown Prosecution Service (CPS)
Cretienne, Jean 101
'criminal act' 135
'crisis of hope' 24
critical consciousness 12, 15, 23, 50
critical economics 7, 68–70
'Crown Jewels' of English education 10
Crown Prosecution Service (CPS) 8
crude evolutionary approach 103
cultural capital 48, 118, 123, 125
cultural imperialism 14
'cultural literacy' 49, 144
'culture of dependency' 60
Cummings, Dominic 46

Davidson-Harden, A. 100, 101
Dawid, J. 52
'Death of Evidence March' 101
decolonisation 107, 139, 140, 146; of curriculum 81–82, 88–90; demands for 81–82; process 140; of society 77
decolonised curriculum: Africa and Britain 87–90; multiculturalism and revival of nationalism 87; #RhodesMustFall Oriel College Oxford 90–92
decolonised neoliberal university 106–108
decolonised university 102–106
Decolonising SOAS: Confronting the White Institution 91
dehumanisation 22
Dei, G.J.S. 15
democratic socialism 138
democratic systems 132
democratisation 99
dependency theory 82
deregulation 66, 113
Dewey, J. 98
'dialectic of emancipation' 26, 28, 30

Dialectic of Enlightenment (Horkheimer & Adorno) 26
dialectic of freedom 30
Dibley, A. 30
The Dispossessed (Le Guin) 29
doctrine of neoliberalism 71
'domestic terrorists' 134
Duggan, Mark 8
Duncan-Andrade, J.M.R. (2009) 113, 114
Durkheim, E.: *The Elementary Forms of Religious Life* (TEFRL) 103, 104
dystopia 28, 29

economic capital 43, 120, 123, 125
economic ideology 108
economic liberalism 138, 140
'economism' 4
The Economist (2013) 7
educating hope 15, 23
education 48, 50–51; banking model of 14; banking system of 44, 147; degradation of 6–9; of desire 28–29; free public 138, 139; higher (*see* higher education); impact on 64; international market in 127; investment in 141; liberal 65, 97; market 125; in neoliberal context 43–44; non-exclusionary system of 143; notion of 12; policy 4, 5; popular 12, 13; post-school 99; progressive 45; public 65, 67, 115, 116, 138, 139; quasi-market in 41, 118, 127, 142; in reproducing class privilege, role of 9–10; state (*see* state education); system 4, 8, 10–11, 16, 48, 116; traditional 80; variety of alternative approaches to 12–13; and welfare in a neoliberal world 40–41
Education Act (1993) 118
Education Act (2002) 80
Education Act (2010) 118
educational attainment 9, 117
educational inequalities 45, 120
educational performance of schools 127
educational philosophy 43
educational system in England 127
education and healthcare plans (EHC) 119
'education of desire' 26
Edwards, K. 81
Eisinger, J. 7

The Elementary Forms of Religious Life (TEFRL) (Durkheim) 103, 104
elitist education system 137, 142
emancipation, dialectic of 30
Empire 76, 78, 80, 87; academic legacy of 87–90; enduring power and nostalgia of 77
Empire 2.0 78
'endless experimentation and incompleteness' of Utopia 30
'endlessly defers utopia's realization' 30
'enemies of hope' 113
Engels, Friedrich: *Communist Manifesto* 27
English education system 11, 122, 123, 126
English History National Curriculum 144
English National History Curriculum 87
Enlightenment belief 100
environmentalism 29
environmental pollution 30
epistemological disobedience 102, 104
'epistemological equity' 15
'epoch of rest' 27
An Epoch of Rest (Morris) 28
Equality Act 2010 90
equality of educational opportunity 137
equality of opportunity 48, 114, 127, 137
ethics/ethical 21, 49, 57, 67, 109, 136, 143; of excessive wealth 57–58; guidelines 133; obligation on economic actors 59; principles 10; questions 3; void 5–6
'ethno-racial' discrimination 145
Eton 126, 142
Eurocentric curriculum 80
Eurocentric knowledge 15
European settlement 34
European Union (EU) Referendum 76
'evidence-based politics' 5
'exacerbating poverty' 42
exceptionalism 81
excessive wealth, ethics of 57–58
exclusions 108; of alternative or Indigenous forms 100; policies 118, 142
extreme food insecurity 42
EXXON 109
Eze, Chukwudi 106

'false caring' 114
Fanon, Frantz 85, 88
Fauci a 'Fraud-ci' 115
Fauci, Anthony 115
feminism 51
Ferguson, Niall 77, 80
finance capitalism 5, 7
financial crash of 2008 7–8
financial services sector 133
First Nation Canadians 45
fiscal policies 6
Floyd, George 90, 133–135, 143
food banks 42, 43, 120
food insecurity 42, 52
Ford, D. 47
'foreign threat' 2
for-profit organisations 46, 66
Foucault, Michel 96
Franco, General 132
Frank, Andre Gunder 82
free market 21, 58; economy 6; fundamentalism 41; liberal capitalism 138; restrictions and regulations in 58
free movement of labour 2
free public education 138, 139
free school 45, 118
free society 3
Freirean pedagogy 12
Freire humanisation 8
Freire, Paulo 12, 14, 15, 25, 43, 49, 91, 110; *Pedagogy of Freedom* 23
French sociology 105
Friedman, M. 6
Friedman, R. 6
Fromm, Erich 49, 109
'full privatisation of all public enterprises' 41

Gaia 33
Gardner Kelly, M. 116–117
Garton-Ash, Timothy 90
Garuba, H. 88
Gates, Bill 58, 113, 116
Gates, Melinda 113
'gentlemanly' professions 124

Gharbzadeghi (Al-e Ahmad) 35, 83
Giddens, Anthony: *Capitalism and Modern Social Theory* 83
Gilman, S.L. 105
Giroux, H. 14–16
The Giving Pledge 62, 113
global capitalism 24
global economic system 7
global egalitarian system 146
global knowledge economy 102
global pandemics, threat of 146
Goldacre, M. 42
Golden Age of Islam 99
Golden Age of Philanthropy 62, 63
'golden age of social democracy' 67, 139
Gossling, S. 33
Gove, Michael 5, 9, 49, 50, 52, 80, 114, 115, 122, 143, 144
governmentality 99, 117
Gramsci's concept of hegemony 70
Gray, J. 22
Great Depression of the 1930s 138
'great meritocracy' 121–123
Great Transformation (Polanyi) 138
Green, Francis 142
Guest, William 27

Hall, S. 24
Hancock, C. 42
'handout culture' of state welfare 60
Hardy, K. 34, 36
Hargreaves, Peter 57
Harper, Stephen 101, 109
Harvey, D. 66
Hasan, R. 108
Hay, I. 62–64, 113–114
Heath, Deana 77
Heath, Edward 79
Hegel, Georg Wilhelm Friedrich 106; *Philosophy of History* 105; *Philosophy of Spirit* 105
Heleta, S. 89
Hendricks, C. 87
heterodox economic thinking 68
heterodox thinkers 70

higher education 96–97, 108; decolonised neoliberal university 106–108; decolonised university 102–106; hegemonic Western knowledge through knowledge economy 100–102; knowledge economy 100; modern university 97–99; Northern hegemonic knowledge 102; universities and reproduction of inequality 99–100
higher education institutions (HEIs) 13
Hilton, Paris 33
Hinds, Damian 47
Hirsch, E.D. 49, 144
History National Curriculum 49
Hitler, Adolf 78
Ho, J. 86
'hokey hope' 113, 122, 123, 137
homo economicus 69
hooks, b. 13
Horkheimer, M.:*Dialectic of Enlightenment* 26
human behaviour 69, 70, 146
humane social philosophy 140
human intellectual endeavour 98
humanisation of the nation 3
humanist education 133
humanist principles 133
'humankind's central problem' 8
human rights obligations 42
Human Rights Watch 42
Humboldtian model 97
Hwang, A. 57
hypercapitalism 67–68, 132, 137, 140–141

The Idea of a University Defined and Illustrated (Newman) 97
ideology 4, 15, 16, 29, 46, 140, 147; amoral 8; of completeness 110; economic 108; of Empire 77, 87; extreme right-wing 63; of inequality 67; of meritocracy 9; nationalistic 115; neoliberal 6, 60; patriarchal 51, 52; political 141; of racism 146; regressive 140
Ideology and Capitalism 67
'ignorance squared' 69
imagined community 79
'imagined' concept of community 2
income 3, 5, 6, 48, 58, 120, 124; distribution 140; equality in countries 5; inequality 57; progressive taxation on 139; wealth and 61, 97, 114, 138
independent sector 114, 118, 126–127, 142
Indigenous community 104
Indigenous cultural and intellectual development 83
Indigenous traditional knowledge 102
Indigenous voices 34–36, 85–86
'indiscriminate' charitable giving 59
individual freedom 6, 9
inequality 4, 5, 9, 14, 21, 25, 41, 44, 60, 69, 97, 121, 122, 127, 139, 140, 146; class 16, 143; economic 120; educational 45, 120; in educational progress 51; extreme 6; gender 26, 49; global 66, 108, 113; in health 133; income 57; injustice and 61; and injustices 2; knowledge and 107; neoliberal 141; regimes 67, 138; social 1, 46, 114, 128; tackling injustice of 137–138; universities and reproduction of 99–100
infinite wealth 3
Initiative for Pluralism in Economics 70
institutional racism 26, 89, 133–135
intellectual openness and freedom 98
intellectual thinking and political life 23
intentional utopian communities 32
international energy corporations 133
international human rights organisations 42
international market in education 127
international organisations 47
International Popular Education Network (PEN) 13
Inuit of the Canadian Arctic 45
Iranian Revolution in 1979 35

Jacques, M. 24
Jameson, Fredric 24–26
JBS *see* John Birch Society (JBS)
Jerrim, J. 48
John Birch Society (JBS) 65
Johnson, Boris 21, 46, 59, 79, 126, 127, 140
Joseph Rowntree Foundation 122
judicial activism 32

Kabyle 85
Kant, Immanuel 97, 106
Katz, L. 14
Keen, Steve 70

Kendrick, A.H. 48
Kenyan education system 88
Khaldun, Ibn: *Muqaddimah* 84
Kim, Dae Shik Jr. 134
Klineberg, O. 45
Knights, Emma 120
knowledge 43, 84, 96, 97, 105, 110; academic 86; acquisition of 98; collective 146; colonial-based 107; content-oriented skills and 44; economy 100–102, 113; Eurocentric 15; Indigenous traditional 102; and inequality 107; in neoclassical economics 108
Koch, Fred 65
Kolderie, E. 116, 117
Kurak, M. 61, 62
Kwoba, Brian 77, 136

Labour government 57, 121, 122, 141
labour market 9
Labour Party 3, 139
laissez faire approach 9
Lampl, Peter 127
Lane, J. 85
'language of possibility' 1–2
Lansdown, G. 51
LDCs *see* less developed countries (LDCs)
'leave' campaign 76
left-wing authoritarianism 26
legal rights 51
Le Guin, Ursula: *An ambiguous utopia* 29; *The Dispossessed* 29
Leibowitz, B. 87
Leopold II 134
less developed countries (LDCs) 67
Levin, K. 30, 146
Levitas, R. 25, 31
Lewis, Clive 57
Lewis, S.L. 146
liberal education 65, 97
liberal market capitalism 138
liberation 15, 26, 99, 105
'lifestyle choices' 2
Lightowlers, C. 8
Local Government Act 63
The Logic of Practice (Bourdieu) 85

long-term national crises 61
Lovelock, James 33

Macron, Emmanuel 145
mainstream economics 67, 68
mainstream education, role of 1
Manicom, L. 13
Manifesto for New Times 24
Manzoor-Khan, Suhaiymah 126; *A Fly Girl's Guide to University: Being a Woman of Colour at Cambridge and Other Institutions of Power and Elitism* 126
market capitalism 21, 99, 138, 140
market democracies 21
Marsh, H.W. 48
Marsland, David 60–61
Martin, A.J. 48
Marx, Karl 24; *Communist Manifesto* 27
Maslin, M.A. 146
Maxwele, Chumani 89
May, Theresa 5, 9, 50, 119, 121–123, 127
Mbembe, A.J. 100, 102, 105
McCarney, J. (2003) 106
McCowan, T. 98
'McDonaldisation' of childhood 5
McIntyre, N. 118
medicalisation 5
mental health of children 5
mental illness 5
meritocracy 9, 114
'meritocratic myth' 141
meritocratic society 9, 119
messianic movement 34
#MeToo movement 32
Metropolitan intellectuals 84
metropolitan sociology 85
Michel, Charles 134
Mignolo, W.D. 102
minimal state 60–61
minority ethnic groups 2
The Mismanagement of Learning 47
modern university 97–99
monarchy 4, 10, 76, 142
Monbiot, George 33
Mondragon Corporation 133

'monological principle of utopian socialism' 28
Montessori Method 12
Mooney, G. 59
morals/morality 6, 7, 21, 48–50, 59, 62, 67, 69, 136; consciousness of society 25; guidelines 133; obligation on economic actors 59; panics 115; principles 10; problems 109; questions 3; void 5–6; weakness 57
More, Thomas 25
Morrison, Scott 32, 50
Morris, William: *Being Some Chapters from a Utopian Romance* 28; *An Epoch of Rest* 28; *News from Nowhere* 27–28, 30
Motes 27
Muller, S. 62–64, 113–114
Mulroney, Brian 101
multiculturalism 87
Muqaddimah (Khaldun) 84
Murray, Charles 60, 61
mythical community 10
'mythical hope' 114
myth of care 114–115

NABST *see* National Advisory Board on Science and Technology (NABST)
Nadir, C. 26, 29
NAHT *see* National Association of Head Teachers (NAHT)
National Advisory Board on Science and Technology (NABST) 101
National Association of Head Teachers (NAHT) 119
National Curriculum 135, 143
National History Curriculum for England 80
nationalism 87
national myth 77, 91
National Union of Teachers 47
'natural consciousness' 105
'naturalise' inequality 140
Nazi threat 144
'necrophilous' mechanisms 49
Nelson, C. 32, 80
neoclassical economics 7, 67–70, 108; principles 82; theory 101
neo-colonialism 35, 36
neo-imperialism 82

neoliberal austerity 41–42
neoliberal capitalism 5, 16, 108, 109, 113
neoliberal capitalist path 21
neoliberal countries 2
neoliberal doctrines 64
neoliberal economics: ideological commitment to 11; moral and ethical void 5–6; policies 59; and welfare policies 25
neoliberal efficiency 119
neoliberal free market fundamentalism 41
neoliberal governmentality 96
neoliberal hypercapitalism 137, 146
neoliberal ideology 6
neoliberal inequality regime 141
neoliberalisation 66–67
neoliberalism 4–7, 36, 41, 43, 46, 60, 66–67, 97, 101, 108–110, 114, 146, 147; continuing threat of 66; encroachment of 6
neoliberal organisations and foundations 65
neoliberal policies 4, 41, 43, 45, 60
neoliberal policymakers 117
neoliberal principles 100, 106
neoliberal reform, policies of 5
neoliberal regime of governmentality 99
neoliberal state 10, 11, 16, 106, 124
neoliberal system 23
'New Jerusalem' 139–140
New Labour governments 41, 119
Newman, John Henry 98, 99; *The Idea of a University Defined and Illustrated* 97
News from Nowhere (Morris) 27–28, 30
Ngugi, wa Thiong'o 105–106
'No Cop Co-op' 134
non-charter public school 116
non-dominant groups 14
non-exclusionary system of education 143
non-Indigenous academics and intellectuals 36
non-Northern sociological thinkers 83
non-privileged groups 14
non-selective state schools 125
non-Western utopianism 35
Northern epistemologies 84, 100, 105
Northern hegemonic knowledge 102
Northern intellectuals: and researchers 83; tradition 35

Northern knowledge systems 106
Northern sociology 83, 84
Northern theories of modernisation 82
Northern/Western knowledge 100
Nothing Left in the Cupboards 42
Nozik, R. 6
nurturing freethinking in pupils 12

Oakley, A. 51
OCP *see* Oxford and Colonialism Project (OCP)
Odo, Laia 29
Odonianism 29
OECD *see* Organisation for Economic Co-operation and Development (OECD)
Okri, Ben 134
Olufemi, Lola 126; *A Fly Girl's Guide to University: Being a Woman of Colour at Cambridge and Other Institutions of Power and Elitism* 126
Olusoga, David 77
'opening doors, breaking barriers' 9
The Open Society and Its Enemies (Popper) 22
Organisation for Economic Co-operation and Development (OECD) 43, 44, 46–48, 68
Osborne, George 119
Oxford and Colonialism Project (OCP) 91
'oxidation' 35

Parekh Report 80
parliamentary sovereignty 142
PDC organisation *see* Production and Distribution Coordination (PDC) organisation
'pedagogical action' 15
pedagogy for change 4; allure of nation 10–11; alternative approaches to education 12–13; arguments for change 5; classroom, critical pedagogy in 13–14; confused and confusing system 11; contemporary era, critical pedagogy in 14; degradation of education 6–9; education 12; free society 3; 'language of possibility' 1–2; moral and ethical void in neoliberal economics 5–6; perverse logics 3–4; raising critical consciousness 15; role of education in reproducing class privilege 9–10
Pedagogy of Freedom (Freire) 23
performance criteria 8, 110

performance-driven reforms 47
performance-driven regimes 43
perverse logics 3–4, 9, 16, 32, 122, 132, 142
Peters, M.A. 96, 97
Pettifor, Ann 70
philanthrocapitalism 62–63, 65, 114; growing evidence against 64–66; threat posed by 63–64
philanthropic declarations 113
philanthropic foundations 62
philanthropic organisations 61
philanthropic relationships 62
philanthropy 59, 61, 64, 66
Phillips, Melanie 50, 52
'philosophically incoherent' concept of welfare state 60
Philosophy of History (Hegel) 105
Philosophy of Spirit (Hegel) 105
Pickett, K. 5, 21
Piketty, Thomas 138–142, 145; *Capital and Ideology* 137; *Capital in the 21st Century* 67
piliriqatigiingniq 45
PISA *see* Programme for International Student Assessment (PISA)
Plato 10; *Republic* 22
Polanyi, Karl 140; *Great Transformation* 138
police racism 8
political freedom 41
political rights 51
'the politics of envy' 21
Popper, K.:*The Open Society and Its Enemies* 22
popular education 12, 13
possessive individualism 109
post-Brexit agreement 81
post-Brexit free trade policy 77
postcolonialism 32–34
postcolonial scholarship 35
postcolonial theory 34, 35
Post-Crash Economics Society 7, 147
'Post-Fordism' 24
'post-invasion theory' 35
post-school education 99
post-war devastation 139
post-war political consensus 60

poverty 3, 25, 32, 40, 41, 46, 58–60, 62, 79, 100, 109, 114, 127, 135, 137, 139; child 2, 43, 47, 51, 52, 121, 122, 141; exacerbating 42
Powell, Enoch 79
pragmatism 52
Praxis 15, 23, 52
Prebisch, Raúl 82
prime *raison d'état* 108
primitive societies 104
principles of liberal philosophy 97
principles of market capitalism 99
private schools 10
privatisation 3, 46, 60, 66, 117, 119
processual utopianism 25
Production and Distribution Coordination (PDC) organisation 29
'professional neutrality' 1
Programme for International Student Assessment (PISA) 43–48
progressive education 45
progressive secularist intelligentsia 35
progressive taxation 61, 68, 138; and pension reform 67; system 139
public education 65, 67, 115–116, 138, 139
public goods 8, 11, 40, 59, 62, 63, 110, 117
'public schools' 142
punitive sanctions 42
punitive strategies 52
punitive tariffs on Indian exports 78
punk learning 49
Purtschert, P. 105

quasi-market in education 41, 118, 127, 142
Quirk, H. 8

race 43, 88, 89; and ethnicity 125–126; and racial segregation 81
racism 106, 134, 144, 146; casual 79; ideology of 146; institutional 26, 134, 135; structural 133, 141
radical critical teaching 14
'radical subversives' 3
raison d'état 99, 108
Rawls, J. 6

Rayner, Angela 127
re-centring Africa 106
'reduction of inequality' 138
Reece-Mogg, Jacob 78
REF *see* Research Excellence Framework (REF)
regressive ideologies 67, 140
Reich, Robert 64
'reification of impossibility' 24
Remain campaign 119
'remoralization' 59
'Renewing Democracy in Scotland' 13
Republic (Plato) 22
research 98–103, 105, 107–109
Research Excellence Framework (REF) 107
resilience 47, 48
Resolution Foundation 121
Rethinking Economics 7
'revolt against utopia' 24
Rhode, David 115
Rhodes, Cecil 64, 81, 87, 89–91
#rhodesmustfall campaign 81, 87, 89, 143
rickets 42
right-wing governments 46, 115
right-wing politicians 68
right-wing think tanks 5, 60
'rivers of blood' speech 79
Robbins, Lord 6, 110
Robson, J. 126
Rogers, John 116, 118
'rogue traders' 8
Rose, Nikolas 40
Rostow, W.W. 82
Rudd, Amber 42
Russell, Bertrand 12, 143
ruthless colonialism 134

Sahlberg, P. and Hargreaves, A. 45
Sandbrook, Dominic 144
Sargent, L.T. 25, 32
Sarkozy, Nicolas 105
Satterthwaite, David 33, 137
Saunders, Peter 60
Savage, M. 48, 120, 123–127
SCC *see* Science Council of Canada (SCC)

Schleicher, Andreas 43
school funding 44, 127
School of Oriental and African Studies (SOAS) 91
school-related factors 44
Schultz, J. 81
Science Council of Canada (SCC) 101
Science Innovation and Technology Council (STIC) 101
science policy in Canada 102
Scientific Integrity Policy 101
Scottish independence referendum 52
Sebatindira, Waithera: *A Fly Girl's Guide to University: Being a Woman of Colour at Cambridge and Other Institutions of Power and Elitism* 126
selection, impact on social justice 118
self-regulating market 146
settler utopianism 34
Shapps, Grant 76
Shor, I. 14
A Short History of Sociological Thought (Swingewood) 83
SMC *see* Social Mobility Commission (SMC)
Smith, Duncan 61
SOAS *see* School of Oriental and African Studies (SOAS)
social capital 123, 125, 127
social class and social mobility in Britain 120
social classification system 123
social democracy 67, 138, 140
social inequalities 1, 46, 114
socialisation process 40, 83
socialism 24, 27, 28, 82, 138
social justice 13, 48, 67, 107, 118; ancient educational institutions 142–143; assault on state education 116–117; constitutional safeguards 141–142; continuing myth of social mobility in neoliberal times 119–120; education 141; false hope 113–114; global demand for justice 134–135; great transformation 138; impact on vulnerable children 118–119; independent sector 126–127; inheritance of privilege 124–125; injustice of inequality 137–138; Mondragon Corporation 133; myth of care 114–116; 'New Jerusalem' 139–140; problem of elitism 125; race and ethnicity 125–126; selection and social justice 118; time of opportunity and hope 139; utopian visions and the education of hope 132; youth activism and pedagogy through activism 144
'socially embed' market capitalism 138
social mobility 9, 11, 119–121, 127
Social Mobility and Child Poverty Commission 121
Social Mobility Commission (SMC) 121
'social organic utility' 29
socio-economic class spectrum 8
Souter, Brian 63
Southern sociology 84
Southern theory 86
Soviet communism 60
Soviet-style communism 21, 23, 139
Soviet-style socialism 138
Soviet-style 'utopianism' intellectuals 24
Spanish Civil War 132
Spencer, H. 103
Stakhanovites 59
Stanford, Jim 58
state education: assault on 116–117; marketisation of 119; system 63, 65
state-imposed curriculum 49
state public services 117
Steiner schools 12
Steiner Waldorf education 12
STIC *see* Science Innovation and Technology Council (STIC)
Stiglitz, Joseph 64
structural inequalities 137
structural racism 133, 141
structural vulnerability 51
student-led groups 7
'super-philanthropy' 62
super wicked problems 25, 30, 146
Sutton Trust report 125, 127
Swedish system of free schools 118
Swingewood, Alan: *A Short History of Sociological Thought* 83

Tamimi, S. 5
Tax Cuts and Jobs Act of 2017 66

'teaching universal knowledge' 98
Tell Mamaorganisation 79
terra nullius 103
testing 45, 47, 52; in neoliberal context 43–44; PISA 46; standardised 12
Tharoor, Shashi 78
Thatcher, Margaret 59, 60, 66, 117, 140
'There is no alternative' (TINA) 3
Third Reich 23
This Is Race (Count) 106
Thomassen, B. 104
Thompson, H. (1997) 68–70
Thunberg, Greta 31–32, 49, 50, 133
The Times Higher Education (THE) ranking system 107
traditional agrarian societies 82
traditional education 80
traditional state communism 24
'tragedy of Africa' 105
Traianou, A. 109
transformational education system 13
trickle-down theory of wealth distribution 64
Trudeau, Justin 101
Trump, Donald 6, 32, 79, 115, 134
Trussell Trust 43, 62
Tunzelmann, A. 81

UCT campus *see* University of Cape Town (UCT) campus
UK-based higher education 13
ulama 35
UN Convention of the Rights of the Child 147
unequal societies 21, 61
UNHRC *see* United Nations Human Rights Commission (UNHRC)
United Nations Declaration on the Rights of the Child 51
United Nations Human Rights Commission (UNHRC) 42
university 96, 108–109; decolonised 102–106; modern 97–99; neoliberal 107; and reproduction of inequality 99–100
University of Cape Town (UCT) campus 89
unlimited wealth without responsibility 59

unrealistic romanticism 22
UN's Special Rapporteur on Extreme Poverty and Human Rights 42
US healthcare system 80
utopian chains 132
utopia/nism 21, 26, 28, 32–34; Abensour 26; abstract 31; ambiguous 29; blueprint 22, 25; and colonialism 36; non-Western 35; Popper's approach to 22; production 132, 133; revolt against 24; traditional approaches to 27, 28; and 'wicked' problems 30
utopian literature and education of desire 28–29
'utopian marvellous' 28
utopian method 31, 32
utopian niches 132
'utopian party' 30
utopian spirit: adopting 22–23; and education of desire 26–27; renewal of 25–26
utopian thinking 23, 30, 31
utopia production 132, 133
'Utopie et démocratie' 26

van Gennep, Arnold 103–105
Verkaik, Robert 142
Vertigan, M. 32, 80
Virgil 79
Vogel, P. 61, 62
voice 3, 4, 9, 33, 50, 51, 80, 87; counter hegemonic 32; indigenous 34–36, 85–86; of victims 90, 91, 135
Volante, L. 48
von Humboldt, Wilhelm 97
vulnerable children 118–119, 137, 142

Walford, G. 117, 118
Walters, S. 13
Walton Family Foundation 116
Warner, Marina 109
Warren, Earl 65
weak and vulnerable group 3, 8, 26
Weal, S. 118
wealth: austerity ethics of excessive 57–58; distribution, trickle-down theory of 64; ethics of

excessive 57–58; and income 61, 97, 114, 138; infinite 3; without responsibility 59
'wealth creators' 57, 58
Weber, M. 25
welfare 51; benefits 114; children 47; democracy 67; internal markets in 113; neoliberal governments' policies on 52; in neoliberal world, education and 40–41; policies 25, 43; progressive 66; provision 67, 68; society 138, 139
Welfare Reform Act of 2016 121
welfare state 61–62
Western academic and cultural values, domination by 44–45
Western capitalist economies 24
Western colonialism 34, 81
Western Europe 24
What Are Universities for? (Collini) 98
White, I. 47
Whiteman, Paul 42, 119–120
Wilkinson, Richard 5, 21
'willed transformation' 29, 31
Williams, J. 31
Windrush scandal 135
Wittrock, B. 99
working-class children 117, 119
World Inequality Database 67

YouGov poll 76
Younge, Odelia: *A Fly Girl's Guide to University: Being a Woman of Colour at Cambridge and Other Institutions of Power and Elitism* 126
young people 43, 44, 49, 50, 52, 64, 65, 68, 69, 71, 81, 97, 108, 117, 125, 143, 147; activism among 144; mental illness among 5; physical and educational development of 46; vulnerability of 51
youth climate activists 133

'zealous advocacy' 8
Zero Hour movement 49
Zuckerberg, Mark 113